An Introduction to Childhood

For my sister, Claire

An Introduction to Childhood
Anthropological Perspectives on Children's Lives

Heather Montgomery

WILEY-BLACKWELL

A John Wiley & Sons, Inc., Publication

Blackwell Publishing was acquired by John Wiley & Sons in February 2007. Blackwell's publishing program has been merged with Wiley's global Scientific, Technical, and Medical business to form Wiley-Blackwell.

Registered Office
John Wiley & Sons Ltd, The Atrium, Southern Gate, Chichester, West Sussex, PO19 8SQ, United Kingdom

Editorial Offices
350 Main Street, Malden, MA 02148-5020, USA
9600 Garsington Road, Oxford, OX4 2DQ, UK
The Atrium, Southern Gate, Chichester, West Sussex, PO19 8SQ, UK

For details of our global editorial offices, for customer services, and for information about how to apply for permission to reuse the copyright material in this book please see our website at www.wiley.com/wiley-blackwell.

Library of Congress Cataloging-in-Publication Data

Montgomery, Heather (Heather Kate)
   An introduction to childhood : an anthropological perspective of children's lives / Heather Montgomery.
        p. cm.
   Includes bibliographical references and index.
   ISBN 978–1–4051–2590–1 (pbk. : alk. paper) — ISBN 978–1–4051–2591–8 (hardcover : alk. paper)   1. Children—Cross-cultural studies.   2. Children—Social conditions—Cross-cultural studies.   3. Child development—Cross-cultural studies.   4. Child rearing—Cross-cultural studies.   5. Children—History.   I. Title.

   HQ767.87.M66 2009
   305.231089—dc22

                                                                    2008013080

A catalogue record for this book is available from the British Library.

Set in 11/13pt Dante by Graphicraft Limited, Hong Kong
Printed in Singapore by Fabulous Printers Pte Ltd

1   2009

CONTENTS

ACKNOWLEDGMENTS

This book has been several years in the planning and writing and I am extremely grateful to the many people who have listened so patiently to me talking about it for so long. In particular I would like to thank Amanda Berlan, Laurence Brockliss, Phil Burrows, Helen Carr, Marina de Alarcon, Ollie Douglas, Maria Francis-Pitfield, Clare Harris, Mary-Jane Kehily, Mary Kellett, Mercia Mathew, David Messer, Ian, Tessa, and Claire Montgomery, John Oates, Fiona Raje, Gary Slapper, Catherine Sutton, and Martin Woodhead.

My editors at Blackwell have been consistently helpful and encouraging from the very beginning and I would like to thank Jane Huber, Deirdre Ilkson, and Rosalie Robertson very sincerely. I am also most appreciative of Justin Dyer, who copy-edited the manuscript. My very grateful thanks also go to the three anonymous reviewers who saved me from some glaring errors, suggested work I didn't know, and gave of their time and expertise so generously. The mistakes and omissions remain mine.

The staff at the Open University library also deserve great thanks for uncomplainingly ordering obscure volumes with dubious-sounding names every week for the last five years. Without their prompt and efficient help, this book would have been much harder to write.

Finally Peter Rivière, despite his reservations, has shaped much of my thinking and deepened my understanding of both childhood and anthropology. His intellectual rigor and way of seeing the world have been a huge influence and I remain deeply indebted to him.

INTRODUCTION

In 1909 the Swedish reformer Ellen Key claimed that the 20th century would be the "century of the child." She believed that there would be radical changes in the ways that children were conceptualized and treated, and that during the century children's welfare would become a social and political priority. Looking back a hundred years, she has in many ways been proved right: children's welfare and children's rights have become increasingly politically important and, within academia, children and childhood have become significant areas of study. From the late 19th century onward, research on children has moved steadily from the margins to the center of academic interest and it now makes sense to talk of a distinctive field of childhood studies which has been characterized by its interdisciplinarity, bringing together insights from psychology, law, sociology, children's rights, social policy, sociology, and anthropology. (For one of the best collections of articles in childhood studies see Jenkins 1998, which encompasses all these disciplines as well as history and literary studies.) Childhood studies has coalesced into a wide-ranging and significant subject area, which acknowledges that children undergo recognizable patterns of physical and psychological development and growth, but argues that the meanings given to these vary enormously within and between cultures. Furthermore, it has called for categories such as "the child," "childhood," or "children" to be critically examined and rethought (Pufall and Unsworth 2004; Kehily 2004; see also James 2004 for an overview of the origins and history of childhood studies). Anthropologists have made a significant contribution to this debate, especially in their insistence on the importance of cultural difference and cultural relativism. They have shown consistently that the idea of a universal child is an impossible fiction and that children's lives are influenced as strongly by their culture as by their biology. There are now enough ethnographic studies of children, and enough theorizations of childhood, for there to be a distinctive sub-discipline of anthropology which focuses on children, their role in society, and their place in the life-cycle, and it is time for this contribution to be documented and celebrated.

This book has arisen after ten years' work as a researcher and lecturer on anthropology and childhood. Over the years I have regularly been asked to recommend a book aimed at a mid-range undergraduate audience which wanted an overview of the specific ways that anthropologists have studied children's lives and their ideas about childhood, and I have been unable to do so. I found that many other books on childhood studies were either for more theoretically advanced students or on more specialized topics. There have certainly been influential books and articles which have discussed ideas about children and childhood, as well as seminal monographs on particular aspects of children's lives, but when I started to write this one there had not been a book that placed these within the history of anthropology, which linked up previous studies and descriptions of children, or one which looked at the thematic issues that have increased our theoretical understandings of childhood. Given the contemporary interest in children, it is hardly surprising that I have not been alone in this idea and that others, too, have brought out introductory guides to children and anthropology. David Lancy's *The Anthropology of Childhood: Cherubs, Chattel, Changelings* (2008), which is based on a review of material from anthropology, history, and primatology, is a very welcome addition to the field, dealing with childhood in its broadest, and most interdisciplinary, sense. Similarly Robert LeVine and Rebecca New's edited volume *Anthropology and Child Development* (2008), which brings together some of the key anthropological texts on child development into one reader, also makes a valuable contribution. In this book, however, I wanted to go back to original ethnographies, and look at them in context, finding out what anthropologists in the past had written about children and how this could inform future work. I was less interested in cross-cultural theories or worldwide surveys and more in detailed ethnographic descriptions which illuminated children's lives and which could open up areas of inquiry for students to pursue, enabling them to fashion their own papers and areas of potential research.

One of the very first questions such a book needs to deal with is the definition of a child. International law defines childhood as the period between the ages of 0 and 18, but, like others who have written on the subject, I have found this far too limiting. Biology is not particularly helpful either, although there are obvious markers such as conception, birth, or first menstruation. As an anthropologist, however, I am less interested in chronological or biological markers than in the social significance given to them, and, as I will go on to discuss throughout the book, children may be recognized as children long before birth, or sometime afterward. They may still be considered a child until after initiation, marriage, or indeed until their own parents die. One of the most important conclusions for any anthropologist studying childhood is that there is no universal child and that the concept of the child is one that must be defined internally and in its own context. I quite deliberately offer no definition of childhood, in order to show, through the use of different ethnographic evidence, quite how diverse and elastic a concept childhood can be.

I had originally intended to limit this book very specifically to *anthropological* understandings of childhood. I felt that psychologists, and more recently sociologists, had dominated the field, and I wanted to redress the balance, looking at anthropology's unique and substantial contribution. Immediately I realized that this was an impossible task. Trying to uncover a "pure" anthropology of childhood is impractical, especially in relation to North American anthropology, which was constructed as interdisciplinary from the start. Restricting the scope of this book only to social and cultural anthropology would mean ignoring the fields of psychological, biological, and linguistic anthropology, which have made such important contributions to the study of childhood, as well as downplaying the fact that most of the social anthropologists in North America who have studied and published on childhood since 1950 have also been involved in the field of child development. Nevertheless, I have tried to concentrate as far as possible on anthropological work on children, and where I have used the work of authors from other disciplines, I have mentioned their disciplinary background.

An issue that quickly became problematic in the research for this book was the large, and sometimes irreconcilable, differences between British and American anthropologists who have been interested in childhood; it would be possible to write two completely distinct histories of ideas about the ways that anthropologists in each country have thought, and written, about children. The emphasis on psychology, for instance, which has been such an important part of American anthropology, has been treated with suspicion, and even hostility, in the UK. The Human Relations Area Files, such a rich source of data for many American anthropologists, were received with distrust and derision in certain anthropology departments in the UK and are used only very rarely by British anthropologists (see the following chapter for more detail on this). At many British universities it is possible to gain an undergraduate degree purely in social and cultural anthropology, and many British students who take doctorates in social anthropology have not gained a first degree in the subject, making social anthropology in the UK a highly specialized area. In contrast, most North American universities operate a "four fields" approach to anthropology, where equal emphasis is given to archaeology, linguistics, sociocultural anthropology, and biological anthropology. This, as I will go on to argue in the next chapter, has led to very different traditions in studying childhood in the two countries.

Another important area of difference is the relationship of folklore to anthropology. While folklore is a thriving and respected discipline in North America, in the UK it remains marginalized and very much separated from anthropology. The most important center for the study of English folklore, Sheffield University's National Centre for English Cultural Tradition, operates under the auspices of the English faculty, and in Edinburgh, folklore comes under Celtic and Scottish studies. Although there was a close relationship between folklore and anthropology in the 1880s and 1890s in the UK, by the 1930s they were two very distinct fields of inquiry, and many anthropologists today treat folklore with a degree of embarrassment. Despite the influence of the work of folklorists Iona and Peter Opie and their studies of children's games, rhymes, and many other aspects of children's culture, few British anthropologists, including those specializing in childhood, wish to call themselves folklorists or view studies of folklore as worthy or relevant.

In most modern anthropological writings it has become traditional for the author to situate herself in the text, discussing how her own gender, ethnicity, and age have an impact on her work. I have mentioned my own fieldwork briefly in chapter 7 without commenting on my background, but for this section of the book, I should state it. After a first degree in English literature, I took a master's and Ph.D. in social anthropology. In many ways I am a very typical product of the way in which anthropology is taught in the UK. I do not have a first degree in it and I have never formally studied biological anthropology, archaeology, or folklore. Classes in cognitive or linguistic anthropology were optional and rather marginal to my studies, and while the following ten years researching children have meant that I have had to engage with ideas outside British social anthropology, I am very aware that certain prejudices remain. I have tried, throughout this book, to set out as fairly and impartially as possible the major schools of thought in anthropology, as well as the work which has been done on particular issues related to childhood, but I am aware that readers may disagree with my interpretations, accuse me of omission, or feel I am too dismissive of particular ways of understanding childhood. It is not my intention to be so; one of the reasons I have long been fascinated by childhood studies is the enormous depth and breadth of the subject and the exciting possibilities that analyzing childhood from different perspectives can offer.

When I first started my doctorate in 1992, the number of people working specifically on childhood was still very small. Conferences on the role of children in anthropology were few and far between and there was a limited amount of theoretical literature on the subject. At the time there was also a sense that children were not a completely legitimate topic of study; Elizabeth Chin has claimed that "despite anthropology's strong – although uneven – tradition of studying children (or, more commonly, childhood), children are a topic that is both overtly and covertly regarded as less than serious" (Chin 2001:134). There is certainly some fairness to this complaint; indeed on my first day in a new job, in the late 1990s, a senior colleague told me that he regarded my work, on children in Thailand, as "comparative social work" rather than "proper" anthropology. Since then, however, the field has blossomed: specific master's courses on anthropology and childhood have sprung up, international conferences, or specific panels within conferences, devoted to childhood are regularly organized, ethnographic monographs which take children as their central focus have increased exponentially, and almost all university departments can claim at least one or two students working on projects directly related to children's lives. Children and childhood are now generally recognized as being worthy subjects of study, and it is no longer possible to agree with those who make the claim that children are not taken seriously in anthropology or that those who study children are not taken seriously as anthropologists.

Although many anthropologists have studied children's lives and deconstructed ideas about childhood, and have done so for a long time, there has been a growth in the numbers of academics focusing primarily on children in the last thirty years. Those who have recently specialized in the study of childhood have argued that, in the past, children have been under-represented in both anthropological theory and ethnographic description. They have attempted to rectify this by looking at the ways that children themselves create meanings and form their own belief systems, as well as examining the ways that they negotiate and shape social attitudes about childhood. This analytical approach to children's lives might best be described as "child-centered" or "child-focused" anthropology and it demands the use of children as primary informants and focuses on children's voices and children's agency. This new theorization has been given impetus by the United Nations Convention on the Rights of the Child (UNCRC), which was opened for signature in 1979, came into force in 1989, and is the most widely signed rights treaty in the history of international law, with only Somalia and the USA not ratifying it. It is made up of 54 legally binding articles which aim to protect and promote children's rights in the fields of health, education, nationality, and the family. It is no coincidence that the rise of child-focused anthropology is contemporaneous with the Convention and that anthropologists who work in this field critically engage with the UNCRC and its provisions, and take a rights-based approach to childhood which insists that children's importance as agents and informants be recognized.

The vision of childhood enshrined in the UNCRC is one where childhood is a separate space, protected from adulthood, in which children are entitled to special protection, provision, and rights of participation. The UNCRC emphasizes that the proper place for children is at school or at home with their families. Indeed while there is an article stating that all children have an inalienable right to go to school, there is no corresponding right *not* to attend. The idea of childhood reflected in the Convention privileges education over work, family over street life, and consumerism over productivity. The child envisaged by the Convention is an individual, autonomous being, an inheritor of the liberal, humanist ideals of the Enlightenment, a view which has caused problems for universal interpretation and implementation (see Burman 1996; Cowan et al. 2001; Montgomery 2001b). Against this backdrop, it is perhaps not surprising that many anthropologists interested in studying children in non-Western contexts have been drawn toward those children who exist as anomalies in the new globalized notion of childhood (Hall and Montgomery 2000). They have often studied children who are out of place physically in that they are neither at home or at school, such as street children (Baker 1998; Hecht 1998; Panter-Brick 2000, 2001, 2002; Burr 2006). Alternatively they have turned their attention to children who act in ways contrary to accepted ideals of childhood, such as child prostitutes (Montgomery 2001a), child refugees (Hinton 2000), and child soldiers (de Berry 1999; Rosen 2007). Examinations of these groups of children have challenged universal notions of the child implicit in the UNCRC and profoundly complicated understandings of concepts and categorizations such as childhood or youth.

The political aspects of childhood are never far from such discussions, and the ways in which the notion of the child is discussed, invoked, and contested by politicians, the media, and within families has produced rich ethnographic and theoretical work. Nancy Scheper-Hughes and Carolyn Sargent (1998) and Sharon Stephens (1995a) have contributed important edited collections to the debate over the cultural politics of childhood in which they insist on both the importance of childhood as a political and social construct and the necessity of emphasizing the lived reality of children's experiences (Ennew and Morrow 2002). They make the case that studying children is fundamental in understanding any society or culture and for any meaningful analysis of social change. In Sharon Stephens' words:

> As representatives of the contested future and subjects of cultural policies, children stand at the crossroads of divergent cultural projects. Their minds and bodies are at stake in debates about the transmission of fundamental cultural values in the schools. The very nature of their senses, language, social networks, worldviews, and material futures are at stake in debates about ethnic purity, national identity, minority self expression and self-rule. (1995a:23)

Such authors have argued powerfully that an understanding and examination of children's experiences should be seen as central to anthropology and, furthermore, must be viewed in the context of conflicting and contested ideas about children and the sort of childhood they should have. In Scheper-Hughes and Sargent's words: "Childhood also involves cultural notions of personhood, morality, and social order and disorder. In all, childhood represents a cluster of discourses and practices surrounding sexuality and reproduction, love and protection, power and authority and their potential abuses" (1998:1–2). As more anthropologists begin to question ideas about modernity and the contemporary world order, childhood is one of the central issues with which they must come to terms.

Despite the UNCRC's pivotal role in shaping recent understandings of childhood, I am not suggesting a radical or insurmountable split between child-focused anthropology and a more general anthropology, especially as the conclusions from each can usefully inform the other in a number of ways. Anthropologists who have carried out ethnographic work on children's lives have pointed out many problems inherent in the philosophies and goals of the UNCRC. By setting universal standards for all children, and defining childhood so definitively as the period of life between birth and the age of 18, the UNCRC takes little account of cultural relativity, and anthropologists have regularly pointed out the discrepancies between the realities of children's lives and the universal ideals enshrined in the UNCRC. Even while acknowledging that the UNCRC may be an idealized vision, rather than a blueprint of practical policy, many have shown that it does not work on a local level. They have also critiqued the very nature of the UNCRC, arguing that it is fundamentally flawed and based on a Western ideal of an autonomous rights-bearing citizen that has limited applicability outside the industrialized West (Montgomery 2001b). In many cases they have found that neither the children themselves, nor their families, see them as the bearers of rights, and that looking at indigenous concepts of childhood means analyzing children as incomplete or subordinate in many cases (this point will be expanded in chapter 2). In critiquing notions of universalism, child-focused anthropologists have reinforced many of the points made so explicitly in older work, and there is a large overlap between these two sets of studies. The heterogeneous nature of childhood, the impact of gender, age, birth order, and ethnicity, as well as the problems defining childhood, have, as this book will show, been long-time concerns of anthropology, as have ideas about where life begins, what makes personhood, and how social competency is defined.

Another reason not to view child-centered anthropology as a radical break from the past is that the role and importance of children in fieldwork have been previously recognized, even if not always explicitly acknowledged (there are of course exceptions to this such as Bohannon 1954). When discussing this book with various colleagues, I was struck by how often they recounted anecdotes of how they had been befriended by children who acted as willing research assistants, who answered questions, showed patience with a socially inept foreigner, and acted as important sources of information. Unfortunately, on reading their monographs, this acknowledgment was not always there, even though children were discussed, analyzed, and sometimes even quoted (Rasmussen 1994). Inez Hilger, for example, in her exhaustive description of Araucanian children's lives in Chile and Argentina, gives frustratingly fleeting glances of children's own voices, even though she clearly canvassed children's opinions and was given a great deal of help by them. Her published work, however, relied almost entirely on what adults told her, and it is adults rather than children whose views are quoted and analyzed (Hilger 1957). Looking back now on older ethnographies, it is true that references to children's lives are often incomplete, but nevertheless children and ideas about childhood are there. Discussions of social roles, gender, and the making of persons all touch very directly on fundamental issues of childhood, what makes children children, and what separates them from adults. Indeed the ways in which adults become social persons cannot be understood without an analysis of what they were before.

I found that drawing a distinction between child-centered and older ethnographies was an unhelpful and limiting one, which seemed to create a dichotomy between understanding children as human beings and as human becomings. Anthropologists specializing in children have tended to reject the notion that they are human becomings, arguing that they should be seen in their own terms and not as incomplete or incompetent adults. They have emphasized the importance of children's experiences here and now, rather than seeing children as being of interest for what they will become. As such they have rejected other studies which have looked at socialization or seen children as anything other than possessors of a valuable, complete culture. Ideally, however, an anthropology of childhood should see children as both beings and becomings. Children can be of interest for what they are now, and the many new ethnographies that appear each year on children's everyday lives have shown this, yet children are also becoming something else, they change and transform from the socially immature to the mature. Childhood is a time of transition and change, and despite the enormous variations in the ways in which childhood is understood, there is no society that does not acknowledge that children (however they are defined) are very different from adults, have different needs, and have different roles and expectations placed on them.

When I first imagined this book, I envisaged it as having a dual purpose. The first was as a summary of previous anthropological work, looking at the multiple ways that childhood has been conceptualized and what insights into children's lives such work could reveal. I had become used to hearing students who wished to focus on children dismiss any previous work that did not deal directly with children as irrelevant, and I wanted to challenge this idea. I hope this book will help such students negotiate earlier monographs, showing them where the ethnographic record can guide them, suggesting further reading, and warning them against dismissing too carelessly older works that would have value to them. The second purpose is to place the study of children more firmly in a tradition, to show that there need not be a great separation between child-centered anthropology and the work that has preceded it. I want to show that childhood had a history in anthropology, that children have not simply been ignored or neglected, and, for British readers, that American anthropology, with its long interest in child-rearing, had to be included in any history of anthropological ideas about children. I wished to challenge the notion that only those who talked to children themselves, used them as informants, or discussed their lives in great detail could contribute to the debate about childhood as an area of study. I wanted to show that those who are interested in a variety of other topics, such as birth practices, marriage, gender, education, or economics, have much to say about children, and that their insights are crucial for a full understanding of children's lives. I believe that it is not possible to study, for example, child labor in Africa without a thorough knowledge of social life described in earlier ethnographies. Despite the enormous social, political, and economic changes seen in African societies over the last fifty years, the insights from work into social structures and familial organization are as relevant and useful to an anthropologist looking at child labor from a child's perspective as are the ideals laid down by the UNCRC, which is now more commonly used as a starting point. Similarly I would argue that anyone wishing to study children's lives or ideas about childhood in Melanesia would find as much that is of interest in the work done on gender, initiation, or personhood, but which refers only indirectly to children, as they would in the work of Margaret Mead, despite her direct interest in children and their lives.

In writing this book, I have chosen particular aspects of children's lives that had previously been studied by anthropologists. Some of these were obvious: initiation, for instance, seemed the most appropriate way to end the book, and there was an enormous amount of material to examine. Similarly discussions of unborn and newly born children, although hampered by problems of definition and distinctions between embryos, fetuses, and children, have attracted much anthropological attention and made an obvious body of literature to review. It also seemed useful to give an overview of the place of children within the anthropological tradition, looking at the various ways they have been understood. Other chapters were more problematic. Some, such as chapter 7 on sexuality, reflect my own interests, but, more broadly, the idea of the sexually innocent child is so central to Western beliefs about appropriate childhood experiences that the idea of writing a book about children's lives which failed to engage with discussions about their sexuality and sexual experiences would seem incomplete. Yet, devoting a whole chapter to the study of children's sexuality when there has been such silence on the subject within anthropology was difficult, and the chapter ended up focusing as much on sexual abuse as it did on sexual experience or sexual enjoyment. Given the cultural baggage of so many anthropologists, this may not be surprising, but it does suggest that studying childhood often reflects the prejudices of the ethnographer as much as it illuminates the lives of children themselves.

Patterns of child-rearing and the ways in which children learn to play and work have been important sources of theory and data, and it would be impossible to look at traditions of studying children without commenting on these. Other themes were less obvious. I had not planned to focus an entire chapter on discipline and abuse, and had assumed that it could be included in more general discussions of child-rearing, but in many ethnographies punishment was the sole occasion when children were visible. Children who had been unmentioned before in monographs suddenly came into focus in descriptions of the punishments inflicted on them, especially when these were seen as cruel or in any way unusual.

There are, inevitably, problems in my approach. The vast numbers of ethnographies published means that writing an all-inclusive account of everything ever written about children would be impossible, especially given that anthropology as a discipline is now over a hundred years old and the number of monographs alone published in this period runs into several thousands. I am not attempting to write a comprehensive or definitive volume about children therefore, but trying to pick out certain key topics and use them to illustrate important issues in the anthropological study of children and childhood. There are certain ways of understanding aspects of children's lives that I have not discussed, including archaeological approaches to childhood, or studies from biological anthropology, including those of primates. I have also mentioned medical anthropology only briefly and the anthropology of education in passing. These other, substantial subdisciplines of anthropology do, of course, influence studies of childhood, but in order to keep the book manageable, I have been forced to be selective. Within each chapter I have identified several themes relevant to the study of childhood and discussed particular ethnographies in the context of those themes. Some of these ethnographies are extremely famous, others are less well known, or chosen because they illustrate a point particularly well. Some are included as a result of my own partisanship and favoritism, and it will not be hard for any reader to note my obvious affection for the warmth and humanity I have always found in reading Meyer Fortes and Raymond Firth. Obviously readers of this book may well have other favorite ethnographies and will be surprised and disappointed not to see them included. My aim is that a student who knows little about the relationship between anthropology and childhood, or does not know where to begin to find out how anthropologists have studied childhood in the past, can pick up this book and come away, not with a complete knowledge of all previous ethnographic work on children, but with an understanding of where analyses of childhood and children's lives might be found in this literature, as well as suggestions for further reading. I hope that people interested in the social and cultural worlds of children will recognize that other bodies of literature can broaden and deepen their understandings of childhood. I would also hope that those anthropologists who do not profess an interest in childhood might see how their work could contribute to ways of studying childhood. I do not want to claim that the majority of anthropologists, past and present, have been secret anthropologists of childhood without knowing it, or to coerce them into a specialty with which they have no affinity, but by emphasizing the continuities and areas of overlap between childhood and other subjects of interest, it should be possible to open up a conversation between the various subdisciplines of anthropology.

A pitfall of which I was very aware while writing this book was the difficulty of making comparisons across time and place without ending up producing a modern-day version of *The Golden Bough* where cases and themes are picked up out of context and compared with other examples without any regard for the circumstances in which they occurred, or the time at which they were written. It is very easy to cherry-pick from the literature, drawing false comparisons by selective use of ethnographies. The claim that children were conceptualized one way among the Tikopia of Polynesia in the 1920s and very differently among the Nuer of southern Sudan ten years later, or that Margaret Mead found very different understandings of adolescence among people in the USA and in the south Pacific island of Samoa is liable to be extremely trite unless a deeper analysis can be uncovered. This difficulty is not helped by the convention of using the ethnographic present in monographs, which means that they appear to be written about the way the Tikopia or the Nuer live today, rather than how Raymond Firth or Edward Evans-Pritchard, with all the baggage of their age, gender, class, and background, described them seventy or eighty years ago. Despite these potential problems, it is possible, I believe, to draw useful comparisons between descriptions of children, wherever they live, whatever the background of the people writing about them, and whenever they were described.

Childhood remains an emotive subject and, especially when faced with childcare practices that seem outlandish or even dangerous to outsiders, it is easy to condemn parents as unenlightened or ignorant. Looking at how children are conceptualized within their own cultural contexts, and the consequent implications this has for the ways that they are treated, avoids value judgments and the demonization of parents elsewhere. It allows the anthropologist to recognize when behavior is occurring toward children that is not acceptable and does deserve condemnation. Looking at different forms of punishment, for example, does not simply set up a comparison between hitting children and reasoning with them, but allows an examination of wider questions about how children are dealt with, what is unacceptable in their treatment, and the point at which harsh discipline becomes improper abuse.

Chapter 1 of this book begins with a history of childhood studies within anthropology. Taking the late 19th century as its starting point, it looks at how children have been used by anthropologists in a variety of ways to better their understandings of society in general. It examines various modes of thought within anthropology, all of which explicitly use ideas about childhood to discuss other topics, such as the relationship between primitive and childish thought, the evolution of humankind, the connections between culture and personality, the importance of examining child-rearing practices, the role of women and other "lost tribes" of anthropology, and finally the move toward child-centered anthropology and the recognition of children as active informants and meaning-makers. Chapter 2 discusses the question, "what is a child?" and examines the multiple and various ways that children have been conceptualized, including the claim that childhood is a recent invention in the West. It starts with the premise that while children are usually acknowledged as being different to adults, there is no such thing as a common childhood, characterized by universally recognized developmental markers or similar attitudes. The singular category of childhood, especially when it is used to refer to a large age range, may not be meaningful elsewhere, where the period of social immaturity is characterized by different stages, each having different social responsibilities and each being classified by different terms which may, or may not, correspond to Western ideas of childhood. Children reach adulthood in a number of ways and by a variety of paths, and the divide between childhood and adulthood is complex and permeable. The Western notion that children are weak, dependent, and vulnerable is culturally specific and several other ways of understanding childhood and analyzing children's lives are presented.

Chapter 3 looks at the very beginning of childhood. Contemporary anthropologists have shown convincingly that the idea that childhood ends at 18 is a bureaucratic fiction with limited applicability outside the West. The idea that childhood may also have a beginning has been much less well explored, even though it relates to long-standing anthropological concerns about birth, conception, and personhood. This chapter draws on literature that is not usually considered when discussing childhood and looks at how, and when, children at the very beginning of their lives are socially recognized as humans.

Chapter 4 turns to children's daily lives, their immediate carers, and the kinship connections between children and their families. Kinship has been of central importance in anthropology, and it is in the context of family relations that much information on children's daily lives is to be found. Who children acknowledge as their kin, and by whom they are acknowledged, and the subsequent responsibilities that children and adults have to each other as a result of this recognition have been central to the development of theories about marriage, lineage, and gender. In this process of recognition and claiming kin, children are rarely passive, and several ethnographies have noted the active role that children play in forming and shaping their families.

The study of how children learn language, and the ways they are socialized though language, has formed a distinct sub-field in anthropology, and the importance of this in understanding children is discussed in chapter 5. The role of play, what it teaches children, and how they learn through it have also attracted a great deal of anthropological attention and notions of work and play are examined in detail. While play is sometimes seen as the epitome of childhood and childish behavior, anthropologists have shown that there is not always a clear-cut distinction between play and work, and in the lives of children outside the modern West, where the former ends and the latter begins can be hard to tell.

Another aspect of child-rearing which has received much anthropological attention is the disciplining of children. Chapter 6 examines this issue alongside recent understandings and concerns about child welfare. The spectrum of punishments meted out to children is great, ranging from very harsh beatings that have shocked observers, to the complete absence of physical punishment. This chapter relates these discussions of punishment back to ideas about the nature of childhood and how much children are perceived as knowing or understanding. The issue of abuse has been the focus for much contemporary child-centered anthropology, but the differences between what is truly abusive and what might appear unkind or cruel to outsiders is a difficult one, and so this chapter finishes with a discussion of how to differentiate between acceptable discipline and unacceptable abuse.

The ideal of a sexually innocent childhood is one of the primary sites of contestation in contemporary Western constructions of childhood. Freudian claims of a sexualized infancy come into direct conflict with the ideal of a child as innocent and unknowing about sexuality. Chapter 7 examines this issue using ethnographic accounts of children's sexual experiences and knowledge about sex to argue that this ideal is a product of a culturally specific matrix of social, economic, and cultural ideas about childhood, the body, and sexuality. Sexuality is a relatively recent topic for anthropologists, but work on this subject has shown that sexual acts do not carry the same meanings cross-culturally and that certain acts which may be sexual in one context may not be so in another. In terms of children's sexuality, these understandings are vital, even though this has been much less discussed and there are still almost no analyses of children's own views of their sexual experiences. A horror of child sexual abuse in the West has meant that it is an extremely problematic area to explore, especially for an adult, foreign anthropologist, and much of the work that has been done on children's sexual experiences has focused on abuse rather than enjoyment.

The final chapter, chapter 8, looks at the end of childhood and at initiation. Adolescence is often seen as a concept invented only in the 20th century, yet many societies have intermediate states between adulthood and childhood. Furthermore, globalization has led to the export of the idea of the teenager and increasingly a Westernized notion of adolescence has become a worldwide phenomenon. If birth has sometimes been understood as the beginning of childhood, then initiation has been seen as its end, marking the transformation from socially immature child to fully mature adult. This chapter will concentrate on what initiation rituals can tell us about the end of childhood; whether they really do mark its conclusion, or whether they are simply one process among many that continually change people and which occur throughout the life-cycle.

1

CHILDHOOD WITHIN ANTHROPOLOGY

Introduction

Looking back on the ways that children and childhood have been analyzed in anthropology inevitably reveals gaps, but it also shows that anthropologists have a long history of studying children. This chapter will give an overview of several schools of anthropological thinking that have considered children and used ideas about childhood to contribute to holistic understandings of culture. It will examine how anthropologists have studied children in the past and what insights these studies can bring to more recent analyses. Although not always explicit, ideas about children, childhood, and the processes by which a child becomes a fully socialized human being are embedded in much anthropological work and are central to understanding the nature of childhood in any given society. Work on child-rearing has also illuminated many aspects of children's lives and is vital to understanding children themselves and their wider social relationships. Having discussed these, this chapter will then turn to newer studies of childhood, based around child-centered, or child-focused, anthropology with the assumption that children themselves are the best informants about their own lives. This has been presented as a radical break with the ways that anthropologists have studied children previously, when, as Helen Schwartzman has argued, anthropologists "*used* children as a population of 'others' to facilitate the investigation of a range of topics, from developing racial typologies to investigat[ing] acculturation, but they have rarely been perceived as a legitimate topic of research in their own right" (2001:15, emphasis in original). This chapter will examine the history of studies of children and childhood within anthropology, evaluating the extent to which Schwartzman's view is correct.

Children: The First Primitives

Children have been continual motifs since the earliest days of anthropological writing, the savage and the child existing in parallel to explain social and cultural development. It was through understandings of childhood that early British anthropologists such as Edward Tylor, John Lubbock, and C. Staniland Wake examined the nature of human society and the development of humankind. Before the advent of sustained fieldwork, the child, like the savage or the primitive, stood in opposition to the rational, male world of European and North American civilization. Children were of central importance to these theorists because they provided a direct link between savagery and civilization. The child came to prominence in 19th-century anthropology because of contemporary theory that linked ontology and phylogeny: the view that the transformation of an individual was mirrored in the development of the human race, so that the development of the child from infancy to maturity could be seen to parallel the development of the human species from savagery to civilization. Tylor argued that in children, and in particular in the games that they played, there were echoes of the ways in which our human ancestors lived. "As games thus keep up the record of primitive warlike arts, so they reproduce, in what are at once sports and little children's lessons, early stages in the history of childlike tribes of mankind" (Tylor 1913[1871]:73–74). Children were, he claimed, "representatives of remotely ancient culture" (1913[1871]:73) and analyzing the child alongside the savage was a way to understand the condition of contemporary humanity.

The idea of "the savage as a representative of the childhood of the human race" (Tylor 1913[1871]:284) was elaborated by other anthropologists. John Lubbock, for example, argued that

> the close resemblance existing in ideas, language and habits, and character between savages and children, though generally admitted, has usually been disposed of in a passing sentence, and regarded rather as a curious accident than as an important truth. . . . The opinion is rapidly gaining ground among naturalists, that the development of the individual is an epitome of that of the species, a conclusion which, if fully borne out, will evidently prove most instructive. (1978[1870]:360)

The stance of both Tylor and Lubbock was explicitly evolutionary: the highest stage of evolution was the European adult male while the savage and the child were at the bottom of the hierarchy. This theory was further developed by C. Staniland Wake, who developed a complex theory of the stages of human evolution that corresponded directly to the observable stages of development in children.

> It has become a familiar idea that mankind, as a whole, may be likened to an individual man, having, like him, an infancy, a childhood, youth, and manhood. In the early ages of the world mankind was in its infancy, and from that stage it has progressed, by gradual steps, until now it may be said to have attained, in peoples of the European stock, at least, to a vigorous manhood. (1878:4–5)

In *The Evolution of Morality* Wake attempted to trace these stages in relation to understandings of morality in both children and savages. He identified five stages in moral development, which he characterized as "the selfish, the wilful, the emotional, the empirical and the rational" (1878:6). Each of these stages corresponded both to a stage in a child's development and to particular groups of people who represented different developmental states of the human race. Wake argued that the first stage of development, shown both in infants and in the Australian Aborigines, was that of "pure selfishness" because it was characterized by "an entire absence of moral principle, and a disposition which seeks its sole satisfaction in the gratification of the passions" (1878:7). The next stage of development could be seen in North American Indians and slightly older children and was characterized by an innate cruelty characteristic of a pre-civilized state of being.

The third stage of moral development was shown after the age of puberty, when the child entered the emotional period. In this his development mirrored that of the Negro, who was represented as "a creature of passion, which leads him to abandon himself to sexual excesses, and an indulgence in intoxication . . . he has a disregard for human life, and when his passions are aroused he is utterly careless about inflicting pain" (1878:8). While Wake acknowledged that education had a restraining effect on the European young man, "*subjectively*, the youthful phase of the civilised mind is exactly similar to that which is observed among the negroes as a race" (1878:8, emphasis in original). The empirical stage was shown by older youths and by the Chinese and the Hindus, who, while imaginative and clearly of a higher order than others, still had, Wake claimed, an incomplete control over their emotions and a limited grasp of morality. It was only when a child finally reached the rational stage, with a fully formed moral character, that he became an adult. Similarly, in Wake's view, it was only when the races had reached rationality, characterized as being when "imagination comes to be controlled by the reflective or regulative faculty; and when reason has established its influence" (1878:6), that they were fully civilized. This stage was attained, of course, only by members of Northern European and American societies, and only by men.

In 1906 the first monograph specifically on childhood was written by Dudley Kidd, called *Savage Childhood: A Study of Kafir Children*, which examined aspects of black South African children's lives. Deeply imbued with racist attitudes, Kidd found in "kafir" children a charm and interest that he claimed had vanished from adults, even though he also saw them as lagging far behind European children in intellectual and moral development. Yet Kidd did acknowledge the importance of studying children's lives, claiming that "childhood, so far from being beneath our notice, is the most important, instructive, and interesting period in the life of a savage" (1906:viii). It is possible to dismiss such comments, along with the views of Tylor, Lubbock, or Wake, as rather unpleasant anthropological curiosities. Indeed Laurence Hirschfeld has suggested that because of the offensive early parallels drawn between savages and children, anthropologists have been reluctant to look at childhood for fear of resurrecting these embarrassing antecedents.

> Like Sartre's anti-Semite, who, as a result of a disagreeable encounter with a Jewish tailor, despised Jews but not tailors, anthropologists uncomfortable with their predecessors' awkward comparisons of children's and primitive thought did not end up abandoning the study of native populations, only children. (2002:613)

It goes without saying that the ideas of Tylor, Lubbock, and Wake are outdated and discredited, despite C. R. Hallpike's recent (1979) revival of some of these long-dead debates to draw parallels between the mentality of "primitive" people and children. What is interesting, however, is not so much the prejudices of the time, as the importance placed on children in understanding humanity in general. Without wishing to rehabilitate the conclusions of these authors, ideas about the nature of children were central to the development of early anthropology. Before fieldwork, children were the only observable "others"; they were the savages at home, and as such they could be studied and observed and their development charted and noted. Children enabled anthropologists to write in a way that familiarized the strange and that domesticated ideas about savages.

In the USA such explicit evolutionary frameworks were rejected, and children had a much more prominent role to play in the development of anthropology, as sources of data rather than as providing close-at-hand parallels to exotic primitives. Franz Boas in particular challenged the idea that race was linked, in a hierarchical manner, to language and culture. He criticized the idea of an evolutionist scale with "the savage," represented by children and primitives, at one end and civilization, evidenced in European culture, at the other. He also rejected any idea of racial descent being linked to perceived biological superiority, claiming that "the old idea of absolute stability of human types must, however, evidently be given up, and with it the belief of the hereditary superiority of certain types over others" (1974[1911]:218). In "The Instability of Human Types" (1974[1911]), he used studies of child development to chart the environmental impact on human physiology among immigrants to America. By comparing parents and children of Eastern and Southern European descent, and the observable differences between their children born in Europe and those born in their new homeland, he demonstrated how phenotypes such as face shape changed. This, Boas (1916) suggested, meant that the most important differences between people were not biological or racial in origin but environmental. Boas argued that the changes and adaptations in immigrants could be best noted in children and their bodies, as it was during childhood that the most important physiological changes took place.

> Thus at the time of birth the bulk of the body and stature are very small, and increase with great rapidity until about the fourteenth year in girls, and the sixteenth year in boys. On the other hand, the size of the head increases rapidly only for one or two years; and from this time on the increment is, comparatively speaking, slight. Similar conditions prevail in regard to the growth of the face, which grows rapidly for a few years only, and later on increases, comparatively speaking, slowly. . . .
>
> It is a well-known fact that the central nervous system continues to develop in structure longer perhaps than any other part of the body, and it may therefore be inferred that it will be apt to show the most far-reaching influences of environment.
>
> It follows from this consideration that social and geographical environment must have an influence upon the form of the body of the adult, and upon the development of his central nervous system. (1974[1911]:215)

Children, in this understanding, are not simply primitives by another name and the stages of their development are not analogous to any sort of racial typographies. Instead they are valid sources of data and one of the ways in which the impact of environmental factors can be seen in human populations. Child development was thus an integral part of US anthropology from the beginning, a point emphasized in LeVine and New's recent (2008) reader on child development and anthropology, in which Boas's 1911 article is the first in the collection. Boas's interest in children, and young people, also had a profound influence on one of his most famous students, Margaret Mead, who became such a prominent figure in the anthropological study of childhood, and to whom we now turn.

Culture and Personality

It was with Boas's encouragement that Margaret Mead began her famous studies of Samoa and the South Pacific. Like Boas, she viewed the differences between various peoples as cultural rather than biological. In particular she focused her attention on children and young people, looking at how they were brought up, and the effects that their upbringing had on their adult personality and behavior. Mead's thesis was a direct challenge to psychologists such as G. Stanley Hall, who had argued in his influential 1904 book, *Adolescence: Its Psychology, and Its Relations to Anthropology, Sex, Crime, Religion and Education*, that adolescence was a transitional process in the life-cycle between childhood and adulthood, characterized by particular traits and behaviors brought on by the biological changes at puberty. Most famously Hall described adolescence as a time of storm and stress, when young people were in the grip of powerful biological changes they could not control. He wrote that "every step of the upward way is strewn with wreckage of body, mind, and morals. There is not only arrest, but perversion, at every stage, and hoodlumism, juvenile crime, and secret vice" (Hall 1904:xiv). Although he acknowledged that adolescence could be a time of creativity, and saw it as crucial to the later development of personality, he also saw it as a time of instability and extremes.

Mead set out for Samoa with the explicit aim of disproving this universal, biological determinism. In *Coming of Age in Samoa* (1971[1928]) she analyzed the daily lives of Samoan girls from infancy through early childhood until adolescence. She rejected the idea that adolescence was necessarily a stressful and disruptive experience for both the child and the society and claimed that behavior in adolescence was caused by cultural conditioning rather than biological changes. Based on close observation and discussion with young women and girls in Samoa, Mead found none of the tensions inherent in the lives of American adolescents. She pointed to two factors that caused adolescence to be so stressful in the USA, and which created tensions between society and its young people: the large variety of choices in religious and moral matters in the USA and the repressive attitudes to sex and bodily functions. In contrast she found that adolescence in Samoa was not characterized by stress and strain because of the different cultural expectations about appropriate behavior for children and the ways that these notions of appropriateness were transferred to children. From an early age, children were taught to be demure, courteous, quiet, hard-working, loyal to their families, and obedient. The expectation that children would conform to these norms was made easier by the lack of choice. The society was homogeneous, believing in one religion and attending one church. There were no alternative belief systems or models that children could follow and rebellion was not an option. Boys and girls avoided each other when very young, playing only with members of their own sex. As they grew older they started to come together again until girls began to take lovers. As long as these lovers were within certain social groups (i.e., not family members), these sexual affairs were tolerated or ignored.

Mead subsequently came in for a great deal of criticism concerning both her methodology and her interpretation, but *Coming of Age in Samoa* placed children on the anthropological agenda and Mead remains one of the first anthropologists to take children, as children, seriously. She was also one of the most significant members, along with Edward Sapir and Ruth Benedict, of the Culture and Personality school of anthropology, which was concerned with how the child became a cultural being. Sapir (1949) in particular argued that anthropologists should study child development in order to understand the relationships between the individual parts of a culture and the whole. This insight was taken up by Ruth Benedict, who stressed the necessity of anthropologists engaging with psychology, and famously wrote that "cultures . . . are individual psychology thrown large upon the screen, given gigantic proportions and a long time span" (1932:24). She also emphasized the importance of understanding the entire life-cycle and the ways in which children became adults, as well as the interdependence between child and adult. In "Continuities and Discontinuities in Cultural Conditioning" (1938) she identified a paradox at the heart of American society, in which the features favored and promoted in boys' childhoods – irresponsibility, submission, and sexual ignorance – were the very ones that had to be inverted and suppressed when a boy grew up and his role was transformed from son to father and he had to take on the attributes of responsibility, dominance, and virility. Children were encouraged to act in particular ways until they reached adulthood, when they were explicitly discouraged from displaying any of these behaviors. Benedict claimed that this change of role might well be a universal "fact of life," but how this change was managed varied greatly cross-culturally and there was nothing natural about particular paths to maturity. By using ethnographic evidence from non-Western societies, she argued that children outside Europe and North America had to undergo much less dramatic discontinuities in their cultural conditioning, and that through institutions such as age-sets and initiation into secret knowledge, people could pass from role to role without the stress and strain of Western adolescence.

For Mead, Benedict, and their colleagues, one of the important questions for anthropology was how an infant became a cultural being and what impact early childhood experiences had on adult personality, as well as on the collective culture of a society. Developing the work of psychoanalyst Abram Kardiner and the anthropologist Ralph Linton, Cora Du Bois conducted fieldwork on the Indonesian island of Alor between 1937 and 1939, which she published as *The People of Alor* (1944). Kardiner and Linton had proposed a specific link between culture and personality, arguing that any given culture had a "basic personality," which Kardiner defined as "that personality configuration which is shared by the bulk of the society's members as a result of the early experiences which they have in common. It does not correspond to the total personality of the individual but rather to the projective systems or, in different phraseology, the value-attitude systems, which are basic to the individual's personality configuration" (1945:viii). Studying the early experiences of children allowed anthropologists to look at the individual members of a society and to compare shared characteristics and traits in order to propose a "basic personality" for each culture. Du Bois modified this idea with her concept of the "modal personality," which, while based on an assumption of a "physic unity of mankind" (1944:2), allowed for individual variations within a culture. She understood the infant as a blank slate on which the effects of aspects of childcare would have observable effects. She argued that each culture promoted the development of particular personality types which would occur most frequently within that culture and claimed that the most common personality structure in any society was "the product of the interplay of fundamental physiologically and neurologically determined tendencies and experiences common to all human beings acted upon by the cultural milieu which denies, directs and gratifies these ends very differently in different societies" (1944:3). Basing her work heavily on Freudian psychoanalytical theory, Du Bois used life histories, Rorschach blot tests, children's drawings, and participant-observation in order to arrive at a particular personality type for the Alor. She concluded that Alorese were insecure and fearful, had low self-esteem, and suffered from greed, dislike of the parental role, and negative feelings about human relationships. This could be traced back to their earliest experiences, when the discipline of children was inconsistent, veering between harsh and indulgent, and the fact that mothers returned to work in the fields a couple of weeks after giving birth, leaving the child in the care of others, thereby causing him or her frustration and dissatisfaction.

Since its heyday the Culture and Personality school has come in for much criticism. It has been attacked for using children to discuss adults rather than in their own right, for isolating specific practices and looking for their long-term impact while ignoring others, for implying that adults are no more than the sum of their earliest childhood experiences, and for suggesting that there can be such a thing as a national character, which, following Du Bois, was understood as a result of early childhood experience and was unrelated to later developments or intervening events (Harkness and Super 1983:222). National character studies in particular, based on Du Bois's modal personality type, sometimes carried out by those who had not done fieldwork, were condemned as crude, unhelpful, and of limited interest in understanding children, adults, or social institutions. Despite the criticisms, however, the Culture and Personality school remains a pioneering, if flawed, way of understanding children's lives and ideas about childhood. For all the problems inherent in her work, Margaret Mead "broke the stranglehold [that] biology and genetics held on studies of child development" (Langness 1975:98) and Coming of Age in Samoa remains in print to this day. The Culture and Personality school envisaged an interdisciplinary anthropology that drew upon, but also challenged, the universalist premises of developmental psychology. Yet psychology itself has changed, and as Robert LeVine has argued, child psychologists have re-evaluated their own theories and understandings throughout the 20th and into the 21st centuries, leaving the theories of the Culture and Personality school open to further criticism.

Anthropologists are at least partly dependent on developmental knowledge from other disciplines in their assumptions about how children experience their environments – including the environmental features to which they are sensitive and their age-related concepts for understanding – and they have often turned to psychology and psychiatry for guidance in making these assumptions plausible. For much of the 20th century, however, this guidance was unreliable, as one developmental theory followed another into the trash heap of history. (LeVine 2007:249)

Cross-Cultural Studies of Child-Rearing

Although Margaret Mead's influence declined in American anthropology in the 1950s, the attempts to integrate psychology and anthropology continued, and the work of John Whiting and others developed out of the Culture and Personality school and focused on particular aspects of child-rearing and cross-cultural child development. After fieldwork in Papua New Guinea, John Whiting turned his attention to cross-cultural research, focusing his anthropology on broader patterns of human behavior, and their links to childhood experiences. Using material from the Human Relations Area Files (HRAF), the immense database of ethnographic information based at Yale University and set up in 1949 by George Murdock as a way of making statistical cross-cultural comparisons, Whiting and his collaborators set out to undertake systematic analyses of childhood experiences and the effects that they had on adult society. He later recalled: "I decided to carry out a cross-cultural study to explore the basic assumption of Freudian theory that childhood experiences are a powerful force in shaping adult personality and behavior" (1994:24).

Child Training and Personality, published in 1953, attempted to apply Freudian theories about the stages of a child's psychosexual development to ethnographic data. Using information from 75 societies, Whiting and his co-researcher Irvin Child focused on three particular aspects: weaning from the breast, toilet training, and sex training – stages which Freud had labeled oral, anal, and phallic, and which, he claimed, always occurred in that order. In looking at the ethnographic evidence, however, Whiting and Child found that these were not salient variables in many societies, and while all societies dealt with issues of weaning, toilet training, or the management of sex, these stages did not always occur in the order Freud had suggested and there was evidence from many societies that toilet training preceded weaning (Whiting and Child 1953). Furthermore, in many cases, weaning from the breast or toilet training were regarded as relatively unimportant while "weaning from the back" (when a child was no longer carried by the mother or caregiver) and the management of aggression were considered greater issues in the socialization of children. Whiting and Child concluded that parents in most cultures were more concerned with interpersonal relations than they were with bodily functions. They dropped the idea of temporal stages in favor of behavior systems, which they defined as "oral, anal, genital, training for independence and for the control of aggression" (Whiting 1994:24). They found correlations between each of these behavior systems and other factors such as the degree of initial indulgence, the age at onset of socialization, the severity of socialization, and the techniques of punishment used by parents (Whiting 1977:32). Whiting, however, called these results only a "crude beginning" (1977:32) and spent the next four decades studying child-rearing and socialization in as scientific, and comparative, a way as possible. Throughout his work, Whiting was concerned with testing specific hypotheses about the links between particular aspects of social life: for example, he looked at how a combination of practices such as a boy sleeping exclusively with his mother and a taboo on sexual relations between parents for a substantial period after birth might lead to a boy's strong identification with his mother and a hostility toward his father; an Oedipal situation which could only be resolved by elaborate rituals at puberty such as circumcision (Whiting et al. 1958).

One of the most important projects initiated by Whiting and his wife Beatrice was the Six Cultures study (Whiting 1963). Rather than relying on other people's data, Whiting and his collaborators set out to compare six different cultures using the same methods, and to look at the same problems of child-rearing and socialization. Their fieldwork sites were Japan, the Philippines, North India, Mexico, Kenya, and New England. In each instance a male and female ethnographer simultaneously went to each community and carried out systematic observation and data collection, based on instructions from a single field manual, on children and child-rearing behavior in each community. The Six Cultures study allowed for certain conclusions to be drawn about the interplay between cultural variations in child-rearing, the later personality of the child, and wider aspects of society. One of the most important of these conclusions was the level of complexity of the society, and the Six Cultures surveys showed that children in complex societies tended to be less nurturant and more egotistical than those in simple societies. They found that girls, in all six cultures, were more nurturant than boys and that children of nuclear families were generally low on aggression and high on sociable interaction, while the opposite was true for children of polygamous households (Whiting 1977). Perhaps the most important aspect of the Six Cultures study was, as pointed out by Robert LeVine (one of Whiting's collaborators, who worked among the Gusii in Kenya, see below), the fact that it introduced the "systematic naturalistic observation of children – that is, [the] repeated and aggregated observations of children in their routine 'behavior settings' as a method for recording the interactions of children with their environments in diverse cultures" (2007:253). The Six Cultures study provides a wealth of detail about children's lives, how they were treated, and their place in the life-cycle. There were problems with the implementation of some of the psychological tests, as both Whiting (1977) and LeVine (2007) point out, and some of the methods were later discounted as unreliable. However, the data from this project are still used and developed (see, for instance, Whiting and Edwards 1988) and it has remained one of the most comprehensive studies of child development within anthropology.

The work of John Whiting and his co-researchers has been extremely influential in North American anthropology. It has proved that there is nothing natural, or universal, about the ways in which young children act and that their lives are defined as much by their culture and environment as by biology. Much of the work influenced by Whiting has been explicitly comparative, showing how childcare differs across societies, how children are socialized through these practices into full membership of the group, and how these practices are optimally developed to ensure the continuation of certain behaviors and belief systems. It has also been longitudinal, looking at infants within the life-cycle and analyzing the long-term effects of caregivers' behavior. One of the pioneers of this type of work was William Caudill, who first conceived of a longitudinal, comparative study of infant care and child-rearing in the USA and Japan. His study insisted on the importance of in-depth participant-observation and on the symbiosis of anthropology and psychology. Caudill was concerned with the cultural goals of parenting above and beyond survival: what parents wanted their children to be like, and how they achieved this. Caudill and his co-researchers observed women in both Japan and America, looking at the care they gave to their babies, the ways they interacted with them, and the effects this had on the infants' behavior.

He examined which behaviors were valued in a society, which were discouraged, and how mothers communicated this. He hypothesized that American parents would value independence-related behavior more than Japanese parents, who emphasized interdependence and the importance of harmonious social relationships. His observations and statistical analysis confirmed this, and he found that American children were more active, more vocal, independent, and able to manipulate their social and physical environment, while Japanese children were quieter, displayed fewer extremes of emotion, but were more socially skilled (Caudill and Weinstein 1969; Caudill and Schooler 1973). Self-reliance and independence were not goals of Japanese child-rearing and the promotion of the individual was valued less than the collective. As Robert LeVine concludes of these studies:

> The importance of these findings does not depend on an assumption that the child behavior patterns observed are fixed psychological dispositions that will maintain themselves regardless of environmental support. Rather, the findings indicate that the direction of child development, and the behavioral contexts of early experience, vary by culture according to adult standards of conduct. They also show that children of different cultures acquire different interpersonal skills and strategies, differing rules for emotional expression, and differing standards by which to judge their own behavior. (2003:202–203)

Robert LeVine has analyzed child-rearing practices and child socialization extensively in the decades since he worked with John Whiting as one of the Six Cultures researchers and he remains at the forefront of research on children and the interface between anthropology and psychology. For him, studying child development cross-culturally is central to studying children within anthropology, and such work forms the backbone of an anthropology of childhood. He claims that "socialization research is not a complete 'anthropology of childhood,' though it is an indispensable part of one and has laid the basis for the other parts by describing the environments of children throughout the world" (2003:5). His work has illuminated the differences between child-rearing practices cross-culturally and shown how these are adaptive processes which are rational within their own situations (even if parents do not or cannot articulate why they act as they do) and which enable children to grow up effectively, understanding the norms of their society. From the earliest days of a child's life, LeVine and his collaborators have shown the impact of cultural beliefs

on child-rearing and looked at the interplay between the cultural, the biological, and the environmental. In 1977 LeVine identified three universal
goals of child-rearing which parents strove to fulfill:

1. The physical survival and health of the child, including (implicitly) the
    normal development of his reproductive capacity during puberty.
2. The development of the child's behavioral capacity for economic self-
    maintenance in maturity.
3. The development of the child's behavioral capacities for maximizing
    other cultural values – e.g., morality, prestige, wealth, religious piety,
    intellectual achievement, personal satisfaction, self realization – as for-
    mulated and symbolically elaborated in culturally distinctive beliefs,
    norms, and ideologies. (1977:20)

LeVine went on to argue that there is a "natural hierarchy" among these
goals, so that goal one is the most fundamental priority because it is a
prerequisite of the other two goals. In situations where parents are not
assured of the survival of their children, they may well postpone the other
two goals until the first is secured. In other instances, such as modern
America, or Europe, the survival of children is taken as implicit, so parents are more likely to devote time and energy to the second and third
goals. Parental child-rearing and childcare are necessarily adaptive to the
environment. In African societies, where infant mortality is high, and the
early years of life the most dangerous, mothers are likely to keep their
children in very close contact with them, carrying them everywhere, and
breast-feeding them for up to two years. They will feed them on demand,
but generally do not treat them as emotionally responsive individuals they
should make eye contact with or talk to, or about whose behavioral development they should be concerned (LeVine 1977). It is not that they are
uninterested in their long-term development, or have not made explicit
plans for events later on in life such as betrothal or initiation, but they
are less concerned with shaping their behavior at this point.

By contrasting Gusii mothers in Kenya and middle-class mothers in the
USA, where he and his colleagues have carried out long-term observa-
tional research, LeVine is able to analyze two fundamentally different
models of child-rearing and childcare, which, although they have the same
ultimate aim of socializing the next generation, challenge ideas about the
universal needs of infants. He terms the two models of development
the pediatric, practiced by the Gusii, and the pedagogic, undertaken
by Americans, viewing the first as being concerned with protection and

survival in the early years and the second as more concerned with learning and behavioral competencies (LeVine et al. 1994:249). There are very different parental strategies at work here and very different conceptualizations of the relationship between the child and the parent. LeVine describes this, in the African case, as parents expecting to be "united with their children in a long-run relationship of 'serial reciprocity' " (2003:92). In this model, the care given to infants by parents is reciprocated by children working on the family land and supporting their parents in their old age. Obedience is a crucial factor in this, the teaching of which to the growing infant is one of the main goals of child-rearing. A child must learn to be quiet, make few demands, and must not be allowed to disrupt the hierarchical basis of society. Gusii mothers explicitly discourage praise as they think it would make even a compliant child conceited and disobedient and therefore a threat to the social order. American mothers have no such expectations and they praise their children, engage in protoconversations with them, and encourage them to walk and talk early (LeVine et al. 1994). LeVine's work clearly shows that infant care is not simply about ensuring that a young child's basic needs for food or shelter are met, but is part of much larger systems of cultural practice which ensure that, even from the earliest days of a child's life, he or she is socialized and enculturated into the social values of the society.

This emphasis on infant enculturation and the plasticity of human behavior has also been used to challenge the universalist tendencies of developmental psychology, which has insisted on, for example, optimal forms of attachment between infant and mother (or maternal caregiver), regardless of cultural background (Levine and Norman 2001). Attachment theory, as first formulated by John Bowlby, suggested that "it is essential for mental health . . . that an infant and young child should experience a warm, intimate, and continuous relationship with his mother (or permanent mother-substitute – one person who steadily 'mothers' him) in which both find satisfaction and enjoyment" (1953:13). Bowlby went on to conclude that a baby would become distressed and resist separation from his or her mother, and that this was a biologically adaptive, species-wide, mechanism that had evolved to protect vulnerable young humans by ensuring that mother and infant remained in close proximity.

Detailed studies by anthropologists have challenged these findings and shown enormous variations in ideas about attachment and the ways in which mothers promote certain values, such as independence, in their children. LeVine and Norman (2001) have argued that data from

Germany have shown that self-reliance and learning to play by themselves are valued cultural attributes of babies and that German mothers are not always responsive to their child's cries or demands for attention and are less likely than American mothers to pick up a crying child simply because he or she wants attention. Infants would therefore be seen as insecurely attached compared to their American counterparts, whose mothers are more responsive to their children and do not promote a tolerance of being left alone. LeVine and Norman conclude that relying too heavily on Bowlby's theory of attachment, or taking American patterns as the universal norm, might lead to some dubious conclusions which suggest

> the secure attachment pattern found in the majority of American one-year-olds is adaptive for all humans and that other patterns jeopardize the child's mental health. From this perspective, the findings from German samples in which a majority of infants are classified as insecurely attached could be interpreted as indicating that the majority of German parents are raising emotionally disturbed children. Attachment researchers have understandably refrained from that conclusion, but without offering a satisfactory alternative explanation of the results. (2001:101–102)

This work has also been developed in other very different settings. In his extensive work with Native American Navajo infants, James Chisholm has looked at whether their mothers' use of the cradleboard had any noticeable long-lasting impact on a child's attachment. (A cradleboard is the wooden board on which the Navajo strapped their babies. They were carried by the mother while she traveled or was working and were generally used from birth until the child could walk.) His hypothesis was that the cradleboard might be a source of "perturbation" for children, interfering with their attachments to their mothers by reducing their arousal and activity levels, which would lead to less interaction with their mothers. According to Bowlby, this would have long-lasting effects on the child's later behavior. Chisholm found, however, that while a cradleboard did reduce a child's activity and the mother's responsiveness, the effects were transitory. After a session on the cradleboard, mothers would be particularly responsive to their children and there would follow a very intense period of interaction. Chisholm concluded that infant behavior was more changeable and malleable than Bowlby's theories would allow, and that, furthermore, the differences in the ways that infants responded constituted an adaptive process which showed "an evolutionary trend toward increased plasticity" (1983:216).

Building upon this work on infant socialization, other anthropologists have examined a variety of infant behaviors, and caregiver responses, looking at the impact of interactions between environmental, biological, and cultural factors (e.g., Hewlett and Lamb 2005). Some of the most striking work has been done on crying patterns in infants. It is widely assumed in the West that all young children cry for hours, sometimes without cause, and that there is nothing that parents can do to assuage this crying. This crying is even pathologized and described as "colic," although in other settings such a label does not exist (Small 1998). Cross-cultural studies have shown that this behavior is far from universal, and several anthropologists and pediatricians have noted significant variations in the intensity, amount, and even time of crying in infants, so that while all babies do cry, the patterns of crying are very different. Some of the most detailed work on this has been carried out among Kalahari !Kung babies in sub-Saharan Africa in comparison to infants in Western societies such as America or Holland. There appears to be a crying curve, found in both Western and !Kung babies, in which the crying reaches a peak at the end of the second month and gradually decreases by the age of 12 weeks (Barr 1990). However, within this general pattern, there are observable differences: !Kung babies cry with much less intensity and for shorter periods than do American or Dutch babies (Konner 1976; Barr 1990; Barr et al. 1991).

One explanation for these differences is the very different patterns of caregiving in a child's earliest years. Melvin Konner describes the earliest cultural life of a !Kung infant, noting the sacrosanct nature of the mother/child bond, and the fact that the baby stays in close physical contact with the mother at all times. Infants live in a sling on the mother's hip, where they manage their own feeding by sucking at the breast when they are hungry. They are also allowed a great deal of room to wriggle and move around and their mothers actively encourage them to move at an early age, so that generally !Kung babies have more advanced motor skills than their Western counterparts (Konner 1972, 1976). Similarly studies of Korean infants have shown that they are left alone much less than American babies and show significant differences in crying patterns, with no crying peak at two months and less evening crying. Meredith Small cites one study in which Korean babies at one month were left alone for only 8.3% of their time, while American infants at the same age spent 67.5% of their time on their own. Furthermore, parents in America deliberately ignored infants in 46% of crying episodes (Small 1998:154).

Longitudinal studies have shown how practices of childcare have changed. Looking back at 30 years' work on infant care in the Indian city of Bhubaneshwar, Susan Seymour (1999) has described how patterns of infant care have altered in response to changes in social and economic conditions. She describes how, when first doing fieldwork, she found that among upper- and middle-status Indian families, children were raised in a way to encourage interdependence and submission to authority. Children had multiple caregivers to meet their emotional and physical needs and intense dyadic relationships between mothers and infants were discouraged. Children were socialized "to identify with the family as a whole and to put the interests of that collective unit ahead of their individual interests" (1999:268). They were discouraged from thinking of themselves as individuals, and for the first year of their lives they were referred to by a kin name rather than a personal one. Over time, as women have become more independent and educated, children are less likely to live in the multi-generational, hierarchical, and interdependent families into which their mothers and grandmothers were born. Seymour notes that a shift has taken place in attitudes and that the idea of putting the collective before oneself is being challenged. Young women are more likely to challenge tyrannical mothers-in-law and not all family members fulfill their duties to parents and siblings. As families become smaller and there are fewer caregivers available to look after children, mothers, with some help from fathers, have taken on more childcare. Thanks to their education, they are also more likely to apply different models of education to children, tending more toward the pedagogical model, where children must be taught, talked to, and stimulated, rather than the pediatric, where they are simply looked after.

Children in British Anthropology

The study of children in British anthropology has followed a different trajectory to that in North America, and for many years it was possible to talk about two distinct, and sometimes antagonistic, traditions. The role of psychology, so central to American anthropology, never had the same prominence in the UK, nor did cross-cultural, comparative surveys. While children had first been used as a way of understanding the primitive by Edward Tylor and others, such ideas were soon discredited by first-hand study. Boas had shown in the USA that ideas about evolutionist racial hierarchies could not stand up to data brought back from fieldwork, and within British anthropology also, studies had changed from broad generalizations based on second-hand sources to in-depth, ethnographic studies, supported by sustained fieldwork and participant-observation. Holistic studies of small-scale societies such as those pioneered by Bronislaw Malinowski (1922) described and acknowledged children's role in the family and detailed particular aspects of their lives such as their role in kinship or political systems.

It was Malinowski's insistence on the importance of describing all aspects of life which meant that in the works of his followers there are descriptions of children's lives, the relationships between parents and child, and accounts of the ways in which childhood is conceptualized. Raymond Firth's work on the Tikopia of Polynesia (1936) is particularly rich in this regard and children are described and discussed in some detail. Similarly, in the work of Audrey Richards (1956), another student of Malinowski, issues such as the end of childhood and children's place in society are analyzed and children are an important element in her ethnography. By the late 1940s the study of relationships between children and adults was central to Meyer Fortes's work, and over a third of *The Web of Kinship among the Tallensi* (1949) is devoted to a study of parent/child relationships and their mutual dependence and ambiguities, among the Tallensi of northern Ghana. In his historical survey of children in ethnography Robert LeVine comments:

> These works by a generation of anthropologists influenced directly by Malinowski leave no doubt that by the 1930s childhood was an established topic of ethnographic description, often in the context of kinship or ritual, sometimes in relation to education or socialization, only occasionally with psychological interpretations. Childhood was part of their anthropology, not a topic borrowed from developmental psychology or other disciplines (although Richards and Fortes knew the child development literature of their time). (2007:251)

Generally, however, developmental psychology played a much lesser role in British ethnographers' views of children. Malinowski had looked to Freudianism to understand the psychology of non-Western peoples and found difficulties in applying ideas such as the Oedipus complex to cultures that had very different ideas about kinship. Meyer Fortes (1974) also, a psychologist turned anthropologist, brought the insights from his former discipline to his studies of parent/child relationships, but as Richards (1970) pointed out, British anthropologists tended to see certain practices, be they weaning or initiation, as having normative functions. In general, she argued, most British anthropologists, especially in the period when A. R. Radcliffe-Brown's theories of structural functionalism dominated, were more concerned with social institutions such as age-sets or kinship systems than with psychological interpretations of child-rearing or how children became adults. She commented on the decline in interest among British anthropologists in the subject of child socialization since the 1930s, when many had tackled the subject under headings such as education or child-rearing. She suggested this was due to a deep-seated suspicion shown by many British social anthropologists toward psychology and she encouraged anthropologists who wished to study children to learn from developmental psychology. She wrote that "an institutional study of socialization is a field of inquiries which I believe the social anthropologist is particularly fitted to carry out. Child-rearing practices properly belong to it, but lack of comparative knowledge of child growth and development would probably hamper the ordinary field ethnographer. He or she would require specialist training or alternatively the help of a child psychologist" (1970:9).

Despite the early interest by British anthropologists in children's lives, by the 1970s studies involving children were relatively uncommon (there were, of course, exceptions, such as Goody and Goody 1967 or Read 1968). The rejection of psychology, and the influence in the 1960s of Lévi-Strauss and structuralism, shifted the emphasis away from detailed studies of communities in which children were a visible, if marginalized, part. Furthermore, the large-scale, cross-cultural comparative work that had revealed many aspects of children's lives in American anthropology was treated with suspicion and some disdain amongst certain British anthropologists. The work of George Murdock, starting with *Social Structure* (1949) and continuing on into the Human Relations Area Files, was a source of particular ire. E. E. Evans-Pritchard wrote of Murdock's cross-cultural comparative approach:

> Its arid classifications and terminological definitions seem to me to be of very limited value . . . it is full of contradictions and of assertions and suppositions without supporting evidence. The statistical survey covering two hundred and fifty societies displays in addition to . . . poor sampling, crude itemization, arbitrary and inadequate criteria of classification . . . an almost unbelievably uncritical use of sources. For the most part only one authority is used for each people, and good, bad and indifferent authorities – most conspicuously only in English – are all lumped together

as though they are of equal value as sources; and the same source is used, without any attempt to estimate its value, for several peoples. (1965:26)

Edmund Leach dismissed the Human Relations Area Files as "tabulated nonsense" (1964:299) and Peter Rivière, as chairman of the UK Social Science Research Council's Social Anthropology Committee in the early 1970s, was instrumental in blocking an application for funding from a British university to buy data sets from the HRAF (Rivière, personal communication, October 20, 2007). It was not until January 2007 that Oxford University's Bodleian library acquired access for its readers to the HRAF.

In 1973 there came a limited revival of interest in ideas about children in the UK and Charlotte Hardman published a ground-breaking article in which she claimed that children's lives were as worthy of study as any other section of society, and, furthermore, that a focus on children could reveal aspects of social life not found in most conventional ethnographies. She posed the question as to whether there could be a meaningful anthropology of childhood and concluded that there could, basing her argument on two sources. Firstly, she was inspired by a quote from Iona and Peter Opie, the folklorists who had collected children's rhymes and games throughout Great Britain and who wrote:

> And the folklorist and anthropologist can, without travelling a mile from his door, examine a thriving unselfconscious culture (the word "culture" is used here deliberately) which is unnoticed by the sophisticated world, and quite as little affected by it, as the culture of some dwindling aboriginal tribe living out its helpless existence in the hinterland of a native reserve. ... The worldwide fraternity of children is the greatest of savage tribes, and the only one which shows no sign of dying out. (1977[1959]:1–2)

Hardman proposed that children, as the Opies had suggested, existed within a separate subculture, and had their own ways of thinking, their own worldviews, and their own cultural understandings in the form of games and rhymes. Secondly, she drew heavily on the newly emerging anthropology of women and, in particular, Edwin Ardener's concept of "muted voices" (1975). Following Ardener's work, she concluded that, like women, children did not have access to power and had to use the language of patriarchy, and were consequently dismissed as incomplete or incompetent adults rather than being looked at in their own terms or as possessing different, but equally valid, competencies.

By drawing attention to the importance of children's views, Hardman staked a claim to childhood and children's worlds as valid subjects for ethnographic research. She also made the point, which has been taken as axiomatic by later anthropologists, that "children [are] people to be studied in their own right" (1973:87). She viewed children as having their own autonomous subcultures that existed outside of, and sometimes in opposition to, adult society and which positioned children as a new "undiscovered and pristine tribe" that had to be uncovered and documented. She argued that "if we conceive of society as a group of intertwining, overlapping circles, which as a whole, form a stock of beliefs, values, social interaction, then children . . . may be said to constitute one conceptual area, one segment of this stock. The children will move in and out of this segment into another, but others take their place. The segment still remains' (1973:87).

Such a stance was also an explicit rejection of the work on children pioneered in the previous decades by the Whitings, Caudill, or LeVine. Hardman uses theorists from psychology, such as Jean Piaget or Lev Vygotsky, but does not cite any work from American anthropology, except for Margaret Mead, who merits only the briefest of critical mentions. Hardman claims that

> those anthropological fields concerned with children [such as Culture and Personality or studies of socialization] . . . view them, to a greater or lesser extent, as passive objects, as helpless spectators in a pressing environment which affects and produces their every behaviour. They see the child as continually assimilating, learning and responding to the adult, having little autonomy, contributing nothing to social values or behaviour except the latent outpourings of earlier acquired experiences. (1973:87)

In the new anthropology of childhood proposed by Hardman, children were seen as the best informants about their own lives as well as the creators of a complete culture that they passed onto other children without adult intervention.

The Gendered Child

Hardman's use of Ardener's concept of "muted voices" drew attention to the ways in which women and children could be similarly constructed and understood by anthropologists, and how the study of women's worlds, and gender relations, could inform understandings of childhood and children's experiences. The type of anthropological interest in children proposed by Hardman can be seen as being closely related to the challenges by feminist anthropologists in the late 1960s and 1970s who argued for the necessity of including women in ethnographic descriptions and anthropological theory (Reiter 1975). Children were a part of this, but the focus on family relationships, and particularly motherhood, left studies of children themselves sidelined, or, more usually in anthropology and sociology, delegated to psychologists and psychoanalysts, who focused most explicitly on the gendered child. Psychologist Nancy Chodorow (1978), who had studied under John and Beatrice Whiting, looked at how the relationship between mother and daughter taught girls to grow up to aspire to become mothers themselves. She claimed that the role of gender was crucial in studying children, and she examined this difference in gender roles as being shaped by patterns of human child-rearing. Women, she argued, always took on the care of children, and even when a mother was absent, this work was done by stepmothers, grandparents, aunts, or paid female help. Both infant boys and girls were overwhelmingly dependent on these female caregivers and identified strongly with them, showing anxiety when they were separated from them, but as they got older, they began to break away from this primary caregiver. For boys this process involved devaluing the feminine and identifying with the independence and autonomy of their fathers, while girls never lost their dependency, according to Chodorow, and did not develop a strong sense of separateness or boundaries. After they reached maturity, this manifested itself in a desire for motherhood. Chodorow concluded that "growing girls come to define and experience themselves as continuous with others; their experience of self contains more flexible or permeable ego boundaries. Boys come to define themselves as more separate and distinct, with a great sense of rigid ego boundaries and differentiation. The basic feminine sense of self is connected to the world, the basic masculine sense of self is separate" (1978:169). Although there is some discussion about whether it is more difficult for boys or girls to form these new identities, a theme which will be returned to in chapter 8, Chodorow's work is important in psychoanalytical theory because it shifted attention away from the classic father–son relationship that Freud privileged to a new emphasis on mother–child dynamics and a new understanding of how the child is gendered.

Feminist sociologists, while acknowledging that studies of women, by necessity, had to include studies of children, saw the relationship between women and children as complex and possibly conflictual. Drawing on Marxist criticism, and the work of Friedrich Engels in particular, it was argued that women and children were equally subordinated under patriarchy, both taking on the role of an oppressed proletariat in the household. Yet it was equally clear that women and children did not have the same interests and that while, in some circumstances, children and women might be allies, they could also be enemies, their interests inimical to each other. Shulamith Firestone, for instance, argued that "the heart of women's oppression is her childbearing and child rearing role" (1970:81). She focused on the practical restraints that children put on women and argued convincingly that until children and their care were seen as a social rather than a maternal issue, women could not truly be liberated, and would remain, with children, in "the same lousy boat" (1970:102).

Anthropologists acknowledged the political and social subordination of both women and children, but some, like Eleanor Leacock (1981), drew heavily on Marx and Engels to argue that the subordination of women (and by implication children) was not universal but a product of particular social and economic capitalist systems (see also Sacks 1974). She claimed that women's status was not necessarily related to giving birth and that women in nonindustrial and pre-capitalist societies held important positions of power and prestige. Others, most famously Sherry Ortner (1974), analyzed the symbolic parallels between women and children, examining the ways in which universal dichotomies of nature/culture mapped onto structural inequalities. Ortner claimed that, universally, women were subordinated to men, and given that there was no inherent biological reason for this, the answer must be found in cultural ideologies and symbols, especially in the universal denigration of nature and the admiration for culture. Women, in this analysis, were devalued because of their close association with nature and, in particular, with the messy, "uncivilized" demands of child-rearing, giving birth, and the bodily functions associated with menstruation. Furthermore, they were confined to the domestic domain, along with children, and thus excluded from positions of power, which were associated with the public world of men (see Moore 1988 for a fuller account of the debates of the 1970s and 1980s around gender within anthropology).

Such reasoning had a powerful impact on studies of women in anthropology, and yet these theories continually came up against the difficulty that although they gave cultural and symbolic reasons, rather than biological ones, as to why women should be subordinated, explanations for this inequality continually seemed to hinge on the biological facts of reproduction, and the ways in which these were culturally constructed (Collier and Yanagisako 1987). Children, and how to explain their relationship to women, remained a problem, and children's lives and needs, as well as ideas about childhood, remained largely unexamined. At best, the rise in feminist analyses of women politicized the role of children, but it had little interest in them as subjects for research. As sociologist Ann Oakley argues:

> What happened was that the deconstruction of notions of "the family" and the uncovering of biases in theoretical assumptions made about women, resulted in an emphasis on *women's* experiences of children rather than *children's* experiences of women (or of anything else). Children came to be represented as a *problem* to women. This reflected the political concerns within the women's movement to do with freeing women from compulsory motherhood and childcare work. (1994:22, emphasis in original)

The idea of an anthropology of women eventually proved problematic because of its need to look for universals, particularly those related to women's oppression and subjugation. In doing so, not only did it set up a false dichotomy between men and women, but it also set up a false alliance between women and children and constructed them both in opposition to men (Oakley 1994). The project of discovering women's worlds and hearing their "muted voices" in anthropology was deeply political. Whereas women had often been excluded from earlier monographs, and their work and ideas dismissed as inauthentic, the new anthropology of women took women's worldviews as serious and important. However, privileging sex above all other factors meant that issues such as age, class, ethnic background, and position in the life-cycle were overlooked or relegated to secondary importance. Similarly, while there may be some parallels in the social and political position of women and children in relation to patriarchal social organization, in reality they have vastly different access to political, social, and economic structures both within the family and outside, and the power that women have over children, as adults, is rarely explored, as both Jill Korbin (1981) and Judith Ennew (1986) have pointed out in their studies of child abuse (see also Malkki and Martin 2003).

The use of dichotomies between nature/culture and public/private began to break down as non-Western feminists challenged universal models of subordination and the complexities of social systems and the interactions between gender, class, and ethnicity became subjects of analyses. Gender difference was increasingly understood as one difference among many and straightforward parallels between women and oppression became harder to maintain. Olivia Harris (1980), for example, challenged the straightforward binary opposition proposed by Ortner by looking at children among the Laymi of the Bolivian Andes, where distinctions were made not necessarily between male and female but rather between the wild and the cultivated, and women and men were equally represented symbolically in both categories. Children, on the other hand, were viewed as undomesticated until they learnt to speak. Before they had language, their hair was left uncut and they were understood as wild. Likewise, unmarried people were seen as undomesticated and the married couple who worked, produced, and consumed together represented the core of the social system. The symbolic and social organization of the society was based around dichotomies other than age and gender, and Harris's work showed the problems of using external categories to discuss these issues.

The use of binary opposites, be they woman/man or adult/child, became seen as less important than the interplay and complementarities between these categories, an insight well illustrated by contributors to Jean La Fontaine's edited volume, *Sex and Age as Principles of Social Differentiation* (1978). Enid Schildkrout, for example, analyzed the economic value of childhood in Hausa communities in Nigeria and looked at how that intersected with, and supported, women's role. She argued that

> children and adults [are] complementary participants in the social system. In Hausa urban society, although most children do not play a significant role in providing basic subsistence, they are crucial in social structural terms: the social, economic and political definition of adult roles, particularly those based on gender, cannot be understood without taking account of the roles of children. (1978:133)

In her chapter Schildkrout looked at the variety of childhoods that existed in Hausa society, recognizing that boys and girls had very different roles and that age hierarchy was as important as gender. Women and children could not be placed in the same conceptual category and social organization could not be seen only as a dichotomy between men and women or even between adults and children; each category was informed and made more complex by the interplay of age and sex and the interaction between people of different ages.

The importance of La Fontaine's book for an anthropology of childhood was in its linkage of childhood to a much wider pattern of age-sets and social differences based on generation and stages in the life-cycle. Children were viewed neither as a subculture nor as an undiscovered tribe, nor were they of interest only insofar as they related to women. In her introduction, La Fontaine set up the most sophisticated analysis so far of the role of gender in childhood, and while not denying links between women and children in structural terms, she rejected any easy conflation of the two.

> The two principles of social differentiation that are the subject of analysis in this volume [age and sex] show many features in common. They are both constructed of selected elements drawn from the processes of human physiology and as formal systems have certain logical properties. These differ in that sexual differentiation is based on the unity of conjoined opposites, while differentiation by age creates a hierarchy out of ordered divisions of the human life span. Both principles exercise direct constraints on human behaviour in that they present clusters of attributes which by association with the "natural" origin of the differentiating structure are ascribed to individuals. (1978:18)

Child-Centered Anthropology

Since the early 1970s there has been a noticeable shift in studies of child hood, especially in the use of children as informants and as the central participants in ethnography. Despite the long tradition of studying children in the USA, and the popularity of books such as Never in Anger (Briggs 1970), which showed how important childhood was in understanding the whole life-cycle, it was European anthropologists and sociologists who began to conceptualize studies of childhood politically. As Allison James argues, "given this much longer U.S. anthropological tradition of work with children, it is rather curious, therefore, that in the 1970s the loudest rallying call for exploring 'children's perspectives' – perspectives that could be articulated through the 'voices of children' when positioned as social actors was from Europe" (2007:263). In the UK Jean La Fontaine (1986a), Allison James and Alan Prout (1997), and sociologists Chris Jenks (1996), Berry Mayall (1994), and Frances Waksler (1991) all argued that childhood must be understood as a culturally constructed, social phenomenon which changes over time and place and that it should not necessarily be seen as a time of universal dependence and powerlessness, although this is often how children experience it. In particular they examined how childhood came to be understood in contemporary Western society as a time of separation from the adult world, where children were sent to school rather than staying with their families, where they were characterized as weak, powerless, dependent, and vulnerable, and as beings who must be protected rather than empowered. La Fontaine argued explicitly that children should be studied as worthy subjects in their own right, not as unshaped cultural beings. She wrote that "in general, anthropology has retained an outdated view of children as raw material, unfinished specimens of the social beings whose ideas and behaviour are the proper subject matter for social science" (1986a:10). She went on to claim that childhood, like adulthood, "is always a matter of social definition rather than physical maturity" (1986a:19) and therefore that anthropologists should be interested in childhood as a social construction, as a way of ordering culture, and as important a variable as gender.

Child-centered anthropology was seen as a corrective to the previous neglect; it supported the notion that a child's perspectives and understandings should be taken seriously and rejected the idea that children were in any way incomplete or incompetent. Emphasizing children's voices challenged the perception that children did not know what is happening, even on issues such as education or initiation, about which they might be expected to have a certain expertise. However, this gap had not gone entirely unnoticed, and, writing in the 1950s, Audrey Richards, in her work on girls' initiation rites among the Bemba of Zambia, had commented:

> A striking gap in my material is the absence of any comments made by the girls themselves. This is, I think, significant. These girls, who are obliged to remain silent, often covered with blankets, seem to lose all personality for the observer as the rites follow one after the other. They are both the centres of the ceremony, and yet the least interesting of the actors in it. However, I consider my failure to arrange for longer conversations and more intimate contacts with the two girls to have been a serious omission. It leaves an element of uncertainty in my interpretation of the educational function of the rites. (1956:63)

Although a few anthropologists such as Mary Ellen Goodman (1957) did put forward the suggestion that children could be useful as informants and that their worldview should be of concern to anthropologists, it was over twenty years before the idea that children were the best informants about their own lives came to the fore.

One of the earliest examples of anthropologists using children as informants was Myra Bluebond-Langner's study of children in American hospices (1978). She worked with terminally ill children, comparing their knowledge of and reactions to their illnesses with those of their parents and doctors. Her child informants understood very clearly that they were dying, even though their parents and doctors had specifically kept the information from them. By looking at the condition of other children and noting the gestures and attitudes of the people caring for them, the children understood that their illnesses were terminal but tended to shield their parents from this knowledge. By talking to children directly, Bluebond-Langner showed the ways in which children understood and interpreted their parents' attitudes toward their own illness and demonstrated the desire on both sides to protect shared ideas of innocence and ignorance. She also showed that knowledge was a negotiation between parents and children and that children were not just the passive recipients of the information that their carers wanted them to have.

By the 1990s, children's lived experiences, as described by children themselves, had become the focus of several anthropologists, who studied issues such as the nature of children's friendships in British schools (James 1993), their daily lives at home in Norway (Gullestad 1984; Solberg 1997), and playground injuries and sickness in Denmark (Christensen 1999). There was also an acknowledgment of the many ways that anthropologists had been befriended and taught by children in the field (Bird-David 2005). Children's daily lives and concerns were central to these studies, all of which took children's participation in research, and their role as informants, as vital, rejecting the idea that childhood could be seen simply as an "epiphenomenon of adult society and concern" (James et al. 1998:197). This new perspective entailed changing the emphasis within studies of childhood from socialization, and how parents raised their children, to how children themselves perceived their lives, surroundings, parents, and upbringing. Taking children themselves as a starting point meant that they could no longer be seen as a homogeneous group with views and priorities that depended only on their physical advancement. Child-centered research firmly rejected the idea that because children's roles were impermanent, they were also unimportant. Furthermore it reflected a recognition that children possessed agency and that they could, and did, influence their own lives, the lives of their peers, and that of the wider community around them (Waksler 1991; James and Prout 1995; Morrow 1995). This vision of childhood is a profoundly political one, which has caused some unease amongst those with a long-standing interest in childhood. Robert LeVine, for instance, rejects the argument that an anthropology of childhood should only be about children as active agents, existing in their own world, and that studies of child-rearing are in some ways redundant or dismissive of children. He argues that studies of socialization do not treat children

> simply as objects rather than subjects, suppressing their voices and taking the perspective of the adults who oppress, victimize and exploit children. These allegations come from those who see an anthropology of child-hood as a political weapon against injustice like political struggles to end the persecution of women and ethnic minorities, rather than a search for knowledge and understanding. One of the strengths of socialization research is that it has resisted this kind of politicization in its pursuit of a deeper understanding of children and their parents. (2003:5)

While the idea of childhood as a social phenomenon has been widely accepted, the use of children as informants, and the problems of doing research with children, have remained more problematic (Friedl 2004). For older children, the issue is to do not so much with methods as with ethics. Working with children necessitates an acknowledgment of power differentials between adult researcher and child informant, and this represents particular problems (Morrow and Richards 1996). In Western settings, children may be asked if they wish to participate, but their ability to refuse is constrained by a number of factors. The fact that much research takes place in schools means that it is harder for children to opt out of a group activity when it has been integrated into their daily schedules. While their parents and teachers might be asked for their consent, often children are not. Similarly, in non-Western settings, permission is often granted to work with the whole community and children are rarely singled out or asked their views on cooperation with the researcher. Even if children do give informed consent, further problems remain, however, as Myra Bluebond-Langner and Jill Korbin point out. Emphasizing children's voices, or their right to participate in research, does not necessarily solve all the difficulties: "In using quotations from children we have to be cognizant of all of the following: selectivity of representation, uncritical quoting, poly-phony of voices, whose point is being made (e.g., the anthropologist's or the children being quoted), and whose agenda is being served (e.g., the human rights community or the people of the community in which the child lives)" (2007:243).

Many anthropologists who work with children have developed specific techniques which take into account children's attention spans and daily activities. Some of these involve interpreting children's paintings and drawings, which allows younger children to participate in research (although these were first used by Margaret Mead in Samoa; see also Toren 1993 and 2007 for a discussion of how children's drawings can be used to understand their ideas about the relationship between space and status). Others entail giving children cameras and asking them to photograph people and places that are important to them and using this to gain insight into their lives. In his work among street children in Brazil, Tobias Hecht (1998) gave some of the children tape recorders and asked them to interview each other, which they did, elucidating information that they would not tell to adults. Rachel Hinton (2000), working with Bhutanese refugee children in Nepal, used "participatory visual techniques" such as drawing and painting to enable her to understand how they perceived health and healthcare. Rachel Baker et al. (1996) worked with street children in Nepal using methods of participatory rural appraisal (PRA) such as "spider diagrams" and photography. Not only do such techniques offer the possibility of new insights into children's lives, they are also very much in keeping with accepted ethical ways of working with children, which encourage them to become active partners and participants in research conducted about and among them.

The question of how to relate to a child as an adult, as well as an outsider, has also been of concern. Given that an adult can never pass as a child, anthropologists and sociologists who wish to work with children have had to pay particular attention to the role that they play as researchers. Sociologist Gary Fine (1987) has suggested that there are four possible roles an adult outsider can play when dealing with children: supervisor, leader, observer, and friend. All these roles need to recognize the power imbalance between adults and children, and while the role of friend may be the most useful way of observing, and even participating in, a child's world, the difference in status, as well as in physical size, between adults and children continues to cause problems. Other ethnographers have acknowledged that there is a distance and discrepancy. Nancy Mandell tried to overcome this by taking on a "least-adult role," in which she "endeavored to put aside ordinary forms of adult status and interaction – authority, verbal competency, cognitive and social mastery – in order to follow their [the children's] ways closely' (1991:42). Although the differences in size could not be overcome, she attempted to suspend other markers of status and difference during her research. Similarly, another sociologist, William Corsaro (1985), has worked extensively with young children in schools in Italy and America, and while he concedes that he will never be seen as one of them, he has found that children are happy to assign a special role of "Big Bill" to him – a non-adult-like adult. Others have tried to deny and diminish the physical differences in size and pass as a child. Anna Laerke (1998), for instance, in her work with British schoolchildren, tried to blend in with them, playing in the sand pit with children, dressing like them, sitting on the same small chairs as them, and allying herself with the children against the teacher.

Children have long been used as researchers by ethnographers, both as informants and as the anthropologist's "significant others" in the field, helping their parents to settle in and making connections with other children and their families. As anthropology has become more reflexive, the importance of the fieldworker's own relationships has come to the fore and the impact of taking a partner or children to the field has been examined (Cassell 1987; Gottlieb 1995; Hendry 1999; Handler 2004). In these studies, the challenges of being a parent and an anthropologist and the conflicts between helping children to fit in and retaining the values of their parents' society are all vividly expressed. Diane Tober (2004), for example, has written of the difficulties and benefits of doing fieldwork as a single mother in Iran. She describes all sorts of tensions as her sons embarrass her in public, and learn language she would not have taught them, but also the ways in which they helped her deal with bureaucracy and gave her a privileged entrance into the school system. Christine Hugh-Jones (1987) has written about the frustrations and concerns she experienced when taking her children to Amazonia, but also the positive impacts they brought, such as the change of status they gave to their parents within their host community. Despite their contributions, however, and the emphasis on their own experiences, children have had limited control over the research process and few opportunities to shape research questions. A future way of integrating children into research is likely to be the use of child researchers and the different perspectives that they might bring. In schools in the UK, Mary Kellett (2005) has trained children in research methods so that they can not only set the agenda of what they think should be studied, but also are given the opportunity to devise appropriate research methods, and Allison James (2007) has suggested that this perspective might transform our understandings of children's own experiences.

Conclusion

By representing a history of childhood within anthropology in this way, I do not mean to claim a teleology in which child-centered anthropology is presented as the best way to understand children, or as the end point for the study of childhood. There can be no neat segmentation of children's issues or children's worlds, and as Bluebond-Langer and Korbin have commented:

> As we study children and childhoods, we need to confront the messiness and untidiness of social reality, not reduce it. Similarly, we need to continue to problematize the nature and development of the individual. . . . we are still struggling with definitions of the terms *child*, *youth*, and *childhood*. In defining these concepts, issues of age, agency, development, roles and responsibilities – not to mention those of essentialization and generalizing – raise their hoary heads. How do we maintain a healthy tension between the individual and the group, the universal and the particular? How do we generalize and particularize in a meaningful way? (2007:245)

The problems of studying children are not necessarily unique, although adults do have particular responsibilities when dealing with children. As Bluebond-Langer and Korbin note, however, the study of childhood is intrinsic to a more generalized study of the life-cycle and of human development. As the numbers of ethnographies of children grow and the theorization of childhood continues, there is now a substantial body of knowledge which rightly claims to constitute a discrete subdiscipline of anthropology (Benthall 1992). Yet an anthropology of childhood has existed for a long time, and however it has been looked at, and in whatever theoretical tradition it has been situated, the study of childhood has always been central to anthropology and has lain at the heart of questions that have been of concern to all. Questions such as: When does life begin? What constitutes a fully human, fully social being? How do children become adults? What is the relationship between child, family and community? The following chapters will examine studies in which children have played a prominent role and which go some way to illuminating these questions.

2

WHAT IS A CHILD?

Introduction

Two key findings that are constantly reiterated among those who study childhood are, firstly, that childhood is a social phenomenon and, secondly, that biological immaturity is assigned social meanings dependent on the cultural setting. The idea of "the child" as representative of a whole category of younger people has been shown to be untenable, and age, gender, birth order, and ethnicity all have an impact on the ways that children experience childhood within cultures. Between societies the variables are even more apparent, and from the earliest monographs onward, the multiplicity of childhoods, and the differences in children's lives, have been recognized and discussed and the myriad ways in which children are conceptualized have been analyzed. This chapter will look at multiple understandings of childhood and the many different answers to the question, "what is a child?" Childhood has been variously claimed as a non-existent stage in the life-cycle, a time of incompetence and incompleteness, or the period in a person's life when he or she is without fault or flaw. Looking at ethnographic accounts of childhood, it is hard to find instances where childhood does not exist in some form, yet a rigid dichotomy between adult and child is not always apparent, nor is a sense that adulthood is the end point of socialization.

Childhood as a Modern Idea:
The Influence of Philippe Ariès

Despite concentrating on work by anthropologists in this chapter, it is necessary to start with the work of French historian Philippe Ariès, whose analysis of childhood as a social and historical construction has had a profound influence on ideas about childhood across the social sciences. In *Centuries of Childhood* (1979[1962]) he claimed that in Western Europe the notion of childhood as a distinct human condition started to emerge only around the end of the 15th century, and that before this people had little conception of childhood as a phase in the life-course. He claimed that "in medieval society the idea of childhood did not exist; this is not to suggest that children were neglected, forsaken or despised. The idea of childhood is not to be confused with affection for children: it corresponds to an awareness of the particular nature of childhood, that particular nature which distinguishes the child from the adult, even the young adult. In medieval society this awareness was lacking" (1979[1962]:128). Ariès's thesis relied mostly on analyses of medieval European art, in which, he claimed, children were depicted as small people, with the posture and muscles of adults. It was not until the 16th century that artists began to represent real children in portraiture and it was possible to see the development of specialized clothing, literature, and toys for children. Ariès claimed that the idea of childhood as a special and separate state from adulthood gained ground during the following centuries and culminated in the sentimentalization of childhood and the "child-centred family" in the 19th and 20th centuries, in which the child was seen as "not ready for life and . . . had to be subjected to a special treatment, a sort of quarantine, before he was allowed to join the adults' (1979[1962]:412).

There have been many criticisms of Ariès from almost all disciplines in the social sciences (Vann 1982), but nevertheless he remains a much-quoted and much-discussed author and many anthropologists who have studied childhood have relied on his insight that childhood is socially constructed and that it changes depending on the historical and cultural setting. Ariès is still the starting point for many of those studying childhood, and there are certainly ethnographic examples that support his stance that parental investment in children is not an unquestioned biological fact but one that varies according to circumstance. Even if the main thrust of his argument is accepted, however, many of the details have been challenged. Although he did use evidence from other sources, such as the absence of childcare manuals, his overwhelming evidence came from paintings. Yet paintings are not produced in a social and political vacuum and a particular person or institution usually commissions them for a specific purpose. Paintings in the Middle Ages were almost exclusively connected with, and painted for, religious purposes. They illustrated religious themes and used symbolism to represent religious ideas and narratives. They were in no way concerned with the lives of real children, but, rather, with what the infant Jesus and child saints represented: innocence, purity, and the soul. The growing wealth of the merchant classes in the 15th and 16th centuries enabled them to commission artists to paint portraits of themselves and of their children in a secular rather than a religious way, using particular symbolism and artistic motifs to convey certain ideas relating to the social and economic position of the child and his or her family. Only specific children were represented in these paintings. Poor children were rarely portrayed and boys were much more frequently represented than girls. Consequently critics have argued that Ariès's thesis did not take into account issues of class or gender (Pollock 1983; Montgomery 2003).

Ariès's reliance on paintings also meant that he ignored other sources of information about children. For example, there were several scientific and medical books on children's illnesses that recognized childhood as a different stage from adulthood, a stage with specific needs and attributes. The legal system of the 15th and 16th centuries also set ages for criminal responsibility (the age at which children could be held responsible for their crimes), implying that children were seen as being different from adults, and not as morally aware. Ariès argued that parents viewed children under seven as being of no importance and until that age more or less ignored them: children under the age of seven simply "did not count" (Ariès 1979[1962]:128). His critics have disagreed strongly with this, claiming that children were much loved, even from infancy. Linda Pollock (1983), for example, has quoted from 16th- and 17th-century diaries, poems, and first-hand accounts of parents' sense of loss and despair over the death of their children. Child mortality meant that parents were only too aware of the fragility of their children and a great deal of emphasis was placed on nurturing and protecting them. Indeed the claim that parents were largely indifferent to their children, and only began to look after them after belated weaning at seven has been described as "biologically almost inconceivable" (Hunt 1970:49).

Conceptualizations of Childhood

In English, the word "child" can refer to anyone between the ages of 0 and 18. Although, at either end of the scale, it may be replaced by more age-specific words, such as baby, infant, toddler, or teenager, generally the word "child" can be used to denote any young person who has not yet reached social maturity. The stages of a Western child's life tend now to be demarcated by bureaucracy (what age a child starts school, or when he or she has certain legal rights), but these change over time and depend on social context, so that, for example, children may start school at five in the UK, or at seven in Scandinavia. Other societies differentiate between children much more explicitly so that childhood is a series of age-related stages which a child must pass through on the way to adulthood (Raum 1940; Gravrand 1983; Ahmed et al. 1999). Passage through these stages occurs with the gradual assumption of responsibilities rather than when a set chronological age is reached.

The impact of gender cannot be overestimated. The child, as Judith Ennew has pointed out, is not some "strange, ungendered isolate" (quoted in Oakley 1994:21), and discussions of the child that do not take gender into account can quickly become meaningless. It is very clear from all the accounts that we have of children's lives, from the oldest to the most recent, that the childhoods of boys and girls are very different and that they often end at very different times. To give but one example; amongst the Akwẽ-Shavante of Amazonia, David Maybury-Lewis discusses the different skills and knowledge that boys and girls are expected to have, and notes that "a girl of about six tends to behave like a small, weak, and underdeveloped woman. A boy of the same age gives the impression of still being a child" (1974:73). Maybury-Lewis does not explicitly state what he thinks a child should be, but because boys continue to do more "childish" things, such as having races and dancing, he implies that he associates childhood with playing, with a lack of responsibility and freedom from work. In contrast, by the age of 6, a girl is expected to have mastered the womanly skills of her mother; she looks after her siblings, accompanies her mother on short collecting trips, and helps in the house. It is an interesting point of discussion as to whether a girl of 6 is in fact a child. She may well be married at this age and will shortly be considered physically ready to live with her husband.

Children are further defined by their place in the wider social and political system as well as by their gender. A poor girl from a marginalized minority has a radically different childhood to a richer, higher-status boy. This may be apparent not only in the way she is treated and the opportunities open to her but also in the very conceptualization of her childhood. In her work on shantytowns in Brazil, Donna M. Goldstein argues that "childhood is a privilege of the rich" (1998:389), with rich children having long, protected childhoods while their poor counterparts are "hastened into becoming adults" (1998:395). So apparent is this discrepancy that domestic workers express a preference for their employers' children over their own, because they are able to retain their childishness for longer. Other factors also have an appreciable impact on the ways that childhood is conceptualized and experienced. Whether children live in a polygamous or monogamous household, the relative status of their mother, whether they have many kin around or whether they are illegitimate all affect their status and the subsequent way they are treated (see Wedgwood 1938 for an account of the impacts of these factors on children in Manam, Papua New Guinea). Their position in the family can also be important. If they are an unwelcome addition to an already stretched family, they may well be treated less well than a firstborn (Firth 1956; Scheper-Hughes 1992). In those societies that practice primogeniture, it is the firstborn child, usually the firstborn son, who inherits from his parents and may well have a totally different childhood from his siblings. With reference to the Tallensi of northern Ghana, Meyer Fortes (1949, 1974) discussed at length the different relationships that a firstborn son and daughter had to their parents and the different ritual obligations that only they can perform after their parents' death. Alternatively the final child may well have a special place within the family and, under systems of ultimo-geniture, inherit family lands and property. In other contexts, children may be seen as having more in common with their age-sets than their siblings and two siblings may belong to very different generations and have very different roles within the community and within the family (Jackson 1978).

The idea that childhood is a specific stage of life, separated from adulthood, does not hold true in many places, where there are many stages of social immaturity that last well beyond puberty and even marriage. It is difficult to talk of a generic concept of childhood, as made explicit by James Chisholm's model of Native American Navajo development (1996), in which he lists eight stages of development which go beyond childhood and which have no direct counterparts in Western developmental models. In this schema, childhood is divided into several stages based on knowledge and social competence rather than age. Social maturity is gained by moving through a progression of stages which are not completed until a person is over 30. Stage One begins when a child is between two and four years old. It is the age at which a child becomes aware and starts to show the first indicators of self-discipline. Between the ages of four and six, during Stage Two, a child begins to learn the importance of kin relationships. Children begin to think during the third stage (six–nine years) and begin the passage to adulthood during the fourth stage (10–15 years), when they learn their responsibilities to their families and also deepen their knowledge of Navajo religious law and clan hierarchies. At Stage Five (15–18 years), they are considered fully adult, other than the fact that they are unmarried and are still expected to help with their parents' households. After this, Stage Six takes place between the ages of 17 and 22, when people begin to marry, raise livestock, and take on the responsibilities of adult life. During the penultimate stage, Stage Seven (22–30 years), people have children, and ideally have material success, until the final stage of life (over 30), when a person's reputation has grown and he or she is considered fully mature (Chisholm 1996:172–173).

Finally the term "child" can be as much a relational term as a description of a younger person at a particular stage of life, so that a person is conceptualized as a "child of" someone, implying mutual support and care throughout life. Nurit Bird-David, in her study of hunter-gatherer childhoods in south India, looks at the relative meanings of the term "childhood" and argues that

> both adult and child tropical-forest hunter-gatherers see themselves as "children" of the forest. The South Indian Nayaka . . . use the word *makalo* (children) to describe themselves vis-à-vis the forest and vis-à-vis all invisible and previous dwellers in their area, whom they call respectively "big parents," or in some cases "grandparents." "Children" is a concept that is central to their sense of themselves, their place in the world, and their relations with their surroundings; it recurs in their moral and ritual discourse. (2005:93)

She goes on to argue that children "cannot be considered a distinct minority group or a subaltern culture" (2005:99) and there are no separate or autonomous categories of adult or child.

Children as Incompetent or Subordinate

The ages at which different societies assign different competencies to children vary enormously. There are many accounts of young girls having full-time care of younger siblings from the ages of five or six and of young boys of this age tending goats or cattle on their own for long periods. Even if they are not thought of as competent in other areas, they are assumed to be able to carry out tasks such as these, jobs that a child in the West would not be considered capable of doing for many years. Historians Barbara Ehrenreich and Deirdre English have argued that "today, a four-year-old who can tie his or her shoes is impressive. In colonial [American] times, four-year-old girls knitted stockings and mittens and could produce intricate embroidery; at age six they spun wool. A good, industrious little girl was called 'Mrs.' instead of 'Miss' in appreciation of her contribution to the family economy: she was not, strictly speaking, a child" (1979:185–186). If children are seen as competent in some areas, however, they are often thought of as lacking a vital component of full adulthood, whether that is a sense of wrong or right, a sense of appropriate behavior, or knowledge of their status and their role in their community. Helen Morton (who previously wrote as Helen Kavapalu) in her study of children in Tonga identifies this as *poto* or social competence. Children are conceptually related to the insane and mentally handicapped because they lack reason and are ignorant. They are also linked to commoners as opposed to chiefs. Even when they are born into chiefly families, there are strong conceptual similarities between commoners and children, both of whom are associated with foolishness, bad behavior, a lack of restraint, and dirtiness. Chiefs, and adults, in comparison, are linked to cleverness, proper behavior, restraint, and cleanliness (Kavapalu 1995).

Children are thought of in Tonga as mischievous; they cry simply because they are naughty. In a society that prizes social competence and where its lack is regarded as shameful, children are at the bottom of the social hierarchy (Morton 1996:72). They are told off for being clumsy, and a child who falls over may be laughed at, or berated, for his or her incompetence. A child learns *poto* gradually; he or she learns appropriate behavioral responses and thus gradually becomes socialized. There is no consensus about when children are no longer considered as lacking in skill. Morton claims that children are not considered capable of "proper" learning until the age of four and that this process goes on until around 11. It might be said about a teenager that "their mind or reason is whole" (Morton 1996:72) and that therefore they have achieved social competence, but until then children are seen as incomplete (see also Kavapalu 1993).

In a similar way the Mende of Sierra Leone view children as lacking in understanding and unable to control themselves in terms of either behavior or their bodily functions (Ferme 2001). They are recognized as real persons but also likened to animals, and before they are initiated they are referred to as "*kpowanga* (pl.), a term that also means 'mad' and 'mentally deficient'. In other words, until children are taught how to use knowledge so that they might achieve real understanding, they are capable only of imperfectly perceiving the world around them and are unable to operate in it according to codes of prescribed social behaviour" (Ferme 2001:200–201). The Fulani of West Africa likewise view children as lacking in self-control and thus unable to show the basic characteristics of *pulaaku* or "Fulani-ness," such as modesty, control, patience, fortitude, care, and forethought (Johnson 2000). Fulani children are viewed as very much subordinate to their parents, who will sometimes insult them and remind them of their powerlessness. A child is understood as being unable to control his or her emotions and is taught that the only acceptable time to cry is when deliberately hurt by another person. Praise of children is discouraged, as are all emotions, and although it is accepted that children have less self-control, they are encouraged to show emotional restraint from as early an age as possible. Until the age of six a child is thought to be lacking in *pulaaku*, and it is only when the child is able to recognize all the extended family members by name that he or she is understood to have passed an important developmental marker and achieved some measure of *pulaaku*. Even so, by the age of four, girls are expected to be competent in other spheres, such as caring for their younger siblings and fetching water and firewood, and by six they will be pounding grain, producing milk and butter, and selling these alongside their mothers in the market (Johnson 2000).

Among Inuit children in Canada, growing up is largely seen as a process of acquiring *ihuma* (thought, reason, and understanding). Young children are treated with a great deal of tolerance and affection, because they are seen as lacking in this quality. They are understood to be easily angered, to cry frequently, and to be incapable of understanding the external difficulties facing the community, such as shortages of food (Briggs 1970). Children are thought to acquire *ihuma* at their own pace, and while they are taught and instructed on appropriate behavior and reactions, it is thought pointless to teach children before they show their innate *ihuma*. Jean Briggs writes that

> growing up is very largely a process of acquiring *ihuma*, since it is primarily the use of *ihuma* that distinguishes mature, adult behaviour from that of a child, an idiot, a very sick or an insane person. *Ihuma* has many manifestations. When a child begins to respond to the social world around him: when he begins to recognize people and to remember, to understand words and to talk, when he begins to be shy and self-conscious (*kanngu*), to learn restraint in self-expression, and to want to participate in socially useful activities, people remark affectionately that the child is acquiring *ihuma*. (1970:111–112)

One of the earliest ethnographic accounts that specifically focused on children was Otto Raum's *Chaga Childhood* (1940). He described how during early infancy children from this East African tribe were called *mnangu* (incomplete) and were never scolded or beaten because they lacked the sense to know any better. Later on in children's infancy, when they were called *mkoku* (little ones who fill the lap), they were seen as beginning to gain sense but were still viewed as liable to make mistakes and be willful and mischievous. If they cried without reason, ate earth, or broke something valuable, they were beaten. Until the age of three, children were known as *mwana* or infants, and regarded as nuisances and regularly beaten in order to keep them in line and their spirits in check. *Manake* referred to children between the ages of four and 14 whose punishments increased in severity, although they became less frequent as they learnt self-control and social competence on the way to adulthood (Raum 1940).

Cultures that view children as subordinate or incompetent give rise to special problems for anthropologists who emphasize the importance of child-focused anthropology. How is it possible to view children as competent informants when they are seen so differently within their own cultures? In her study of Tuareg children in Niger, Susan Rasmussen (1994) looks at the ambiguity of children and their relationships to adults and to those outside their immediate society. She argues that there are close similarities in the ways that children, slaves, and blacksmiths are conceptualized: all three are viewed as low-status and lacking in reserve, shame, and intelligence. One informant said of small children that they are "not people, but children" (1994:350), implying that children are incomplete and lacking in socially prized characteristics, and yet, unlike slaves or blacksmiths, children are also seen as being without sin, which puts them in a unique position. Their behavior can be easily dismissed as simply childish pranks, done without malice or intent, but such behavior can also be manipulated by adults as a form of resistance and dissent. Maintaining social identities and separate social statuses, as well as emphasizing religious purity and descent, means that adults have a problematic relationship with outsiders, whether in the form of development agencies, state officials, or even anthropologists. "Childish" behavior such as pulling up vegetables in the school gardens, daubing graffiti on the state school (although never the Koranic one), or throwing stones at outsiders may be verbally condemned by adults, but it is also tacitly supported, so that Rasmussen concludes: "Children become active subjects rather than passive objects during field research, by voicing adults' true but muted sentiments, as 'exhibits' for moral and political commentaries, as buffers, scapegoats and mouthpieces" (1994:368). Even when children are understood as subordinate, or incomplete, they may not necessarily be passive, and may collude with adults and manipulate their status for other ends.

One final case to look at in this section is an example where children are seen less as subordinates of their parents than as extensions of them. Roger Goodman has written extensively about children in Japan and the relationships between parents and children. He claims that the child is often "described as a *mono* (object) which is an extension of, rather than separate from, the parent" (2000:165). He looks at the issue of *oyako shinju* or double suicide committed out of love. These are cases, most common in time of economic depression, where a parent, usually a mother, kills her children before killing herself. They are never described as murder, and, indeed, there have been harsh criticisms of mothers who attempted to kill themselves without killing their children first. In 1985 a divorced Japanese woman living in California attempted to drown herself and her two children, aged respectively four years and six months, in the Pacific Ocean. She managed to drown them before being rescued herself and was subsequently put on trial for double murder. The Japanese-American community in the USA, with support from Japan, organized a 25,000-name petition arguing that the case was not one of murder but one of *oyako shinju*. "Her supporters argued that there had been no malice towards the children in what she had done; indeed she had done it out of love for them" (Goodman 2000:165). In this instance not only were the children subordinate to their mother, they were part of her and their murder could not be seen as the killing of individual children. As Goodman (1996) explains, there is strong argument that Japanese culture and language generally do not have the notion of a separate and autonomous and individual self, especially where children are concerned.

Ideas about the incompleteness or incompetence of children may not apply to all aspects of children's lives, however, and there may well be ambivalence about the extent to which children are subordinated. In his work on a Taiwanese fishing community known as Angang, Charles Stafford brings this out very well. He writes of the two different roads that Chinese children can take toward adulthood and the contradictions between them. On the one hand, children are seen as persons from before birth, their growth is a natural process, and they need only to be protected so that their natures may grow and mature without being forced; on the other, they are also seen as unformed and incompetent persons who must learn Confucian ideals of filial piety and obedience in order to achieve full adult status.

> There is not so much a problem with Chinese children *becoming* something, as with them *remaining* something. The underlying assumption is that children are, were, and will forever be persons, located in a matrix of human relationships. The emphasis is therefore not on making them social, but instead on protecting a natural process and on emphasising certain forms of identification. However, this exists alongside another more "Confucian" view of things, in which children are in the process of becoming persons, in part through learning and self-cultivation. (Stafford 1995:18, emphasis in original)

Taiwanese children are subject to a variety of contradictory influences: obedience may be valued but parents also admire an independent or willful child. While schooling is promoted because it formally teaches Confucian values, mothers often seem less concerned with educating their sons than with protecting them, although they can simultaneously seem very careless with their children's safety. Schooling, which turns children into model citizens, is both encouraged and undermined by mothers, who resist attempts to take children away from them. Similarly, there is an ambivalence about children that Stafford notes, so that while the birth of children is celebrated, it also raises anxieties over the dependence of the older generations and the "anxiety-making possibility of descent gone wrong" (1995:24). Stafford's book makes the point very powerfully that childhood does not have to be seen in terms of dichotomies – human becomings or human beings – and that the various paths to adulthood may be contradictory but not mutually exclusive.

Children as Equals

Assigning incompetence to children is not universal. In her studies of the Beng of West Africa, Alma Gottlieb (1998) shows how adults assume complete linguistic and social competence among the very young. Children are seen as existing in parallel to the spirit world before birth, where they have complete knowledge of all human languages and cultures (see chapter 3 for a more detailed discussion of this). Growing up is seen as a process of losing this knowledge and, as children grow, they become less competent. On the Indonesian island of Bali, infants are viewed as being divine until 210 days after birth. They are addressed by honorific names, held high, and never placed on the floor, as an indication of their high rank. It is only after the *otonan* ceremony, which acknowledges the child's full entry into the human world, that a child is allowed to take its first steps, and its feet can touch the floor (Diener 2000). Joy Hendry (1986) emphasizes that in Japan children are seen as being born without sin or pollution and that parents and other adults have an overriding duty to protect this natural goodness. In other instances, children are described as small equals who cannot be ignored (Fock 1963). There are hints from earlier ethnographies as well that such views caused some surprise when first encountered. Raymond Firth, for example, noted with mild amazement that, among the Tikopia of Polynesia, "children are often spoken to quite gravely by adults, as if they were fully responsible and competent beings" (1936:145).

Sociologist Jane Ribbens McCarthy (1994), in her study of the way that mothers in the UK conceptualize their children, argues that while many show a classic split between seeing children as "naturally" innocent and good or "naturally" bad and willful, a third group identified their children as "little people." In doing this, the mothers acknowledged the individuality of the child, and supported the idea that it was a person in its own right, although constrained by size, maturity, and adult behavior. At a legislative level, the United Nations Convention on the Rights of the Child (UNCRC) is based on the premise that children are equal to adults and should be seen as persons; increasingly, also, international policies construct children as rights-bearing citizens rather than immature beings. There is not universal agreement on this, however, and the USA has refused to ratify the UNCRC because many US states fundamentally disagree with the idea of childhood that it promotes. Jean La Fontaine (1997) has gone further and argued that, whatever the rhetoric at a legislative level, many in the West still reject the idea of children as persons. In non-Western cultures, the idea of children as rights-bearing persons is even more contested. Psychologist Erica Burman (1996) has argued that the UNCRC is based on the notion that each human is an individual who has the right to liberty, to shelter, and to freedom of expression, yet this understanding of the person as an autonomous individual is very much based on Western, liberal humanist philosophy and does not easily translate into other societies (see also Boyden 1997). For example, Roger Goodman writes that

> when the concept of "rights" was introduced into Japan . . . a whole new vocabulary had to be developed to explain it, as did the idea of the individual who could be endowed with such rights. Even today, individualism has strongly negative connections in Japan and is frequently associated with western concepts of selfishness. (1996:131)

This different way of understanding children and their relationships to others is taken up by Joy Hendry (1986), who studied the worlds of the pre-school child in Japan, looking at how children are socialized, what ethno-theories of child-rearing are used, and what parents aspire to for their children. She found that in many respects young children have a centrally important and honored role in Japanese families, with a great deal of attention being paid to their physical and emotional needs, as well as to their ritual ones, so that there are many ceremonies associated with different stages in their early life-cycle. Babies are seen as being fundamentally good and cooperative and a gift to their parents. The early years of their lives are particularly important as children's characters are thought to be fully formed by the age of three, and in these years happiness and harmony are essential factors in a child's life which protect them from negative influences. Parents are expected to behave in an exemplary manner in order to act as guides for their young children. They are also expected to put their children's needs first, and mothers, in particular, are expected to make children the center of their lives and to respond immediately to children's needs, whether for food, clean clothes, or simply attention.

Despite the importance of attending to the child's needs, the individual is not emphasized and children are socialized to be part of the collective. Hendry stresses the importance of *shitsuke* as a value in Japanese goals of child-rearing, which she translates as "the putting into the body of a child the arts of living and good manners in order to create one grown-up person (literally, one portion of a social person)" (1986:11). Parents are creating a social person through the ways in which they raise their child, attempting to protect a child's goodness while teaching him or her how to participate in wider social life. After experiencing the security and safety of the home, Japanese children are gradually exposed to the world outside, where they are taught the importance of harmony and cooperation. They learn to experience the collective group as a place of security and cooperation where emphasis is placed on conformity, internal cohesion, and working together to attain common goals. At the same time, children are expected to learn about age and gender hierarchies and the correct ways of behaving toward those to whom you should show respect. This emphasis on conformity is not, in Hendry's words, "aimed to turn the children into little robots or automatons, as some Western observers like to see it, but to impress upon the child that the world is full of people just like itself whose needs and desires are equally important" (1986:64). Individual desires in this context are much less important than social cohesion, and the idea of children as beings with rights has been strongly resisted.

Children as a Means of Forming Families and Giving Status

In English, the word "family" almost always implies the presence of children; "family" services at church, "family" films or television programs suggest not that they are aimed at multi-generational households generally but that they are suitable for young children. In Anglo-American society, which has limited recognition of wider kin relationships, it is children who define families. Indeed one of the most significant ways that children are conceptualized throughout anthropology is as the basis of descent and family formation, as the next generation and the way that society will reproduce itself (Fortes 1950; Goody 1971). Children create kinship not only between parents and offspring but also in wider social relationships (Fortes 1950). The Tikopia, when studied by Firth (1936), believed that it was children who bound together affinal kin, especially brothers-in-law. For societies that believe in ancestor worship, it is impossible to become an ancestor yourself unless you have children to carry on your lineage (Fortes 1949; Radcliffe-Brown and Forde 1950). Children are the means by which parents become ancestors and they are also the way that adults understand the relationships between ancestors and mortals in this world. This point is made most explicitly in Robin Horton's account of the Tallensi, in which he views the relationship between ancestors and mortals as analogous to that of parents and children. Children are necessary to continue this cycle and to model the ancestor/mortal relationship on earth. He writes: "Wherever one finds ancestors as the principal gods, attitudes to them tend to be an extension of the attitudes of children to parents; and their supposed attitudes to men tend by converse to be an extension of parental attitudes towards children" (1961:110).

Children are also status-givers and the way in which proper families are formed. In some places, prolific child-bearing is honored and respected. Among the Ashanti of Ghana, for example, a mother of ten children was publicly honored (Fortes 1950). In other instances, the size of the family and the sex ratios of the children are more carefully controlled and having the "right" number of children and the "right" number of each sex is important. Elvira Belaunde (2001) writes that among the Airo-Pai of Peru, three children (two of one sex and one of the other) are the ideal number and composition of any family, and that infanticide may occur if there are too many children of the same sex or if there is insufficient space between the siblings. Niels Fock (1963) also claims that among the Amazonian Waiwai four children of each sex is the ideal, and his informants told him that if five or six children of one sex were born, they would be killed.

It is often children who cement marriage and transform their parents into full, adult persons. Barbara Bodenhorn, in her work on the Canadian Inupiaq, states explicitly that "full adult status entails having children" (1988:9), which includes the raising of children who are not biologically one's own, a common occurrence in this society, in which the sharing of children is widespread and hence almost all families raise children. Janet Carsten (1991) makes a similar point about kinship in Pulau Langkawi, Malaysia. Here it is children who determine full adult status for a couple in a way that marriage does not, and indeed childless marriages may end in divorce. In many cases the birth of a child brings about profound changes in the status of the parents (Fortes 1949). It is sometimes not until the birth of a first child that full adult status is conferred upon a couple; indeed, childlessness and childishness are conceptually very similar. Michelle Johnson notes that among the Fulani, a married woman without children is "neither a full wife nor a full woman" (2000:176), and when a woman is pregnant with her first child, she is known as a "pregnant child" herself, emphasizing the transitional state of her first pregnancy. In some Pacific societies, Christine Salomon (2002) claims that giving birth used to be a prerequisite for being a wife and alliances between families only occurred after a woman had become a mother. Even though this idea has changed, young people still live together for a long time before a formal marriage and it is hoped that a child will be born during this period.

Having a child is not only a means of increasing social status; it also enables women to gain some measure of economic independence. In Thailand, it is motherhood rather than marriage that is a sign of maturity for women, and a woman undergoes an increase in economic and social status on the birth of her first child (Hanks 1963). The number of children a woman has is also important. A Chaga woman, for example, gains increasing status with each child:

It is . . . interesting to see the increasing reverence – as expressed in honorary names – which is extended to the mother as she grows older. When she has borne her first child, she is addressed by the name of her paternal great-grandmother, for it has become apparent that, like her, she will continue the regeneration of the family. When she has three or four children who may be sent as messengers or be of service to neighbours and friends, it is the mother who is praised: "May she live long, the mother of children!" Accordingly, she becomes open-handed to foster the general goodwill toward her offspring. When the number has been increased to half a dozen or more, and the eldest son is able to prove his might and mettle, a woman will be addressed as one who has nursed children not in vain. When asked for a favour and when thanked for one, people give her the praise-name of *moongo* – that is, "nursing mother". When her sons take wives, she is honoured as "the uniter (*makulinga*) of the men", and when her daughters are wanted in marriage she is praised as the uniter of women. During the next phase of her life, when a woman becomes the guardian and tutor of her grandchildren, she is greeted as *makitshutsu*, the exhausted one, intimating that her breasts have been sucked to depletion by her children and grandchildren. (Raum 1940:125–126)

The continuing importance of children as status-givers is also apparent among the Papel of Guinea-Bissau, who acknowledge the social status of a woman who has borne many surviving children (Einarsdóttir 2000).

A woman who has given birth to many children is taken seriously, her opinions are listened to, and she is perceived as being able to wield a great deal of power.

In the above instances, the emphasis is placed on surviving children, as visible symbols of successful motherhood. More ambiguous are cases where it is pregnancy, rather than the survival of a child, that is the marker of adulthood for women, Among the Tallensi, Meyer Fortes reported that when a young woman became pregnant, her mother's co-wife presented her with a perineal belt and told her never to be seen without it again (traditionally she would have been naked until this point). Once a woman was confirmed as pregnant, she was considered a mother, even if the child was not successfully brought to term. "A woman's first pregnancy was thus publicly proclaimed as the proud transition from maidenhood to motherhood. Even if she miscarries, or her firstborn dies in very early infancy, or she never bears again, she is a matron for life" (Fortes 1974:87). The role of pregnancy in determining a woman's status has also been analyzed by Linda Layne (1996, 2000) in her studies of miscarriage and stillbirth in America, in which she presents a diametrically opposed view (see also Scrimshaw and March 1984). She discusses how women in the USA are seen as "mothers in the making" (though not yet mothers), but that if miscarriage occurs, support and social recognition are withdrawn and motherhood is denied.

> Women now may begin to actively construct personhood of their wished-for child from the moment they do a home pregnancy test. . . . Their friends, neighbors, and colleagues may also have begun to participate in the social construction of the expected baby by asking the mother how it is doing, speculating on its sex and personality, buying presents for it, and putting on a baby shower. . . . When the pregnancy ends without a baby to bring home, the very people who have encouraged the mother-in-the-making to take on this role and may have participated with her in the social construction of her "baby" often withdraw their support . . . and act as if nothing of any significance took place. The cultural denial of pregnancy loss challenges the validity of the cultural and biological work already undertaken in constructing that child and belittles the importance of that loss. (Layne 2000:323)

While concentrating on the emotional aspects of pregnancy loss, Layne draws attention to the change in status which is expected but which never occurs. If a woman undergoes pregnancy but produces no child (or a dead one), she is not considered a mother. Layne quotes one informant who ponders this question after her premature child died after 18 hours: "She sometimes finds herself asking am I a mother? and explains that family members tell her 'that I am not a mother because I have never experienced raising a child and all the work that is involved'" (2000:323).

Children as an Economic Investment

It is now commonplace to view children in the modern West as economically unproductive and as consumers of goods and services rather than producers (Morrow 1996). Even when children do work, their work is considered as pocket money rather than as a major contribution to household finances. Historian Viviana Zelizer (1985) has shown how, in less than a hundred years, children in contemporary North America have changed from being producers to consumers, from being economically "worthless" to emotionally "priceless." She contends that the modern North American child is viewed as "a privileged guest who is thanked and praised for 'helping out,' rather than a collaborator who at a certain age is expected to assume his or her fair share of household duties" (1985:209). This attitude toward children is, inevitably, class- and gender-dependent, and certain children whose parents are richer or more privileged have always been shielded from the world of money and work. Nevertheless, the ideal childhood, as conceptualized in much contemporary legislation and set out in the UNCRC, is seen as one where all children are shielded from the workplace and from the necessity to earn money to support a family. In reality, many children do work and are expected to be economically useful, contributing substantially to the household economy from an early age (see also chapter 5).

Outside the West, however, children can still be seen as an economic investment with a specific return, whether this is that they should go to work as soon as they are able to contribute to the family, or whether, in the longer term, they are expected to look after parents in their old age, thereby guaranteeing a safety net for the elderly. As the Gonja of West Africa put it: "In infancy your mother and father feed you and clear up your messes; when they grow old, you must feed them and keep them clean" (Goody 1982:13). In rural Thailand, this reciprocity is both an economic and a moral one because, "according to the Thai Buddhist moral scale, parents are entitled to be 'moral creditors' . . . because of their

presumably self-sacrificing labour of bearing and rearing children . . .
while children are 'moral debtors'. Children are obliged to express their
gratitude by serving and obeying their parents till the end of their lives"
(Tantiwiramanond and Pandey 1987:134). Being born in this context incurs
a debt of gratitude that involves the child in lifelong obligations to his or
her parents and toward the mother in particular. In Thailand, this anticipated return is also highly dependent on gender. Penny van Esterik writes:

> In rural contexts, women express the idea that one raises a child in expec-
> tation of explicit returns. A daughter repays the debt to her mother by remain-
> ing in the parental household to care for her parents in her old age, while
> a son ordains as a Buddhist monk to pay his mother back for her breast
> milk. (1996:27)

In Buddhist Thailand, women are excluded from the monkhood, which
is one of the greatest sources of making merit, and an important way of
improving karma in the hope of a better rebirth in the next incarnation.
Having a son in a monastery brings merit to his mother and is one of
the ways that a boy can repay the debt that he has to his mother for
giving birth to him. As girls are precluded from this, they are expected
to give a lifetime of service to their parents, and the youngest daughter
of the family usually inherits the family house, with the explicit intention
that she remains in it to care for her parents in their old age (Blanc-Szanton
1985). In other contexts in Thailand this anticipated return is also evident.
In studies of both prostitution and factory work, one of the reasons consistently given by young women for undertaking this work is that they
believe they have filial duties and responsibilities to fulfill toward their
families (Phongpaichit 1982; Muecke 1992; Ford and Saiprasert 1993;
Montgomery 2001a; see also chapter 7).

   In older ethnographies, this idea of children as an investment with anticipated returns is also apparent. Elizabeth Colson's description of familial
relationships among the Gwembe Tonga of Zambia is a good example
of a formal statement of perceived economic reciprocity:

> The child's right to support is seen not as an abstract principle, but as a
> repayment for the work which he does for his parents. This is very notice-
> able in the Middle River region where children working in their parents'
> fields speak of themselves as working for clothing. Children who shirk badly
> may be told to be off to their mother's brothers, that a useless child has
> no right to its father's bounty. (1960:110)

Monica Wilson's account of Nyakyusa kinship in southern Tanzania also focuses on the economic relationships between people and the expectations that kinship entails. A girl marries and thus brings bride-price into her family in the form of cattle, while a son stays and works in the fields, or sends money back as a laborer if he is working elsewhere, in order to pay for the cows that he in his turn will have to pay for bride-price. Parents make an economic calculation that it is much better to marry a daughter off sooner and gain her bride-wealth earlier and then to delay a son's marriage so that they have his labor or income for longer. Wilson writes:

> Both boys and girls owe their parents, the Nyakyusa think, a material recompense for the trouble and expense of feeding and bringing them up; while a boy, in addition, must make some return for the cattle his father gives him to marry with. A girl fulfils her obligations mainly by getting and staying married. Since marriage involves a transfer of cattle to her father, and divorce involves their return to her husband, it is above all by behaving well in the relationship of marriage, and so avoiding divorce, that a woman discharges her obligation to her parents. "If a daughter ran home in the old days", we were told, "and said that her husband had beaten her, then her father sent to inquire among the neighbours about the quarrel; if they said that it was she who was in the wrong, then her father would beat her and scold her, saying: 'I thought you were a grown woman and were supporting me, but instead of this you spoil my wealth.'" The word which we translate "were supporting me" is a form of *ukuswila* which usually means "to feed a child", and it thus brings out very precisely the element of economic reciprocity in the relationship of father and daughter. (1950:133–134)

It would be an oversimplification to see children only as a source of income or anticipated return to their parents, or to set up a false dichotomy between Western and non-Western societies where children in the former are valued for sentimental reasons and in the latter for economic ones. The affective ties between parents and children more often than not are very strong and children may be desired for many reasons (Rasmussen 1994). As Firth argued:

> It is a pertinent question, then, to inquire how far children in Tikopia are welcome. In general, the Tikopia do desire children. From the sentimental point of view children serve the Tikopia as objects of affection: they are repositories of family traditions and heirs of family lands and property; they serve a utilitarian purpose in doing some of the work of the household, and later in caring for their parents or other kin in old age. (1956:13)

It is also the case that conceptualizations about childhood and what is good for children change in relation to outside forces and pressures. Marida Hollos (2002), for example, argues that among the Pare of northern Tanzania, there are different sorts of childhood depending on family structure, so that those children born into partnership marriages, where there is a strong emotional bond between parents and where the nuclear family is important, are more likely to have Western-style childhoods in which they play and do little work and attend school. In contrast, those children born into lineage-based families, where the interests of the parents' lineages are placed above those of the immediate family, are likely to be expected to do more work, and a greater emphasis is placed on the child as an economic investment who is expected to provide support for parents in their old age.

Unwanted and Nonhuman Children

Despite some attention from anthropologists such as Raymond Firth, one of the least studied and discussed aspects of childhood is the emotive ties between parents and children and the fact that generally children are desired for themselves, and for the love and affection that they bring to their parents and communities. This is not to claim a universal mothering or parental instinct or to state that all children are wanted in all circumstances. As Firth (1956) pointed out, illegitimate children and those who threaten the survival of the family by becoming one more mouth to feed are not always desired and may be abandoned, killed, or aborted. In other instances, too, certain children may be seen as dangerous or harmful to their communities. However, it is extremely rare that all children appear to be an unwanted nuisance. The only account that exists of such a phenomenon is Colin Turnbull's description of the Ik of northern Uganda. In *The Mountain People* (1994), Turnbull describes a community in crisis, weakened by famine and turning in on itself. The portrayal of the Ik is of a community losing its humanity, destroying the weakest, begrudging children their very existence, and without any sense of compassion or ideals of protection to its youngest, or most vulnerable, members. Turnbull describes how, at the age of three, children are turned out of their mothers' houses and expected to sleep in the open courtyard. Children are seen as "useless appendages" and a "burden and a hazard to the survival of others"

(1994:134). His description of the relationship between parent and child is worth quoting in full.

> So we should not be surprised when the mother throws her child out at three years old. She has breast-fed it, with some ill humor, and cared for it in some manner for three whole years, and now it must be ready to make its own way. I imagine the child must be rather relieved to be thrown out, for in the process of being cared for he or she is carried about in a hide sling wherever the mother goes, and since the mother is not strong herself this is done grudgingly. Whenever the mother finds a spot in which to gather, or if she is at a water hole or in her fields she loosens the sling and lets the baby to the ground none too slowly, and of course laughs if it is hurt. . . . Then she goes about her business, leaving the child there, almost hoping that some predator will come along and carry it off. This happened once while I was there – once that I know of, anyway – and the mother was delighted. She was rid of the child and no longer had to carry it about and feed it, and still further this meant that a leopard was in the vicinity and would be sleeping the child off and thus be an easy kill. The men set off and found the leopard, which had consumed all of the child except part of the skull; they killed the leopard and cooked it and ate it, child and all. This is Icien economy, and it makes sense in its own way. It does not, however, endear children to their parents or parents to their children. (1994:135–136)

This pattern of behavior is not limited only to parents, and Ik children showed an astonishingly high level of cruelty toward siblings and other, more vulnerable, children. There are graphic accounts of children deliberately targeting smaller children and old people, stealing food from them, beating them up, raping girls, or of forcing them to exchange sex for food.

Turnbull's account may well be exaggerated. He is obviously describing a community under unique and extreme conditions when almost all social life had broken down. What remains interesting about this account, however, is that it portrays a situation where children as a group are seen as worthless. Although there are suggestions that at some point children might be seen as an economic investment for parents if they could band together and steal enough food from others, or could find some food among the famine-stricken fields, and thus provide their parents with some advantages, it is hard to see, given the situation described here, why children would feel any obligation at all to their parents, or to anyone else.

Ik children are seen not as an economic investment, a way of continuing the lineage, or even as a source of pleasure to their parents. They are portrayed as being denied humanity by their own families and gradually losing their own in the struggle to survive. In this respect, therefore, there is nothing to differentiate adult from child; Ik children, just like their parents, learn quickly to become "selfish, uncaring, and unloving" (1994:10).

Despite the specific desperation of the Ik community, it is not the only situation when economic circumstances dictate the denial of humanity to children. Susan Scrimshaw (1978) has examined patterns of infant mortality and fertility in both historical and contemporary contexts and in a wide variety of societies. She has argued that when children are unwanted, or there is an acceptance of high levels of infant mortality, then there is likely to be parental "underinvestment" in children, emotionally, physically, and in response to their illnesses, which will inevitably lead to their deaths. Subsequent to this pioneering work she has argued that there are many forms of infanticide, ranging from the overt to the passive, in which children are given "lower biological and emotional support" (1984:449), and that there are many reasons for this, including population control, maximizing reproductive success, and cultural attitudes that require "a 'waiting' period after birth before full membership in society is bestowed on an individual" (1984:461). This insight was carried forward by Nancy Scheper-Hughes, whose account of infant death and child neglect in the *favelas* of northeastern Brazil details, with much sympathy, the same phenomenon of underinvestment in the very young, which she refers to as "delayed anthropomorphization" (1992:413). She identifies great ambivalence about infants among such poor mothers, noting that they do not "trust" these children to survive, and therefore invest little emotional energy in them. Mothers in the *favelas* do not recognize or acknowledge individual personhood, reusing the same name several times over for successive siblings and rarely mourning openly for infants. There is little personalization of the very young, and it is only when children show signs of being active, of having the will to survive, and when they are older and therefore worth investing in emotionally, that mothers acknowledge them as more fully human. Until this happens, mothers tend, so Scheper-Hughes claims, to neglect young children who seem passive or sickly. They feel that some children are not meant to survive and they do not fight to keep them alive, do not give them medicine (and usually cannot afford to), and treat their deaths with indifference and resignation. More actively, some mothers make the decision to withhold food from one child, in order to give to a more favored child, or an older one, who is more likely to survive. Unlike Ik mothers, however, there seems to be no dislike or active hostility to children; indeed mothers rhetorically ask Scheper-Hughes "Who doesn't enjoy a baby?" (1992:415), but this affection is general rather than personal.

The idea that, in some cases, mothers make conscious or unconscious choices about which children to invest in has not gone unchallenged. Marilyn Nations and L. A. Rebhun, who worked in similar *favelas* to Scheper-Hughes, have criticized her work, claiming to have found no evidence of fatalism in mothers and arguing that they strive against all odds to keep their children alive, taking them to traditional healers when bureaucratic and geographical constraints prevent them from accessing modern medical care. They accept that women do not always breast-feed their children, do not always arrange prompt medical care, and that, for some women, "a sort of 'twelve month pregnancy' may exist in which newborns are regarded more like fetuses than like children" (1988:190). However, they deny that this implies infant neglect or underinvestment. They claim that women are deeply attached to infants and that their lack of emotion in the face of their deaths has more to do with socially appropriate stoicism and Catholic folk beliefs about infants being transformed into angels than seeing them as less than human.

Behind both interpretations lie questions about whether or not an infant is human and whether it deserves the full regard and care that a socially recognized person should receive. Whether a newborn baby is a fetus, an angel, an unnatural child not meant for this world, or a fully human being will affect its chances of survival (this will be discussed further in the following chapter). Once recognized as a person, though, a child will generally be protected, although, as the case of the Ik showed, this is not always true. In other instances children can be reclassified as nonhuman as a means of getting rid of them without a stain on the social conscience. Childhood is a status that can be assigned, manipulated, denied, or revoked. It can, in certain circumstances, be taken away from children, leaving them extremely vulnerable. The few documented cases of child witches that exist are a good example of the way in which vulnerable children can be classified as nonhuman and treated with what appears to be great cruelty.

Robert Brain (1970) carried out fieldwork on child witches among the Bangwa of Cameroon in the 1950s. He located the phenomenon of child witches within a wider framework of witchcraft beliefs where illness and misfortune were believed to be caused by the malevolence of witches, in particular those who wished to harm their relatives. Child witches, like their adult counterparts, were believed to be able to change shape and to cause illness and death. Children were encouraged to understand illness in terms of witchcraft, so that "for example the child says that he changed himself into a monkey and caught a fever while in the cold plains of the highlands; or that his were-antelope tripped on a lianna in the forest and gave him a pain in the leg" (1970:166). There were also more serious cases where children were encouraged to confess and embellish their confessions. One 12-year-old boy, Asung, having fallen ill himself, eventually confessed to harming his half-brother by mystical means and to killing another child in the compound. His confession was greeted with both outrage and relief; as a result, the community refused to treat him for his own serious illness and he died.

According to Brain, child witches were a category "set off from the rest of Bangwa children; they are, in a sense, abnormal children, subject to mystical dangers which are only removed through ritual" (1970:163). Brain analyzed witchcraft confessions in terms of repressed aggression within a community that had strong strictures against violence, so that witchcraft accusations reflected the guilt that children felt about their aggressive feelings toward close kin. In polygamous households, tensions between co-wives and half-siblings often came out in confessions, and illnesses in the compound were widely believed to be caused by relatives. Brain also claimed that as it was assumed that children did not lie, their confessions, however ornate, gave credibility to and buttressed adult beliefs in witchcraft.

More recent reports about child witches are harder to come by, but in his study of the phenomenon in the Congo, Philip de Boeck (2005) suggests that evangelical Christianity and social upheaval combined with violence and a rise in deaths from AIDS have meant that children may still be targeted as witches and consequently stripped of their humanity and personhood. Against the background of a war-torn country where one in five people is infected with HIV, and where inter-community fighting is rife, families simply cannot manage the numbers of children who are AIDS or war orphans. Lurid accusations of witchcraft against children have become commonplace, as de Boeck describes:

> Little girls are suspected of transforming themselves into stunningly beautiful women to lure their own fathers and uncles to their bed, to snatch away their testicles or penis, and to cause their impotence or death. This

illustrates the fact that Congo's current societal crisis is, to an important degree, also an etiological crisis. Children are also believed to be at the origin of madness, cancer, or heart attacks amongst their relatives and parents. (2005:194)

In the face of such fears, sometimes brutal exorcisms are performed on children and sometimes they are simply turned out onto the streets.

De Boeck describes a society in which the "second world" of the invisible or supernatural exists in parallel to the material world. Witches bring sickness and misfortune to individuals and are likely to be targeted and persecuted within their communities. The visibility of "child witches" on the streets, often a result of being driven out of their homes, or having nowhere else to go after the death of their parents, has made them a vulnerable target. Christian evangelicals, with a strong belief in the physical manifestations of evil, have encouraged such beliefs, and children themselves are expected to make full and gruesome confessions, such as the following one transcribed by de Boeck.

> My name is Mamuya. I am 14 years old. I became a witch because of a boyfriend of mine, Komazulu. One day he gave me a mango. During the following night he came to visit me in my parents' house and threatened that he would kill me if I didn't offer him human meat in return for the mango he had given me earlier. From that moment I became his nocturnal companion and entered his group of witches. I didn't tell my mother. In our group we are three. At night we fly with our "airplane," which we make from the bark of a mango tree, to the houses of our victims. When we fly out at night I transform myself into a cockroach. Komazulu is the pilot of our airplane. He is the one who kills. He gives me some meat and some blood and then I eat and drink. Sometimes he gives me an arm, at other times a leg. Personally I prefer to eat buttocks. I keep a part of the meat to give to my grandmother who is a witch too. Komazulu is a colonel in the "second world," and he has offered me the grade of captain if I sacrifice a person. That's why I killed my baby brother. I gave him diarrhoea and he died. (2005:192)

Once children are conceptualized in this way, they are put beyond the bounds of humanity. Any treatment of them is justifiable because they are not human and have no claims to the compassion and protection that human children might normally expect to inspire.

Cases of older children who are classified as nonhuman are less well documented, but in some literature from Amazonia it is apparent that orphans, and those without kin to protect them, are vulnerable to accusations of sorcery or witchcraft (Santos-Granero 2004). They are the most likely to be punished, excluded, and even killed by the community because their lack of relatives enforces their status as outsiders. Fernando Santos-Granero's study of historical and contemporary cases of child sorcery among Arawak-speaking peoples in the central region of eastern Peru makes these points explicitly. He argues that by reclassifying children as nonhuman, all sorts of cruelty toward them are permissible because, as witches, they are no longer vulnerable children but "the enemy within" which has to be destroyed. Children are suspected of becoming witches in a variety of ways. Santos-Granero describes the process among two particular groups:

> The Asháninka and Ashéninka believe that child sorcerers (*matsi, máci,* or *machi*) are initiated in the art of witchcraft during their sleep. . . . In their dreams, they are visited by any of a number of demonic teachers (*kamári máci*) who are under the orders of Korioshpiri, the "father" or "ruler" of all demons. These demonic teachers, which include birds (cuckoos, nocturnal swallows), insects (grasshoppers, crickets), and the souls of other live or dead human sorcerers, appear to the sleeping child under human guise. . . . The evil spirits of the dead (*shiretzi*) are also reported as possible teachers of witchcraft. . . . The visiting demons place animal or fish bones, palm-leaf slivers, or any other small object in the child's palm, and then knock them off so that they get buried in the ground. Once buried, these objects cause somebody to fall ill. Demonic teachers urge the child to bewitch someone, likening victims to edible forest animals. They also give them human flesh to eat so that they develop a taste for it. After repeated visitations from demonic teachers, the targeted children begin to dream that they themselves bury these pathogenic objects. With the passage of time, they lose their human nature and become demonic witches. (2004:274–275)

Certain children, such as the bad-tempered, sulky, or disobedient, are most likely to be viewed as potential sorcerers, as are the exceptionally pleasant or beautiful children with attractive eyes. By implication, proper or normal children do not stand out; they are obedient, respectful, and good-natured. Children are believed to be aware of their powers and to use them deliberately to negative effect. Although at first children may be unconscious of them, they gradually develop stronger powers and make a conscious decision to inflict harm. Therefore when another person in the community falls ill or dies and a shaman identifies a child as a witch, a series of harsh punishments are called for, such as putting hot peppers in a child's eyes or hanging them upside down over a fire. Sometimes children are half-drowned, sometimes whipped with stinging nettles. In other cases, children are killed and their bodies mutilated and destroyed so that their demonic helpers cannot come back and breathe life into them again.

There is a marked and vicious cruelty about the punishments handed out to such children, but as Santos-Granero points out, "it is precisely because child sorcerers are considered to be no longer human, in fact, that they are tortured in ways that would otherwise be regarded as extremely cruel" (2004:278). Child sorcerers are a threat to the community and to the idea that there must be unity among close kin. They are believed to bring sickness and evil into their society: "It is because of this that children sorcerers are perceived as the 'enemy within,' the rotten apple that infects the crate. Accordingly, they must be cleansed; if this is impossible, or if it fails, they must be purged" (Santos-Granero 2004:298). The treatment of such children is clearly a sensitive issue and has been used as an example of the innate savagery of these people. In none of the cases examined by Santos-Granero, however, were children actually killed. Instead they managed to escape and make their way to mission stations. He also quotes only half a dozen documented cases, although his informants told him of many more. This ethnography is important, however, because along with the cases in the Congo and among the Bangwa, it points to another, less studied way of constructing childhood: that children are dangerous, disruptive, and the bringers of evil.

Conclusion

This chapter has given an account of the wide variations in the ways that childhood has been conceptualized and the vast differences in ideas about the role and status of children. Childhood may be conceived of as a period of immaturity, of incompetence, of weakness, or it may be seen as quite the reverse. While most societies recognize the need for adults to take care of children for extended periods and that their vulnerability gives them some claims to protection, this is by no means universal, or unchanging. A social catastrophe, such as that undergone by the Ik, or an economic one like the endemic poverty of the *favelas* in Brazil means that it may not always be possible to look after young children and they may be neglected or abandoned. Children may be born for the pleasure they will give their parents or for strictly utilitarian reasons of economic investment, or a combination of the two. Looking at the transactional nature of the relationship between parents and children helps to emphasize the very active role that children play in their families and in their productive and affective relationships with their parents. When a child is born, she or he is born into a complex web of social, economic, and political duties and responsibilities. While individual children may not be aware of these for many years to come, it is impossible to understand childhood as an anthropologist without acknowledging and examining these issues.

3

THE BEGINNING OF CHILDHOOD

Introduction

Trying to define childhood by its chronological boundaries is obviously problematic. Childhood is a social status with multiple meanings and expectations attached to it and no clearly defined end or beginning. The previous chapter discussed how the very earliest stages of childhood raise important questions about social recognition and the acknowledgment of humanity, and how this recognition is sometimes withheld from particular infants. Following on from that, this chapter will look at ideas about the nature and status of unborn and neonatal children, particularly the question of when and how children are first recognized as human. It will focus on the imprecise line between what is human or spirit, child or fetus, person or nonperson. Drawing on ethnographic material from many settings, it will show the variety of ways in which the beginnings of childhood are culturally determined. As Beth Conklin and Lynn Morgan argue: "Every society must determine how its youngest will come to achieve the status of persons, how they will be recognized and granted a place within a human community.... In all societies, the complexities and contradictions in normative ideologies of personhood are heightened during the transitional moments of gestation, birth and infancy, when personhood is imminent but not assured" (1996:657–658).

Fetuses

The boundaries between child, fetus, and embryo are extremely blurred, often representing the distinction between person and nonperson, and in some cases between life and nonlife. Ideas concerning these boundaries are problematic, culturally specific, and deeply contested; as Lynn Morgan puts it, "'the fetus' is a culturally specific conceptual entity and not a biological 'thing,' and . . . is created in particular cultural circumstances" (1997:329). Thus a child may be recognized as fully human from the moment of conception (the position of the modern Catholic Church), or it may be seen as becoming a person more gradually and, in some cases, not recognized as a full human being until several days or months after its birth. It is also important to note that there is often little shared understanding within a society about the status of a fetus and how far it is a person. Even legal definitions are problematic and sometimes contradictory. In the UK, for instance, experimentation on embryos is currently (2008) allowed up to 14 days' gestation on the grounds that there is no primitive streak (the earliest manifestation of a nervous system), even though, as Sarah Franklin (1995) has pointed out, this demarcation is not a biological fact but simply a legal and bureaucratic boundary. Abortion is currently legal in the UK until 24 weeks of gestation on the grounds that, before then, a fetus is not viable outside the mother's body (although advances in medical care have made this problematic), and yet, under English law, a child is not considered to be living until he or she is born. The exact status of a fetus between 24 and 40 weeks gestation is unclear: it has some legal rights to protection, but it is not a social entity or a legally recognized person. For individuals there may be differences in whether or not they acknowledge personhood in a fetus depending on circumstances, so that a child who is wanted is seen in terms of its humanity and potentiality from a very early stage, while a fetus that will be terminated is understood very differently (Layne 1996, 2000). In 2001 in the UK, the Royal College of Nurses, a body which supports abortion, demanded the social recognition of aborted and miscarried fetuses. It claimed that 500,000 fetuses each year were disposed of as clinical waste in a way that was not either "respectful or sensitive" (Carvel 2001:3). It called for an end to this practice and demanded communal funerals for these fetuses, with the possibility of individual funerals if the parents wished (Carvel 2001). This would confer on fetuses a special status as beings that deserve some ceremony of social recognition, even though they have no legal recognition until birth.

The contested nature of the neonatal/unborn child is also evident in the bitterly fought battles over abortion in the USA. The cultural politics of the fetus have interested several anthropologists and have focused on questions of when personhood is conferred on an infant, as well as the role and status of women, and the relationship between an individual and the state (Ginsburg 1989; La Fleur 1992). The social and legal challenges to abortion have produced some interesting debates about personhood and the status of the unborn. The Born Alive Bill, for example, was brought before the American Senate in 2000 and focused on the status of failed abortions – fetuses that were aborted but were somehow still born alive. Pro-life groups wanted assurances from the courts that these babies would be treated like any other premature baby, given immediate medical help, placed in incubators, and treated as full human beings with the same rights to medical care as any other child. The aim of the Bill was to establish, in law, legal personhood for all babies who were born alive, whatever the circumstances of their birth. One of the sponsors, Constitution Subcommittee Chairman Steve Chabot (an Ohio Republican), categorically rejected "the notion that an abortion survivor is not a person" (Palmer 2001:1858). His supporters attempted to bestow full personhood on a child at birth and set birth as the definitive boundary between a child and a fetus. In contrast, critics of the Bill argued that birth was not a particularly significant boundary and that fetuses who survived abortion were not babies but aborted nonpersons who should be left to die. Those who opposed the Bill were thus placed in the position of claiming that it was not birth that represented the boundary between life and nonlife, but that life was dependent on the mother's intention. If she wanted an abortion, her choice must be respected, and the fetus must be left to die (Montgomery 2000).

In Japan and Taiwan, several anthropologists have analyzed beliefs in ghost or haunting fetuses and the rise in shrines and temples dedicated to the spirits of these fetuses (La Fleur 1992; Hardacre 1997; Picone 1998; Moskowitz 2001). They have analyzed the fetus as a cultural as well as a biological entity, looked at its place in Japanese and Taiwanese cosmologies, and examined the role that economics and politics have played in changing understandings of the fetus. Although there are some differences between Taiwanese and Japanese beliefs, both societies have seen a recent rise in the belief that aborted children will come back and haunt their mothers. Women who have had abortions report a variety of symptoms, including illness, the inability to eat, fatigue, and the sense that there is a presence nearby watching them. Fetuses are thought to grow into small children in the afterlife, and some women report hearing babies or young children laughing. These ghost fetuses are assumed to be intelligent but also very dangerous because they do not have the maturity to know what to do with their knowledge. Although they are occasionally benevolent, most often ghost fetuses cause distress and have to be placated though spiritual means. The only way to get rid of these hauntings is to pay substantial amounts of money to certain temples that will perform exorcisms to placate the children (Moskowitz 2001).

There are several ways of interpreting this phenomenon. In Taiwan, although abortion is not a political issue, Buddhist values suggest that the deliberate taking of life is morally wrong and women who do so should suffer spiritually. Therefore the ambivalence that many in Taiwan feel about abortion may mean that ghost fetuses are a means of coming to terms with abortion in culturally acceptable ways. On the other hand, a belief in ghost fetuses can also suggest financial exploitation of vulnerable women who are manipulated into paying large amounts of money to exorcize these ghosts (Hardacre 1997). Mark Moskowitz concludes:

> In exploring the significance of the haunting fetus we can learn how women and men come to grips with abortion and how this affects their relationships with their spouses, lovers, children, and other family members. The appeasement can be financially exploitative, yet it provides important psychological comfort to those involved in the choices that lead to abortions as well as a much needed means to project personal and familial feelings of transgression onto a safely displaced object, thereby bringing underlying tensions to the surface and providing a means of working out those problems. (2001:6)

William La Fleur has also written about this phenomenon in contemporary Japan. As the title of his book, Liquid Life (1992), suggests, his work focuses on the fluidity of life and the ways of pacifying the fetus that was prevented from being born. The malevolence of the fetus is less present in his description, and the mizuko (water-child or aborted fetus) is understood as having the potential to return either to the same family or to the land of the gods; birth is therefore delayed rather than prevented. The fetus is seen as existing in the waters of the amniotic fluid in the womb and its existence is precarious and in flux. A water-child is a "child still in the 'becoming' stage rather than emphatically existing as a discrete entity or 'being.' A water-child is a child who has only just begun to emerge from the great watery unknown; it could just as easily be said to be water that has only just begun to take shape as a human-being-to be" (1992:24).

The history of embryology is a well-established field in both Western and Islamic traditions, with questions concerning the beginning of life and the nature of humanity discussed for millennia (see Needham 1959 for the most comprehensive study of this field; see also Furth 1995 for changing Chinese medical views on conception and the interplay between the cosmic and the individual). Aristotle famously argued that the fetus proceeded through three stages of development: at first, it was plant-like, because it grew but did not feel; then it became like an animal, because it felt and acquired sensation; finally, it woke in the womb and became fully alive, although male and female fetuses developed at different rates, with males becoming formed at 40 days gestation, while females did not develop fully until 90 days (Dunstan 1988). Islamic teaching also talks of the fetus undergoing various stages of development before it becomes a person. In the Hadith (the sayings and actions of the Prophet Muhammad), it is written:

> The prophet said: Each of you is constituted in your mother's womb for forty days as a *nutfa*, then it becomes a *'alaqa* for an equal period, then a *mudgha* for another equal period, then the angel is sent, and he breathes the soul into it. (quoted in Mussallam 1990:39)

Similarly, the chapters of the Qur'an called *The Believers* (Sura XXIII, 12–14) relate that, after man is formed from a "quintessence of clay":

> Then we placed him as semen in a firm receptacle;
> Then we formed the semen into a blood-like clot;
> Then we formed the clot into a lump of flesh; then we formed out of
> that lump bones and clothed the bones with flesh.
> (quoted in Mussallam 1990:38)

Many Islamic scholars have used this passage to argue that the first stage of development, when the fetus is simply semen, lasts 40 days; the second stage, when the fetus is a "blood-like" clot, also lasts 40 days; as does the third stage, when the fetus becomes "a lump of flesh." It is only after this process, at 120 days of gestation, that the soul enters the fetus and it becomes possible to talk about personhood (Mussallam 1990). Erika Friedl, in her study of a village in Iran, discusses the continued importance of such beliefs on children's comprehension of conception and pregnancy. After interviewing children about their understandings of the stages of fetal life, she wrote: "A child comes to life in three stages; from seed-in-the-womb to the first fetal movement felt by the mother, the child grows and differentiates in body, but has no individuality, no character, no soul. A child's first movement in utero, around four months, is a sign that God is giving it a soul (*jun*) at that moment. . . . From then on, it will move and will grow quickly into a person but cannot yet hear, see, talk, or think" (1997:31). In an interesting local variation, children also told her that "if one could look into the womb one could recognize a boy as such already twenty days after conception: he has tiny testicles, shaped like lentils. A girl is a formless lump of meat for sixty days" (1997:31).

In other settings there are differing accounts of the stages by which an embryo becomes a person and the ways in which the fetus is socially recognized depending on its stage of growth (Cecil 1996). In many cases one of the most socially significant stages in the transformation of a fetus into a child are its first movements, often seen as evidence of ensoulment, quickening, or the formation or solidifying of the fetus. In rural North India women distinguish clearly between a delayed period and the point, approximately three months later, when the baby is said to have rooted itself in the womb. Patricia and Roger Jeffry write:

> Women generally note the dates of their menstrual periods and talk initially of "delayed periods" . . . not of pregnancy. Vaginal bleeding at that point would be considered a late period rather than a pregnancy that has ended in miscarriage. Women will say, "there was no pregnancy", merely a "blob of flesh" . . . that broke up into blood clots and caused bleeding. At that stage, there are no limbs or organs, and no baby (*bachā*). It is only after nearly three months have elapsed from the start of the last menstrual period that women talk of pregnancy. At this stage they refer to the baby as such (*bachā*) and consider that it has "adhered". . . . This is the time when the life or spirit (*jān*) enters the baby, its body parts begin developing and its sex is settled. Thereafter, vaginal bleeding is called a "baby falling" or the "belly falling". (1996:23–24)

Personhood is conferred in this case not only through ensoulment but also when the body of the fetus can be recognized as childlike. There is no fixed moment of social recognition of the child; rather it is a matter of individual knowledge, social acceptance of when the pregnancy is likely to be viable, and cultural beliefs about the nature of the fetus. In other instances, this ambiguity is even greater. Women in rural Ecuador, for example, claim that a fetus is a child from the moment of conception, because it is created by God, yet do not always acknowledge it as a social person.

> In the rural highlands of northern Ecuador, the unborn are imagined as liminal, unripe, and unfinished creatures. Nascent persons are brought into being slowly, through processes rife with uncertainty and moral ambiguity. Adults are slow to assign individual identity and personhood to the not-yet-born and the newly born. These unknown, unknowable *criaturas* may teeter on the cusp of personhood for months before being fully welcomed into the human community. . . .
>
> . . . in numbering their offspring [Ecuadorian women] have a great deal of latitude in deciding how to classify and represent the differences among living, stillborn, live-born, miscarried, adopted, and deceased children.
>
> The fact that women can count their *hijos* [children] in so many different yet equally acceptable ways suggests two things. First, it suggests that every pregnancy can be – but is not necessarily – socially significant, no matter the result. . . . Second, it acknowledges that children emerge through a lengthy, gradual process that spans gestation and infancy and that any divisions imposed on the process (such as "trimesters," or "viability") are somewhat arbitrary. (Morgan 1997:329–333)

The fetus here remains ambiguous: it is not yet a child or a full person but has the potential to become so. Potential personhood and full humanity are very different prospects, albeit parts of the same continuum.

In industrialized countries, advances in medical technology and scientific knowledge have meant that fetuses can be assigned the status of persons at significantly earlier stages of gestation than has been previously possible. Some scholars have argued that women's knowledge about their own bodies, their own recognition of the signs of pregnancy, and their own internal acknowledgments of new life, and in particular feeling the first movements of the baby, have been supplanted by medical intervention so that doctors now confirm pregnancy before women themselves know (Rapp 1999). The routine use of scans for Western women early in pregnancy gives them an external view of the fetus and a visual representation of it, possibly before they can feel it. "So convincing is the cognitive and sensual apprehension of the fetus via the electronic mediation of ultrasound technology that women may routinely experience a 'technological quickening' several weeks before they sense fetal movement in their own bodies" (Mitchell and Georges 1997:373).

In the above ethnographic descriptions, ideas about fetal development, and the gradual processes during which the fetus moves toward ensoulment and personhood, take place in an approximate nine-month period, yet, looking cross-culturally, there is no universal understanding of development occurring within the womb or within a specific time-frame. Some children begin socialization long before birth and their incorporation into a wider society is a series of processes which begin in the womb and continue after they have left it. Laura Rival describes how the Huaorani of Ecuador have only one word – translated as "in the process of being born" – for fetus, newborn, and infant (1998:625; see also McCallam 1996; Conklin 2001). The child becomes recognized as a person through social practices such as diet restrictions or couvade, rather than physical transformations (Rivière 1974; see also Morton 2002 for an account of *tapu* or pregnancy prohibitions in Tonga). Rival writes:

> As in other parts of Amazonia, the child is said to result from the coagulation of female blood and male semen. . . . As the clot forms, it is activated – energized – by the Creator's soul matter and becomes a child. So the child is all formed from the start; there is no process of transformation or metamorphosis, only a process of growth. Likewise, delivery is not sufficient to give birth to the child, who is definitively born only when the father and mother have ended the couvade restrictions, and when a classificatory grandparent (a grandmother for a girl, a grandfather for a boy) has given him or her at least one personal name. Going a step further, I would say that the moment of birth is not the beginning of life *per se*, but rather the transfer from one dwelling (the womb) to another (the longhouse). . . . All this suggests that birth is part of a wider process of gradual incorporation by which children, who start their lives in the mother's womb, are progressively integrated within the longhouse sharing economy. (1998:625–626)

In other parts of Amazonia, conception represents only a theoretical possibility of new life; it needs then to be followed by sexual intercourse, which forms the body of a child and transforms the potential human life into an embodied child. Marco Gonçalves (2001) writes that for the Pirahã of Brazil the act of conception is not associated with sexual intercourse. When a woman realizes she is pregnant, because she is not menstruating, she gets together with her husband and close kin and they try to remember recent incidents which could have occasioned the conception; usually some sort of surprise. The causes of this surprise could be very diverse, a fish jumping out of the water, an animal running in front of her, a burn from hot food, or a wasp sting. Conception therefore creates the possibility of the birth of a new human being in the world; only after it has occurred does the process of making the body of a child begin through sexual intercourse. The man's semen creates the bones and flesh of the child, and the women's menstrual blood the internal organs (Gonçalves 2001).

In Tunisia, and other parts of the Middle East, beliefs in the existence of "sleeping children" further suggest that ideas about a nine-month gestational period are not universally shared (Bargach 2002). Sleeping children are those who are conceived normally, develop in the womb for a period of between three and six months, and then, in reaction to a shock or some other external circumstance, such as a death, go to sleep in the womb. They may be born several months later or never at all, and women in their seventies may claim that they are still pregnant and that they still have fetuses in their wombs. In her study of this phenomenon Angel Foster (1991) argues that such beliefs are a way of preserving the centrality of fertility and reproduction in women's lives, even when they are past menopause. They may also be used to legitimize illicit sexual relations, so that a woman whose husband dies and who then gives birth to a child several years later can be said to be carrying a sleeping child. She can claim that grief for the loss of her husband put the child to sleep and it took several months or years to wake up. When it is finally born, it is socially recognized and legitimized as her husband's child.

Spirit Children

The difficulty in knowing where an anthropology of childhood begins, or what it should include, is evident in the case of spirit children, who stretch the category of "the unborn" to the furthest extreme. These are children who are believed to exist in the supernatural world, waiting to be born as embodied children. Their existence is recognized in communities as diverse as the Aborigines of the Kimberleys (Kaberry 1939) and West African societies such as the Yoruba (Beier 1954; Renne 2002; Dopamu 2006), Akan (Ephirim-Donkor 1997), Mende (Ferme 2001), Ijaw (Leis 1982), and Beng (Gottlieb 1998, 2000). The links between newly born children and the spirit world are so strong that it is impossible to study the former without reference to the latter.

Some of the earliest accounts of spirit children among Aborigines are found in missionary accounts from the late 19th century. The Rev. L. Schulze wrote about the souls of infants living in trees and entering the body of a woman when she felt the first pains of childbirth (quoted in Ashley-Montague 1937). These ideas were looked at in much greater detail by Baldwin Spencer and Francis Gillen (1899, 1927), who examined beliefs about spirit children among various Aboriginal communities in central and northern Australia. They reported that among the central Australian Arunta, spirit children were seen as the germ or seed of a completely formed human being and were thought to be the size of a pebble (Spencer and Gillen 1927). In Western Australia, spirit children were described as being like ordinary children, albeit the size of walnuts, playing in pools and wandering over the land. In some places spirit children were believed to live beneath the waves in the care of a mother-turtle and a porpoise and could be seen playing there by diviners. Even after these children had entered the womb, and, in some cases, long after birth, they were still understood as spirit, rather than human, children. It was only when they began to laugh and respond and manifested a personality that they were no longer referred to as spirit children (Bates 1938). Spirit children were believed to have some sort of independent existence, not simply as disembodied spiritual matter but as beings with personal preferences and the ability to make choices. Spencer and Gillen wrote of women running away when they saw a whirlwind because they thought spirit children lived in there, and of women attempting to look old and unattractive when they passed a particular rock because they believed it was a place from which spirit children emanated. They described how spirit children were thought to choose their mothers and appeared to have definite likes and dislikes about potential parents. "The natives are quite clear upon this point. The spirit children are supposed to have a strong predilection for fat women, and prefer to choose such for their mothers, even at the risk of being born into the wrong class" (Spencer and Gillen 1899:125).

One of the most detailed accounts of spirit children among the Aborigines is found in Phyllis Kaberry's work in the Australian Kimberleys. She is more explicit than most about the exact nature of spirit children and how they fit into wider beliefs.

These spirit children, *djinganara:ny*, are not ancestors . . . but were placed in the pools by *Kaleru*, the rainbow serpent in the . . . Time Long Past, before there were any natives. Often they are temporarily incarnated in animals, birds, fish, reptiles, but they also wander over the country, play in the pools, and live on a green weed called *gida:l*. Descriptions vary; some say the *djinganara:ny* are like little children about the size of a walnut; others, that they resemble small red frogs. Conception occurs when one of these enters a woman. Its presence in the food given her by her husband makes her vomit, and later he dreams of it or else of some animal which he associates with it. It enters his wife by the foot and she becomes pregnant. The food which made her ill becomes the . . . conception totem of her child. Scars, moles or dimples are the wounds where some animal or fish was speared by the man. (Kaberry 1939:41–42)

Later ethnographies also report continuing beliefs in spirit children. James Cowan (1997) describes how, among the Ngalia of central Australia, spirit children sit under shady trees, waiting for an appropriate mother to pass by. They eat the gum of acacia trees, drink the morning dew, and have light streaks in their dark-colored hair. When they see a woman they would like to be their mother, they reduce themselves to the size of a termite and enter her body. If they are unsuccessful one day, they return the next.

Despite the differences in the descriptions of spirit children, all these societies recognize the preexistence of children in another form. In some instances, spirit children change into "flesh and blood" children in the womb; in others, they metamorphose from frogs, fish, or birds to children at some point during gestation; in other cases, the process happens after birth. There is, however, no separation between spirit children and embodied children; they are part of the same continuum which links the supernatural and the natural world, and the latter cannot be studied without reference to the former. Malinowski wrote that the Trobriand islanders of Melanesia used the "term *waiwaia*, which means embryo, child in the womb, and also infant immediately after birth, [to apply also] to the non-incarnated spirit children" (1948:191). Children themselves are also well aware of the links between their lives as spirit children and their current existences. Kaberry explicitly interviewed children on this point. She wrote:

Children of eight or nine as a rule knew their [conception totem], and were interested in the fact that they had once been a fish, bird, reptile or animal prior to the entry of the spirit child into the mother. [One child] related to me with pride: "I bin sit down alonga fish first time. Father bin come close alonga water. He bin spear 'em me. Me bin go alonga camp, me bin go alonga mother; me bin come out alonga bingy." (1939:74)

[I was a fish at first. Father came up to the water and speared me there. So I was taken to the camp, and to my mother, and I came out as a baby.] (translations by James 2000:173)

Kaberry further emphasized this point in her discussions about whether or not the Aborigines of the Kimberleys denied physical paternity. She argued that even if the biomedical facts of conception were known, or accepted, it would make little difference to notions of kinship. Fathers would still be the parents to find the "spiritual counterpart, soul or spirit double of the child" (Kaberry 1936:399), and it was this role that was their most important contribution to the reproductive process. The physical child and its spiritual counterpart child were inseparably linked; one could not do without the other, and to study either in isolation was to misunderstand the nature of childhood.

West African spirit children have been the focus of much attention in recent years, but the best-known accounts have come from literature rather than ethnography, most notably Chinua Achebe's *Things Fall Apart* (1958), Wole Soyinka's *Aké: The Years of Childhood* (1981), and Ben Okri's *The Famished Road* (1992) (for literary analyses of these texts see Achebe 1980; Hawley 1995; McCabe 2002; Kehinde 2003). It can of course be problematic to equate fiction and ethnography, but several anthropologists who have worked on spirit children reference these literary texts alongside monographs, suggesting that they do provide a useful source of ethnographic information about these children (Ferme 2001; Gottlieb 2004). Beliefs in spirit children are found in both Yoruba and Igbo cosmology. Known as *abiku* in Yoruba and *ogbanje* in Igbo, these children are believed to be those who die and are reborn several times into the same family and whose time in the world of the living is very short. *Abiku* and *ogbanje* children are seen as physically and emotionally different from other children and are thought to continue to play with their companions from the other world and to divine what others cannot see (Beier 1954; Soyinka 1981). There is no separation in these accounts between the spirit and the mortal worlds, and infants and young children are seen as belonging, and having allegiances, to both worlds and as being constantly torn between the two. Ben Okri's lyrical invocation of the spirit world captures this ambivalence well. *The Famished Road* is narrated by a spirit child named Azaro, and tells of his decision to stay in the world of the living, despite the promises he made to his companions in the world of the unborn to return to them.

> In that land of beginnings spirits mingled with the unborn. We could assume numerous forms. Many of us were birds. We knew no boundaries. There was much feasting, playing and sorrowing. We feasted much because of the beautiful terrors of eternity. We played much because we were free. And we sorrowed much because there were always those amongst us who had just returned from the world of the Living. They had returned inconsolable for all the love they had left behind, all the suffering they hadn't redeemed, all that they hadn't understood and for all that they had barely begun to learn before they were drawn back to the land of origins. . . .
>
> As we approached another incarnation we made pacts that we would return to the spirit world at the first opportunity. We made those vows in the fields of intense flowers and in the sweet-tasting moonlight of that world. Those of us who made such vows were known among the Living as abiku, spirit-children. Not all people recognised us. We were the ones who kept coming and going, unwilling to come to terms with life. We had the ability to will our deaths. Our pacts were binding. . . .
>
> We are the strange ones, with half of our beings always in the spirit world. (Okri 1992:3–4)

There is a deep ambivalence in spirit children's attachment to the world, and their relationships to their parents can be hostile and malevolent. Esther Nzewi (2001) describes *ogbanje* as being motivated by revenge, and the desire for parental humiliation, and writes that they are described by their parents as detached, unemotional, sickly, and withdrawn. Chikwenye Ogunyemi (2002) sees them as being locked in a deadly power struggle with their parents over whether to live or die. Their spirit companions also inspire both love and fear. Ulli Beier (1954) claimed that although his informants remembered playing wonderful games with their spirit companions as children, they were also aware of the dangers that these spirits presented to them. He described how spirit children would try to tempt earthly children to throw themselves into the water or provoke other deadly accidents.

The malevolence and cruelty of spirit children is a recurrent theme in the literature. Timothy Mobolade writes that "it is universally believed among the Yoruba people that a bereaved mother's tears are highly valued in the assembly of the *Abiku* spirits" (1973:62). He also recounts how one of his own aunts claimed to be an *abiku*: "This aunt takes delight in narrating to her mother and other relations how much she used to enjoy seeing her mother weeping and sorrowing each time she died" (1973:62). Despite this malice, and the impossibility of keeping spirit children alive against their wishes, they are often treated with special care and consideration by their parents. Wole Soyinka (1981) describes a childhood companion in his home village called Bukola who was recognized as an *abiku* by the community. This is presented with very little comment, other than a simple acceptance that she was different, that she was constantly being tempted to return to her spirit companions, and that her parents and friends tried to be as gentle as possible with her so that she did not take offense and return to the spirit world. Mobolade described how parents plead and beg these children to survive and give them names such as "*Durojaiye* (Wait and enjoy life): *Pakuti* (Shun death and stop dying); *Rotimi* (Stay and put up with me)" (1973:63).

Ideas about *abiku* and *ogbanje* have been used to explain many phenomena in West African societies. The image of a malevolent or capricious spirit being reborn several times to the same mother has also become a literary trope amongst both African and African American writers. Toni Morrison's *Sula* (1973) and *Beloved* (1987) are both well-known examples of African American literature which harness beliefs about spirit children as a way of emphasizing the West African cultural legacies in US slave society (Ogunyemi 2002; Okonkwo 2004). Another approach has been to analyze spirit children beliefs as a way of coping with the high infant mortality of the region and as an adaptive parental response to the ever-present threat of losing several children (Ilechukwu 2007). Although beliefs in spirit children are changing, recent research shows a significant number of Yoruba women still believe in *abiku*, and use these beliefs to make treatment decisions when their children are ill, an important consideration when it has also been suggested that *abiku* and *ogbanje* spirit children show many symptoms associated with sickle-cell diseases and that the idea of *ogbanje* is used as a metaphysical explanation of a physical imperfection (Nzewi 2001; Ogunjuyigbe 2004). Alternatively it has been suggested that *abiku* or *ogbanje* beliefs are a culturally sanctioned way of talking about certain forms of mental illness (Achebe 1986).

Recent ethnographies have examined spirit children beliefs in other areas of West Africa (Leis 1982; Gottlieb 1998, 2000). Again it is impossible to study the lives of living children without reference to their lives in the spirit world. These links are recognized by their parents and by the community at large, and in these instances all children come from the spirit world.

As the Ijaw view it, the special power that children have derives from their recent arrival from another kind of world. They straddle two worlds, that of the non-living (*duwoiama*) and that of the living (*ex ama*), and they can "see" and interact with entities or beings in both worlds. They can remember their agreements with Wonyinghi, the female creator, about the nature of their future life among the living. Each individual, the Ijaw believe, makes such an agreement and decides himself before birth how long to live, how many if any children to have, whether to be wealthy or not, and the major direction his life will take. He then comes to this world in spiritual form . . . and awaits the time to be conceived. (Leis 1982:154)

The ability that children have, in the spirit world, to decide when they will die means that the length of time they spend in the world of the living is determined by the child. The high rate of infant mortality is explained by the pact that these children have made with their creator to remain for only a short time with their parents, a decision they make in their naïvety because they do not understand the pain and suffering they are inflicting on their parents by choosing not to remain alive. In cases where parents suffer the repeated mortality of their children, it is thought that the same child is coming back again and again and dying each time. In these instances, a father might take the body of the child into the forest and chop the corpse into small pieces to show the child that he or she should not come back into the world of the living without a firm intention to stay (Leis 1982; see also Mobolade 1973).

The existence of children in the spirit world affects the lives of other children who have already been born or are still in the womb. The Ijaw recognize that children might be jealous of their siblings, that they may wish to be the last-born (or an only child). A woman who fails to conceive, or has a miscarriage when she already has a child, may assume that her previously born child is jealous and is killing the child in her womb, or preventing conception. Similarly if her child who is already born is ill while she becomes pregnant, it may be that the child in her womb is harming it or trying to kill it. In these cases, a pact must be made between the fetus and the child, agreeing not to harm each other (Leis 1982). Gradually, as children get older, they forget about their previous existence in the spirit world and they forget about their agreements with their creator. They lose their ability to see and communicate with the spirit world and become adults, existing only in the world of the living.

For the Beng of the Côte d'Ivoire there is also contemporary ethnography on the relationship between children of this world and those in the spirit world (Gottlieb 1998, 2000). The Beng believe in a spirit world, *wrugbe*, where children exist before they are born and where people go after their deaths. Although *wrugbe* is reachable by some adults, especially through dreams or if they are diviners, it is children who are closest to it and to whom it is most accessible. Indeed young children are seen as having only partially emerged from *wrugbe* and are in constant contact with it for several years after they are born. A newborn child belongs completely to the spirit world, and until "the umbilical stump falls off, the new-born is not considered to have emerged from wrugbe at all, and the tiny crea-ture is not seen as a person. . . . Hence if the new-born should die during those first few days, there is no funeral, and the fact is not announced publicly. In this case the infant's passing is not conceived as a death, just a return in bodily form to the space that the infant was still psychically inhabiting" (Gottlieb 1998:124). After the stump has fallen off, the child begins a slow process, which takes several years, of leaving the spirit world behind and becoming more firmly attached to his or her earthly life. A child leaves *wrugbe* behind after a series of rituals are performed on his or her body, such as the giving of enemas and ear piercing, and also when he or she is seen as having grown in understanding. A diviner named Koualou Ba told Alma Gottlieb:

> KB: At some point, children leave wrugbe for good and decide to stay in this life.
>
> AG: How do you know when this has happened?
>
> KB: When children speak their dreams, or understand [a drastic situation, such as] that their mother or father has died, then you know that they've totally come out of wrugbe.
>
> AG: When does this happen?
>
> KB: By seven years old, for sure! At three years old, they're still in-between: partly in wrugbe and partly in this life. They see what happens in this life, but they don't understand it. (1998:125)

The Beng believe that both adults and children can live in *wrugbe* and that a child has both spiritual and earthly parents. *Wrugbe* parents are thought to get angry if the baby is not being properly looked after in its earthly life. If it is being abused or neglected, not fed when it cries, or comforted when in distress, its spiritual parents may decide to take the child back into the spirit world and keep it there until better parents are found and it can be reborn in a different family. In Beng belief, spirit children are seen as all-knowing and all-understanding. One aspect of this is that in *wrugbe* spirits are multilingual and can understand all languages. When they are born they do not learn one language but lose all the others they know. This is a gradual process achieved over time, so that very young infants are thought still to understand everything that is said to them, in whatever language. Babies are thought to be able to communicate and speak directly to their parents or caregivers, but because adults have forgotten the languages they knew when they were in *wrugbe*, they cannot communicate directly with their infants or understand what they want. For this reason parents have to rely on help from a diviner, who can understand what babies are trying to communicate because he, too, is in touch with the spirit world.

All this points to profoundly different beliefs about child development to those found in the West, where children are perceived as being born without skills such as language or understanding and are thought to acquire these skills gradually. In contrast, the Beng, and other West African cultures such as the Mende, do not necessarily conceive of the life-course as being a linear process. They believe that children are born with these skills, but that socialization comes about after forgetting this knowledge, and that while children gain certain powers as they grow, they lose others (Ferme 2001). The Western view that sees infants as unable to communicate is here replaced by a model that sees adults as the ones who do not understand because they have forgotten the knowledge possessed by the baby.

Reincarnation

Beliefs in spirit children suggest that children can exist as individuals in different cosmological time and space. Ideas about individual preexistence are also central to people who believe in reincarnation and attempt to see, in their children, reincarnations of parents, family, or other ancestors. Among the Trobriand Islanders, Malinowski (1948) claimed that the period between death and reincarnation could be many generations, so that children were unlikely to be recognized as particular individuals, although they were always born into the same matrilineal clan or subclan to which they previously belonged. According to Malinowski, the Trobriand Islanders believed in *Tuma*, the land of spirits, where people went after their deaths to await rebirth some time in the future. This world paralleled the earthly world, so that people married and aged in *Tuma*. Eventually, however, it became time for them to be reborn.

> When the *baloma* (spirit) has grown old, his teeth fall out, his skin gets
> loose and wrinkled; he goes to the beach and bathes in the salt water; then
> he throws off his skin just as a snake would do, and becomes a young child
> again; really an embryo, a *waiwaia* – a term applied to children *in utero*
> and immediately after birth. A *baloma* woman sees this *waiwaia*; she takes
> it up, and puts it in a basket or a plaited and folded coconut leaf (*puatai*).
> She carries the small being to Kiriwina, and places it in the womb of some
> woman, inserting it *per vaginam*. Then that woman becomes pregnant.
> (Malinowski 1948:190)

It may take many generations for a spirit to be reborn as a child, and
little is likely to be known about the identity or personality of the child.
Elsewhere the link between the newborn child and the person who
has been reincarnated is much closer and the child will be accepted as
the reincarnation of a person who has recently died in the community,
especially when he or she is recognized by some distinguishing physical
characteristic, or by patterns of behavior that remind observers of the
recently dead.

Among certain Inuit communities in Canada it is believed that if a child
dies young, then the next child will inherit the dead child's spirit, or if a
twin dies, his or her spirit will live on in the surviving sibling (Mills 1994).
Adults, too, may be reincarnated as newly born children after they die.
There is a search for a relationship between the child and the dead person, possibly in the form of a birthmark or in shared memories. Edith
Turner gives the example of an Inuit whaling family:

> A child of three in one whale-hunter's family was watched for significant
> sayings, especially at whaling time, because he was regarded as the rein-
> carnation of his wise uncle Patrick, who in turn had gained spiritual
> powers from his ancestors. "Aapa catch whale," the child announced one
> day to everyone's delight, and indeed Aapa, that is, his grandfather, did
> assist in catching a whale that year. This child, Aaron, was treated with
> unusual respect, indeed reverence, which did not fade after a new grand-
> child was born. (1994:69)

In this case the identity of the child, and the way that he was raised,
depended on who he was believed to be in a former life. He was
expected to take on many of the characteristics of his uncle, including his
wisdom and skill at whaling. His daily life therefore would be influenced
by his existence in a previous one, and to understand his experiences it

is necessary to understand not only his own life, but also that of the uncle of whom he is a reincarnation.

In this case there is a sense that there is no such thing as a new person being born or that a child is a new addition to the community. Mark Nuttall writes of the Inuit of Greenland:

> On an emotional level, when a child is named . . . the bond between deceased and bereaved is re-established. The dead person is said to have "come home" . . . to the bereaved kin. There is a sense that people are not naming a new person, but are welcoming back a member of the family and the community. A child does not take a new name, thus becoming altogether another person in the cosmos, but re-enters an existing order of being, of which their name at least is already a part. (1994:129)

Such beliefs are widespread and, once more, make the idea of an anthropology of childhood infinitely complex. Among the Ndenbu of Zambia, when children are born, they are watched for signs of who they once were. When they cry, the parents and other relatives speak the names of ancestors. When children hear the right one (always a dead relative on their father's side), they will stop crying (Turner 1994). Thus the child is not simply an individual whose daily life and experiences need to be recorded and analyzed, but his or her existence needs to be conceptualized as part of wider cosmologies which look at how and why ancestors return to earth. The Papel of Guinea-Bissau believe that ancestral spirits return in newborns and that a child who cries continually, or shows signs of precocity, is a reincarnation of a near relative. Again physical signs may give a clue as to who the child once was. Jonina Einarsdóttir recounts: "On one occasion I met an elderly man together with his teenage daughter. The girl, who was a little chubby is neatly dressed. I noticed her face was severely deformed and wrinkled, the nose could hardly be seen, and her mouth was just a small, round hole. I asked her father if she got burnt as a child. 'No, she did not. She is a person who died, and that person got burnt' he responded" (2000:103). There are also, of course, numerous other examples from Buddhist and Hindu societies about children who are recognized, as they begin to show a resemblance to those who have died, as the reincarnation of others. In some cases children are the reincarnation of complete strangers and are born thousands of miles away from where they died. The search for reincarnated lamas in Tibetan Buddhism is one of the most famous examples of this, where the reincarnation of the dead lama can occur in a child anywhere in the world. The identified child is expected to know particular signs and understand certain texts, and, once he has been identified as the reincarnation of the lama, is trained in his religious heritage (Gupta 2002).

Anomalies

Other focuses of anthropological attention that relate to the nature of infants and their claims on personhood are the many studies of twins and twinship. Much of this literature focuses on twins' ambiguous nature, whether they have one soul or two, whether they are children or spirits, monsters or people. It is also worth noting that the term "twin" can have very different meanings in different contexts, so that a child may be thought of, or referred to, as a twin not only if it is a multiple birth but also if it is a single, breech birth, or a baby born with a caul (Diduk 1993). "Twin," therefore, can mean any child whose birth deviates from accepted norms. Much of the most famous literature on twins is many years old and ideas about twinship and the status of twins has been changed by colonial intervention, globalization, missionary work, and national policy (Chappel 1974; Bastian 2001; Diduk 2001; Renne 2001). Yet such studies remain of interest, not only because they relate to issues raised in the previous chapter about what is a child (and how should it be treated), but also because a study of anomalies sheds light on the status of "normal" children and the processes by which they are assigned personhood. As Isaac Schapera wrote in one of the earliest comparative studies of twins in South Africa:

> We have to look upon these customs [relating to twins] as a variation from the customs relating to ordinary children rather than as a special series of rites and ceremonies peculiar to twins, and our explanation must be such that it will be capable of satisfying not only the reactions produced by the birth of twins, but also those produced by normal birth. (1927:134–135)

Both Schapera (1927) and, most famously, Evans-Pritchard (1936) used indigenous ideas about twins in order to understand ideas about personhood and identity. Evans-Pritchard described twin beliefs among the Nuer of southern Sudan as follows: "Besides being considered a single personality twins are also spoken of as birds. I have often been told by Nuer,

'A twin is not a person, he is a bird.' ... If a baby twin dies they always say, '*Ce par*' ('It has flown away')" (1936:235). While there has been much debate since about whether or not this association was metaphorical (Firth 1966), and Evans-Pritchard himself points out that this association may not be literal, what is apparent is that twins are often anomalous. The Nuer, according to Evans-Pritchard (1956), believed that twins had only one soul and were "children of God," different from other children. In a society where sibling order was important, twins presented difficulties of succession and they could not be placed in socially recognized and accepted categories. Victor Turner sums up this problem: "Twinship presents the paradoxes that what is physically double is structurally single and what is mystically one is empirically two" (1969:45).

Often twins have powers other children do not have and they are more closely connected with the spirit or ancestral world than other children. Mariane Ferme (2001) writes that many Mende claim to have a twin in the spirit world. Even when only one child is born, there is sometimes an assumption that the other twin died in the womb and now lives in the spirit world, giving the earthly twin particular powers of divination. The presence of twins may be determined by dreams before birth, or alternatively by examining the placenta after birth, and this may be construed not as the by-product of parturition but as the remains of a dead fetus. In other instances a twin can be born several years after its sibling, thereby undermining the idea of twinship being based on simultaneous birth. In Mende society, which emphasizes the relationship between the visible and invisible and the open and the concealed, such ideas about twinship mean that infants have a particular relationship to the spirit world and occupy a liminal and somewhat dangerous position.

This anomalous place in the social order occupied by twins can have various effects on the ways that they are treated. For the Labwor of Uganda, twins were seen as especially troublesome and dangerous. Although not viewed as one person, twins were treated alike, in terms of both reward and punishment. If one twin was given something, the other one was also given something of equal value, and if one twin was punished, the other was as well. Twins could be dangerous because they conspired against their parents, causing them harm if they were displeased with them (Abrahams 1972). In other cases twins are not regarded as humans because they challenge the divine order, where children are born singly and animals are born multiply. As Misty Bastian writes of the 19th-century battles between Christian missionaries and the West African Igbo:

The elders refer to a common northern Igbo notion (one that continues to have power in contemporary Igbo areas) that human beings are manifestly not like animals. Humans, if they are humans indeed, must not demonstrate animal-like traits. In a world where the human form is considered mutable, a mask that can be put on by certain spiritual and animal beings, it is imperative that one be sure that he or she is dealing directly with other human beings and not spiritual tricksters with morally ambiguous or outright evil designs. One of the hallmarks of animality within Igbo cosmological reasoning is bearing litters of young; as a general rule animals bear multiply rather than singly. (2001:16)

In such cases, twins might be exposed or suffocated and their bodies disposed of in the "bad bush" outside Igbo towns. Schapera also gave the example of the !Kung and the Auin in South Africa, where twins signified bad luck for the parents and the senior herdsman and one or both of them were killed at birth. Twins may also be understood as a sign of unnatural or adulterous conceptions, where, for instance, a woman has had a sexual partner other than her husband and conceived children with two different fathers (Bastian 2001). Elsewhere the close proximity of children in the womb, especially those of opposite sexes, can suggest incest and thus becomes monstrous (Errington 1987).

As several anthropologists have pointed out (Chappel 1974; Diduk 2001; Renne 2001), ideas about twins are related to much wider social and political factors, and there are instances where ideas about twins have changed in relation to external forces. The influx of Christianity into parts of Nigeria, and the ideological and cosmological arguments that this process has brought with it, means that understandings about twins have been radically reversed. Elisha Renne (2001) discusses how, in Yorubaland, twins, who were formerly destroyed as witches, are now revered. They are now seen as having special powers, are honored as a link to the ancestors and as intermediaries to the spirit world, and are thought to bring potential benefits, such as great wealth, to their families (Renne and Bastian 2001). In contrast, Bastian (2001) has shown that in areas of Hausa-speaking Nigeria, twins, who were once welcomed, are now sometimes reviled as products of unnatural conceptions. In both cases, the clash of local and Christian ideologies has wrought huge changes in views of twinship, emphasizing once more that ideas about childhood are not natural, biological, or universal but cultural, socially constructed, and subject to change.

Twins are the most obvious anomalous children found in the anthropological literature. Yet there are other instances where the birth of children who are seen as different or unusual can shed light on other ideas about childhood. In rural Jamaica there is a category of "false belly" when a woman is believed to be carrying the result of an unnatural conception after being entered by a *duppie* (ancestral ghost) against her will. When this occurs she will have all the symptoms of pregnancy but at the end of nine months will not give birth to a child or will give birth to a seriously deformed or monstrous one. Elisa Sobo (1996) argues that not only is this a way of women coming to terms with a miscarriage or a deformed child, it is also a way of denying the fetus any humanity, making it easier to terminate the pregnancy. In a society which does not sanction the abortion of healthy fetuses, false belly can be used as a justification in doing so.

The previous chapter discussed how questions about the nature of childhood have profound effects on the ways children are treated. In the case of older children, if they are classified as nonhuman and have the recognition of personhood withdrawn from them, they are immensely vulnerable. In the case of newborn children, this is even more apparent; not only are they most physically vulnerable when in their infancy, but this is also the time when personhood is negotiated and contested most explicitly. It is the time when whether or not they are considered human dramatically affects their life chances. While twins may be at particular risk of being seen as nonpersons, any children born in ways that are considered unacceptable or deviant may arouse suspicions that they are in some way evil or possessed of a nonhuman nature. David Parkin (1985), in his study of the Girama of Kenya, has found historical evidence that children born feet first or whose top teeth came through before the bottom ones were seen as deviant and that such children might be drowned by non-family members worried about bringing evil into the community. In other cases, children's behavior as they grow arouses suspicion that they are not what they seem. Alma Gottlieb (2004) discusses the category of snake children among the Beng. These children are born after a snake is thought to have invaded the mother's womb and dislodged the fetus. When the child is born, its true nature asserts itself, it fails to thrive, and shows signs of snake-like behavior. Diviners are called in and offer the child snake food, which, if it rejects, is a sign of its humanity, while if it likes the food, it is revealed as a snake. Often, however, these children are allowed to live, and while they cannot marry, they are tolerated and enabled to grow up. In other communities snake children are abandoned when their true nature becomes apparent. Kathleen Dettwyler (1994) asked a diviner in Mali about what happened to snake children and how they could be identified. He told her:

They just never grow. They never reach out for things with their hands, they never sit up and walk, they never talk. Some begin to, but then stop. You keep praying and hoping and looking for medicine for them, but nothing helps. . . . Well, if they don't get better after a couple of years, then you know that they are evil spirits, and you give up . . . , you take them out into the bush and you just leave them. . . . They turn into snakes and slither away. . . . You go back the next day, and they aren't there. Then you know for sure that they weren't really children at all, but evil spirits. When you see a snake, you wonder if it used to be your child. (1994:85–86)

Most anomalous, and vulnerable, of all are children born with obvious birth defects or physical deformities. As Nancy Scheper-Hughes argues:

Whereas stigma may consign the spurned adult to a life of exclusion and marginality, the stigmatization of a hopelessly dependent neonate is inevitably a death sentence. The sickly, wasted, or congenitally deformed infant challenges the tentative and fragile symbolic boundaries between human and nonhuman, natural and supernatural, normal and abominable. Such infants may fall out of category, and they can be viewed with caution or with revulsion as a source of pollution, disorder, and danger. (1992:375)

It might be argued that such children are a drain on their families, and on the wider community, and therefore the denial of personhood is a way of protecting the community from the time-consuming work that looking after them would entail. Yet many parents are very reluctant to turn against their children, and within communities there is often great discussion as to what will happen to them. These discussions revolve around the fundamental humanity of these children: are they really human children or are they evil spirits? Jonina Einarsdóttir (2000) carried out work on how high rates of infant mortality were understood and explained among the Papel of Guinea-Bissau and whether there were any circumstances in which, with the survival of infants so precarious, they were deliberately harmed. She discusses a category of children known as *iran*, or nonhuman children. Often these children have physical deformities or obvious discrepancies such as albinism and stand out at birth as being noticeably different. Even so, before children are accepted as *iran*, they have to be identified as such by a diviner, who accesses the true nature of the child and tells parents whether or not their child is a danger to the community. If a child is identified as an *iran*, it is taken to the sea (a euphemism for drowning it), and given the opportunity of returning to its true place in the spirit world. If it disappears, it is truly an *iran*, although if it cries, it might be saved. Alternatively a child might be killed and its body burnt to prevent it returning. Not all children born with a disability are seen as evil or dangerous, however, and Einarsdóttir discusses other cases where even though the child was different, the parents fought to prove that the child was human and therefore entitled to the protection of the community; there are

> disabled children who never become suspected to be an *iran* because their impairment is interpreted differently, and their humanness is never questioned. Truly human children are not killed despite severe physical deformity. To kill such children would be classified as a murder and to be an immoral and dangerous act. Strictly formulated, *iran* children are not to be killed either; *iran* children are erased in a fire or allowed to return to their true home. (Einarsdóttir 2000:191)

Conclusion

The field of ethno-embryology has always been of interest to anthropologists, and from the earliest ethnographies the fascination with ideas about conception and gestation is obvious. In some of these works, we see the beginnings of interest in ideas about childhood and in the lives of children. Often it is oblique and many of the references to children are found buried in texts on spirit children, on conception and reproductive beliefs, or on the couvade. Yet these texts are important for anthropologists discussing childhood in that they point to the necessity of deconstructing ideas about the beginning of childhood in order to understand fully the ways that children fit into social and cosmological systems. This chapter can only give an overview of the complexities, but what becomes clear is that looking at the fetus and the neonatal child means analyzing some of the central questions that have beguiled anthropologists from the beginning. What is it that makes a person? How do adults differ from children, men from women, fetuses from children, persons from non-persons? By examining how a variety of cultures have answered these questions, it is possible to turn now to children once they have been born, and to understand in greater depth the ways in which they are treated, how their roles and statuses are viewed, and how their identity is understood once they have made the transition into the social world

4

FAMILY, FRIENDS, AND PEERS

Introduction

Children are fundamental to the recognition and continuation of kinship, and this chapter will look at a few examples from the vast literature on the subject which examine children's roles within their families. It will focus on the issue of who cares for children and with whom they live, including discussions of adoption and fosterage. It will also examine the significant role played by siblings, friends, and peers in children's lives. The importance of recognizing and acknowledging kinship is often central to children's lives. As suggested in chapter 2, Fulani children are not considered to show sense until they can recognize their extended kin by name. Likewise, Mandinka children in Senegal are expected to learn the names of their kin without direct adult instruction and to be able to place themselves both geographically and socially within the community. In a society in which "physical location is synonymous with identity," children must know their place in several senses of the phrase (Beverly and Whittemore 1993:270). Understanding kinship is a central way children learn to understand their culture. This chapter will begin by looking at the role of parents in children's lives and will be based partly on Esther Goody's discussion of what parenting involves. She begins her book on fostering in West Africa with a discussion of the role of parents, focusing in particular on the idea that "parenthood is about social replacement" (1982:7). While acknowledging that the term "parent" is complicated, and dependent on contextual understandings of kinship and family formation, she identifies five tasks of parenthood: "i. bearing and begetting, ii. endowment with civil and kinship status, iii. nurturance, iv. training and v. sponsorship into adulthood" (1982:8). The final two tasks she identifies will be covered in more detail in chapters 6 and 8, respectively, while the first three aspects of the parenting role will be examined here.

The Role of Parents

The first task of parenting, the begetting of children, as the previous chapter has shown, is far from straightforward. Anthropologists have pointed out a necessary distinction must be made when discussing kinship ties, between the social mother or father – that is, the mother or father who raises the child – and the biological/genetic father or mother – the person who is biologically related and/or gives birth to the child. In social science terms this has been done by referring to the social mother and father as the *mater* and *pater* and to the biological parents as *genitor* and *genetrix*. Until recently, with the advent of genetic testing, paternity was always an ascribed social status, based on a father's social relationship to the mother of the child, and, unlike maternity, it could not be proved. Famously, Malinowski discussed the denial of physical paternity among the Melanesian Trobriand Islanders, who saw no biological link between father and child, but acknowledged a strong social bond, basing claims to fatherhood on the relationship between a man and his wife rather than between a man and the child (see also chapter 3 for a discussion of conception theory). Another equally famous example is the institution of ghost marriage, practiced by the Nuer of southern Sudan, in which the paternity of children is assigned to a dead man, in order to continue his lineage, rather than to his brother who has married his widow (Evans-Pritchard 1951). The role of *pater* need not even be based on gender. Evans-Pritchard (1951) further discussed woman/woman marriage among the Nuer, in which the "female husband" of the pair was understood as the social father of a child, and had responsibilities for it, alongside its biological father. In other instances the roles of fatherhood are split between several people and the child is assumed to have more than one father. In some parts of Amazonia a child is seen as having multiple fathers and the fetal body is believed to be built up through many men's semen (Beckerman and Valentine 2002). After a child is born, social paternity is assigned to some, or all, of the men who had intercourse with the mother of the child and they are understood as having particular responsibilities to that child, such as undertaking couvade restrictions, or naming the child. Fatherhood is based as much on what men do, and the responsibilities they take on, as it is on notions of shared substance.

The second aspect of parenting mentioned by Goody, that of "endowment with civil and kinship status," is equally important in understanding children's position within society. When a child is born it is born into a complex web of social relationships that are further transformed by its arrival. The birth of a child may change the social status of both mother and father; it may legitimate a marriage, trigger the transfer of property from one lineage to another, or transform a married couple into a family. Whether or not a child is active in this is debatable, but it is certainly the transformative agent in all these situations. It is possible to extend Goody's point and say that while one of the roles of parenthood is to confer civil and kinship status on children, one of the roles of children is to confer the same on adults. Ideas about the social or civil status of a child are, or course, predicated on much wider systems of kinship, as well as on economic and political systems. If a child is born to an unmarried mother in a society that strongly disapproves of births outside of marriage, this will determine the social status of that child within the society and affect his or her life-chances, and a child who is orphaned and without the care and protection of relatives may well be viewed with suspicion and hostility. It is equally obvious that a child born legitimately to a high-status couple will be born with higher social and civil status than a child born to socially marginal parents. The implications this will have on a child's life are very profound, and, as argued in chapter 2, poor Brazilian children, for example, may well receive less care and nurturing from their biological mothers than do the children of their mothers' employers, because of their social marginalization and lack of vulnerability and dependence.

The question of nurturance, and its definition, is a vast topic which covers all aspects of children's lives. Children must not only be fed, kept sheltered, and have their physical needs met, but, if parenthood is about "social reproduction," then parents must also bring up children who fit into society and can become active members within it. They must learn the socially approved models of childhood and adulthood, even though they will also shape and change them. They must be nurtured to adulthood from before they were born, in some cases, until they are socially mature and beyond. Anthropologists who have looked at childhood have consistently shown that there is no one universal form of nurturing or correct path to adulthood and that nurturance is as dependent on cultural and environmental considerations as it is on biological ones. Meyer Fortes (1949), for example, spelt out the duties that parents had toward their children, including the duty to provide them with food, to obtain medical help for them, and, for a father, to provide bride-wealth for his son. In return he had rights to his son's labor and property and the expectation of help and support in his old age. Nurturance was multifaceted and involved reciprocal obligations between parents and child, as well as between other kin, such as grandparents.

The giving of care to infants was discussed at some length in chapter 1, which looked at how childcare practices have been analyzed as adaptive ways of rearing the very young in particular cultural and environmental contexts. What was not discussed in that chapter was the question of who provides that care. In studies of hunter-gatherer children in particular, the issue of paternal care has been of great interest, and there has been much work on the amount of time fathers spend with their children and the impact that this high level of involvement has on their children. Barry Hewlett, in his study of Central African Aka fathers, describes a situation where "Aka fathers do more infant care giving than fathers in any other known society" (1991:5). The assumption that a mother, or maternal substitute, is the most "natural" source of care for the very young thus needs to be questioned, although, as Melvin Konner (2005) points out, mothers still spend more of their time holding, and vocalizing to, their infants than even the most involved of Aka fathers. He further notes that, even with multiple caregivers, typical of hunter-gatherer societies, it still appears to be a child's mother who provides the closest physical contact and who is most likely to take care of a child's daily needs.

The number of caregivers available in hunter-gatherer societies has meant that siblings and grandparents also have important roles in nurturing young children. Nick Blurton-Jones and his colleagues (2005) have examined how these roles differ between grandparents among the Tanzanian Hadza and found that a maternal grandmother is more likely to live with her daughter, and provide help in raising her children, than is a woman's father. From an evolutionary, adaptive perspective, a post-reproductive-age woman both better ensures her own fitness by helping to raise her grandchildren, and increases the likelihood of leaving more descendants, compared to a woman who does not help her daughter. An older man has more options to show his fitness through hunting or remarriage, and Blurton-Jones et al. hypothesize that a man who is less successful in hunting may well distribute his help among his offspring in the same way as an older woman.

Adoption and Fosterage

So far, there has been an assumption that those who bear and beget children are also those who endow them with civil status and nurture them. This is not always true, however, and not only have anthropologists distinguished between social and biological parenthood, they have also looked at other methods of family formation and different family structures in which the tasks of parenting can take place, such as adoption and fosterage. Generally, anthropologists have tended to draw a conceptual distinction between the two, arguing that adoption involves a change of identity and a move from one family to another, giving up rights of inheritance and support from the former while gaining new ones in another family. In Western societies it usually occurs when someone is a legal minor and involves a full legal recognition of the change in identity (Modell 2002). It involves "the transfer of an individual from one filial relationship to another, from a 'natural' relationship to a 'fictional' one, but one which is in most respects legally equivalent" (Goody 1969:58). In other contexts adoption may occur when a person is an adult but involves a similar change in identity, particularly in regard to inheritance and legal status. Fostering, on the other hand, involves no such change of identity. Even in cases where children are sent away from their natal parents for long periods, their social and legal status is unaffected. In terms of property or lineage, they remain the heirs of their parents and there is no relinquishment of duties and obligations on either side. This distinction, although conceptually useful, has come under attack from more recent scholars such as Melissa Demian (2004), who argue that it is inadequate as it imposes external categories on indigenous social relations and that such a distinction does not truly exist in many societies. In some cases, children do not give up their obligations even when they are formally adopted, but merge the responsibilities they have to birth and adoptive parents. In her study of adoption in Papua New Guinea, Demian argues that "as the adoptee grows older his or her obligations to both adoptive and natal parents increase accordingly. What is removed from natal parents is not their relationship with the child, but the work they must do to raise the child and the effect that not working, or working less, will have on the relationship" (2004:103).

Similarly work on adoption in the Islamic world has revealed a complex situation where legal adoption may be formally disallowed but other systems, somewhere between adoption and fostering, allow children to be brought up outside their biological families. In Morocco, for example, Jamila Bargach (2002) discusses three different ways of transferring guardianship from biological parents: family or customary adoption, where a child is "gifted" from one family to another; secret adoption; and legal guardianship. In the first scenario close kin or even neighbors may request a child to raise and the arrangement remains an informal tie, claimed as an extended "visit," and the child retains his or her original family name. However, as Bargach comments: "If, outwardly, this seems like a visit, it is from within an 'interminable' visit which entails the inevitable development and entanglement of feelings of attachments, anger, love, and jealousy between children, siblings, and parents, just as if the ties were truly those between natural children and parents" (2002:27). The second type approximates more closely to Western ideas about adoption and concerns a situation where a mother hands over her child, often through an intermediary, to another family. They then go through a fictive process of giving birth to the child and passing it off as their own so that the child is given the identity of its new parents. Although this is illegal, and may cause disputes in the future, it remains a potential method of family formation. Finally, there is legal guardianship of a child who is either an orphan or abandoned and who is formally and legally offered into wardship. Islamic insistence on blood ties as the true marker of kinship mean that legal adoptions, in the Western sense, are not possible, and that genealogical accuracy must be maintained. These forms of guardianship enable this ideal to remain intact while allowing children to be moved between families.

In 1969 Jack Goody published a cross-cultural study of adoption in Ancient Rome, Greece, and modern (1960s) China, India, and certain African societies. He compared the reasons why children were adopted in some societies and not in others, and analyzed the respective roles and duties of adopters and adoptees. He divided adoptions into two types: those done for the child's good, in the case of it being orphaned or abandoned; and those done primarily for inheritance purposes, be they spiritual (e.g. providing a descendant to worship at the family shrine) or material. He emphasized the importance of inheritance and descent in China and India and noted that the Chinese term for adoption, *ssu chi*, actually means "to continue the succession." Goody points out that in China, monogamy and unilineal descent were the norm, so that heirs had to be "bought" in, if they were not produced within the marriage. In contrast many African systems had more diverse patterns of descent and inheritance, so that sisters' children were the inheritors in a matrilineal society and there was no scarcity of heirs. Alternatively a man without children could take other wives, or if he died without producing an heir, social institutions such as ghost marriage enabled him to have children socially assigned to him to continue his line. For Goody there was an obvious split between those societies with a relatively high rate of adoption who practiced it as a means of ensuring that property stays in the family (India and China) and those which were less likely to practice adoption because there were more potential heirs and less emphasis on direct inheritance (African societies).

This emphasis on descent and inheritance may seem a long way from an understanding of children's lives, but these beliefs and value systems affect the care and support children are given and therefore do have significant impacts on their lives. Roger Goodman (2000), in his commentary on the different forms of child welfare provision in Japan, gives an account of current adoption policies which illustrates this point. While adoption in Japan was common in the past, it took place along the lines suggested by Jack Goody (1969) concerning China, so that the majority of adoptees were adults and adopted for inheritance rather than welfare purposes. Children continued to have social obligations to their birth families, regardless of residence or who raised them. In 1988 new laws were passed, specifically with child protection purposes in mind, which allowed an adoptive family to register a child as if it were a natural child. It ended the relationship between birth parents and natural child and specifically ended all forms of obligations between biological parent and child. The child was no longer expected to look after his or her birth parents in their old age, nor could he or she inherit from them (Goodman 2000).

More generally it is worth noting how rarely children's welfare lies at the heart of adoption. Goody noted that adoption carried out for the good of the child is rare in societies such as China or India, even when it is common for inheritance purposes. The need for male heirs in some parts of the world may render girls unwanted and unwelcome, and they are more likely to be abandoned or killed than adopted. Adoption in these instances is for the good of the lineage system and individual children are incidental. In contrast, many African societies which do not have formalized systems of adoption do have extensive patterns of fosterage. Within these, children may be circulated or spend long periods away from their parents, sometimes for the benefit of adults, sometimes for their own social advantage, but they are less likely to be unwanted or abandoned. Fosterage enables quite distant kin to take in children and the cost of raising children to be spread more widely.

There are many types of fostering relationship, ranging from children being sent away at a very early age and not seeing their parents again for years, to those where a family takes in a child temporarily for only a week or two. In between, there are a variety of arrangements between birth parents and foster parents and different duties and responsibilities are expected of both parents and children. In many instances, there are ongoing relationships between the biological and foster parents and children can be called back to their parents' home if they are needed. The reasons behind different fostering practices are also multiple, ranging from the death of parents, or the complete abandonment of children, to arrangements where children are fostered as matter of course and parents may send their own children away to relatives while taking in other people's children themselves. Children may be fostered when their parents' marriage breaks down and it is not appropriate for them to remain with stepparents, or when they are needed in other households as domestic labor, or as a way of compensating for another couple's childlessness. Much of the ethnographic literature on fostering challenges the notion that biological identity lies at the heart of kinship and that children need stable, parental figures throughout their childhood in order to form lasting attachments as adults. The Mende of Sierra Leone, for example, believe that "the truly unfortunate children are those who have not been sent away from home to advance" (Bledsoe 1990a:85), a view echoed in ethnographies from Wogeo island in Papua New Guinea (Anderson 2004) and among the Baatombu in Benin (Alber 2004), for whom adoption or fostering is the preferred method of raising children, not a last resort.

Systems of fosterage are found in many places, but some of the best studied have been those among West African communities. Goody and Goody (1967) examined fosterage in the context of the overall circulation of women and children within different systems, linking it to patterns of marriage and descent. Esther Goody (1982) has focused on this in greater detail, examining fostering arrangements among the Gonja of Ghana at both a national and an international level, looking at the reasons why parents send their children to be fostered and what the benefits are for parents, children, and the wider community. Among the Gonja it is unusual for children to be fostered by nonfamily members, and the preferred option is for a boy to be sent to his mother's brother and a girl to her father's sister. Ideally there is no split between foster parents and natural parents and the latter continue to be involved in the lives of their children. In terms of outcomes, Goody sees these placements as usually successful: children apparently feel no long-term negative consequences of being sent away by their parents, and, in contrast to evidence from Western Europe and North America, they have no obvious difficulties in forming life-long relationships when they grow up. The reasons given for fostering are complex and linked to social and economic factors as well as cultural ones. By fostering children out, families can offset the cost of raising them during periods of economic hardship. The households into which they are fostered gain help and support, particularly if they foster girls, who can then look after smaller children or perform household chores. The importance of fostering as a way of overcoming temporary economic hardship can also be seen elsewhere. Carol Stack (1974) worked on children's residence patterns and their impact on social relations during the 1960s in a poor, African American, urban neighborhood in Chicago which she called The Flats. Here she found groups of women raising their children in a variety of family patterns, swapping and sharing children as their social and financial resources permitted. In this community children were shared between their mothers, their friends, and their female relatives when financial and social circumstances required it. Despite the necessity of this, it was also viewed as a positive care system, which reinforced social ties, rather than a symptom of family breakdown.

In much of the literature on fostering, the same families who foster children out may well take other children in, being both child-senders and child-receivers at the same time, which would appear to negate any economic advantage that fostering might have. Analyzing this requires looking beyond the economic and considering fostering as part of wider cultural beliefs about the relative roles and responsibilities of parents and children and ideas about who are the best people to raise children. In her study of the Ga of Labadi, also in Ghana, and carried out in the 1960s around the same time as Esther Goody's fieldwork, Diana Azu (1974) gives a clear description of the reasoning behind fostering in that community.

> There is a general belief that parents are not the best suited people for the upbringing of their children, that they tend to pamper their children, making it impossible to exercise that little bit of hardness, if not harshness, that Ga believe to be an essential ingredient of the socialisation process.
>
> For this reason children are often sent to relatives or non-relatives for training. . . . It is preferable to send the child to someone of the same sex for training, and, although this is not always followed, it is less often the case that a boy is fostered by a female than that a girl is fostered by a male. A girl may be sent to a paternal or maternal relative who has no children of her own or to a grandmother to help her in the house. She may also be sent to an educated relative or non-relative "to learn to be a lady". The girl goes at the age of seven or eight and may live there until she marries, save for occasional visits to her parents. A girl so sent participates in the

performance of household duties, and sometimes in trading. Where the foster parent is educated, she may be taught sewing as well. She is given food and clothing and where she is dutiful, she may be given money with which to start trading. (quoted in Goody 1982:151)

This description supports much of Goody's evidence. She asked foster parents why they had fostered children and was given a variety of reasons, ranging from reciprocity (they had been fostered by the mother of the foster child and wanted to do something in return), out of love for their siblings, because they had no children of their own, for the child's own benefit, or because they were in a position to offer support, training, or education and they felt it was their duty to help out.

One final example of fostering that Goody (1982) mentions is that of children being sent away to live with other families as pawns for security on a loan, which she refers to as debt fostering (see Fortes 1949 for further examples of this). In these instances, children are sent to live and work for a creditor until the loan is paid off, at which point they are able to return home. At no point do they take on the name or any aspects of the creditor's identity, even though sometimes they may learn a trade with him or her and be looked after within his or her household. Goody cites several examples of this practice in West Africa, among the Yoruba, the Ga, and the Krobo.

> If the loan was granted, he [a Krobo man] gave one of his children, more often a boy than a girl, as hostage or security to his creditor. This hostage was to "serve him . . ." i.e. to work for him up to the day the money was returned. . . . On the appointed day the debtor brought back the amount he had borrowed, together with another bottle of rum . . . and the child was free to return home. (Huber 1963, quoted in Goody 1982:148)

The word "hostage" sounds very harsh in this context, and the extent to which this can be seen as form of fosterage is debatable. Elisha Renne (2005), who has examined child pawning or *iwofa* among the Yoruba, draws on a life history of an old man who had been pawned as a child to pay off a debt incurred by members of his extended family. Although the practice was banned by the colonial authorities in 1928, the ban was rarely enforced and this man remembered the harsh treatment meted out to him in the nine years it took for the debt to be repaid. He claimed that being a pawn was little better than slavery: "My life was a little better than a dead person – I was a dead but living person. . . . It was another form of slavery, no access to one's parents, no care except food to keep me and other people alive" (Renne 2005:69–70). Whatever terms are used, however, the practice of bonded labor persists and parents continue to use their children as bonds in many parts of the world, promising their future labor in return for a loan. In contemporary Thailand, children are still debt-bonded into brothels by their parents and may not return until their debt is paid off (Montgomery 2001a). In these instances the risks of exploitation make it very difficult to view this pattern as a form of fosterage rather than abuse, although, as the next case study will describe, sometimes this line can become blurred.

More recently anthropologists such as Caroline Bledsoe have looked at the reality behind culturally stated ideals of fosterage (see also the contributors to Fiona Bowie's 2004 book on cross-cultural adoption). Based on fieldwork conducted among the Mende of Sierra Leone, Bledsoe describes how fostering arrangements are explained as a way of promoting social mobility, so that children tend to be sent to more powerful or prestigious members of the family. For children themselves, however, the experience may be a miserable one that brings them into conflict with both their birth parents and their foster parents (Bledsoe 1990a, 1990b). Bledsoe cites examples of children being treated harshly and worked hard by their foster parents and of parents being generally unsympathetic to their complaints. There is a clash between children's and parents' views on fostering: it is seen by parents as a way of training children for the future, teaching them that life is a struggle which they must work hard to overcome, but by some children it is regarded as a form of abuse and neglect by their parents. Fostering in Sierra Leone is a political act as well as a social or economic one. Mende society has an elaborate system of patronage, and parents see sending their children off to be servants to their patrons as a way of appealing to an influential supporter who may later be in a position to help them. This traffic is not only one-way and parents may foster children themselves as a way of building up indebtedness. They may send their own children out to others to foster, while taking in other children themselves, thereby accumulating many layers of indebtedness and influence over time. As Bledsoe argues:

> Children are also potential patrons. Especially if sent to higher-status homes and better schools, they may learn sophisticated skills and make important contacts. Later, parents, former guardians and anyone else who helped them can make claims on their monetary and political assistance.

This makes a child's education a means towards the larger end of "developing" a much wider social group, as a common adage states: "A child is not 'for' one person." Even adults with their own children invest in other people's children through fosterage or contributions to school fees in order to widen their network of indebted supporters. (1990b:75)

Both fostering and adoption are usually described in terms of their benefits for adults, whether individual adults or wider demographics (Bledsoe 1990a). Judith Ennew (1980), for example, describes how, in the Scottish Hebrides, until the 1950s, a child might be given to a childless woman to raise in order to keep the woman herself out of trouble. Likewise there are many ethnographic accounts of childless couples raising relatives' children in order to overcome the stigma of barrenness and to have someone to look after them in their old age. There are descriptions from Amazonia of parents giving a child up for adoption specifically so that he or she can live with, and look after, an aged grandparent. Rather than bringing the parent into their household, which would imply a loss of status and authority for the older person, a child is given up to a grandparent in order to look after them (Halbmayer 2004). Among the East African Maasai, a childless woman may ask a pregnant relative to give her a child to raise, and the giving up for adoption of a child is considered an act of generosity on the part of the biological parent (Talle 2004). Children may be adopted across families to balance the sex ratios within them, to ensure access to land utilization rights, or to build alliances between families, as in Papua New Guinea (Anderson 2004). In the context of Cameroon, Catrien Notermans (2004) suggests another reason for fosterage: that it is a woman's way of ensuring the claims and rights of her own lineage and asserting her own and her maternal relatives' identity and control over the child, despite it being a patrilineal society. Marriage is fragile and women are likely to leave marriages or resist them through not allowing the father to sign a birth certificate or by refusing bride-wealth. While one or two children may be assigned to a husband's lineage, the grandmothers often destroy birth certificates, and foster the child themselves, a situation described by Notermans as "foster politics" (2004:56).

Contemporary Chinese adoptions are most usually carried out with specific benefits for the adoptive parents (and society in general) in mind, rather than the needs or wishes of the child. Adopting children has a twofold benefit for the state: not only does it pass on to individual families the cost of raising children, which would otherwise have to be paid by the

state, but it also imposes an obligation on these adopted children to care
for their adoptive parents in old age, thus relieving the state of another
potential request for support (Palmer 1989). Although, ideally, adoptees
in China should be under seven and adopters in good health, government
policy is relaxed on occasions in order to ensure that older people are
provided for and do not become a social burden. Children up to the age
of 20 can be adopted in order to provide care, and the adoption of a child
is often seen as the solution to caring for an elderly or infirm person (Palmer
1989). In South Korea, similar patterns have emerged, and adoption is understood as "parent-centered" rather than child-centered. Adoptions are
primarily carried out to continue a lineage, and may even be carried out
posthumously in order to provide descendants for the deceased (Roesch-
Rhomberg 2004).

There may be, of course, some benefit for the child in all the above
scenarios, and this discussion need not imply that adoption or fosterage is
entirely about adult needs. Children may actually choose to be adopted;
they may gain social advancement, a better education, or greater opportunities, and in the Chinese example discussed above, they may expect
to gain rights of inheritance and stand to benefit financially in the longer
term. Ethnography from the early 1950s suggested that among Singapore
Malays children might be adopted if they were sickly and thought not
likely to survive. Some parents felt that they were not destined to raise
such a child, who was clearly unhappy with them, and that the child would
have a better chance of survival if it was fostered by others (Djamour
1952). Fostering may also be understood as the best way of helping both
mother and child in situations where a young mother is not considered
to have the proper knowledge to be able to raise her child on her own.
Among Xhosa families in South Africa it is often the maternal grandmother
who rears her daughter's child. As one Xhosa woman told researchers:
"In many cases, when you have your first child, you are considered to
be immature, and inexperienced. So [your] mother will bring up the
child for you, and you will be there to see how the child is brought
up. By the time you have your second child, you actually know what
goes into bringing a child up" (Xhosa woman quoted in Burr and
Montgomery 2003:61). Sometimes it is taken as a matter of course that
parents are not the right people to raise their own children (and indeed
go to great lengths to downplay any sense that they do, in fact, "own"
their children). Among the Baatombu in northern Benin, there is a social
distance between parents and children, and numerous rules of avoidance

between them (Alber 2004). Children's education is seen as the responsibility of the entire community and it is believed that parents would be too lenient in raising their own children and would fail to give them a proper education.

Ideas about the correct care of children and the best people to provide it are also subject to change. Among the rural Yoruba studied by Elisha Renne (2005), for instance, ideas about fostering and child-rearing are being reconsidered. Her informants told her of their concerns about sending their own children away or taking in others, despite the long traditions of child fosterage in the area. Numbers of children were running away from what they perceived as abusive foster carers, and certain relatives, particularly grandmothers, were viewed as overindulgent. The younger generation of parents interviewed by Renne argued that they were the best people to raise children and were limiting their family sizes so that they had only those children for whom they could care themselves.

In more rare cases children themselves may choose by whom they wish to be fostered. In the Chicago Flats studied by Carol Stack (1974), older children, especially boys, who had retained links to their natural fathers sometimes chose to live with them if life was difficult with their mothers. Barbara Bodenhorn (1988) also describes a fluid and flexible situation where children come and go between households and are allowed great leeway about where they live. In the Inupiaq communities of northern Canada in which she worked, children are circulated between households for a variety of reasons, including being unsettled in their parental home, possibly as a result of being wrongly named (see chapter 3 for a more detailed account of naming and reincarnation among Native Canadians such as the Inuit or the Inupiaq), or because their animating spirit is unhappy with their parents. They may be adopted because there are too many children of one sex in the family, because a mother cannot conceive, or because it is too difficult to feed any more children. In this case the sharing of children is linked to more generalized cultural patterns of sharing, exchange, and reciprocity, so that children, like food, are shared around the community to provide for all. Children are not passive in this process and may be adopted because they themselves wish it, even if their parents do not. Their own choice and agency are recognized as important, and informants told Bodenhorn about a certain child who "came to stay for a while and liked it so much we adopted him" (1988:14). The choice to be adopted by others and to choose by whom to be adopted is considered a legitimate one for an Inupiaq or Inuit child to make, although at what age a child can make this choice is not known. Despite the high levels of adoption, however, it can also bring problems, and, as Jean Briggs cautions, adoption in mid-childhood "appears to be unhappy more often than not" (1991:261).

Janet Carsten (1991) has analyzed patterns of fosterage and adoption and the ways in which children are fostered by people other than their birth parents in Pulau Langkawi, Malaysia. She examines the flexibility of kinship and argues that kinship can be acquired through the sharing of food or households. Indeed she argues that children who are fostered at an early age are believed to come to look like their adoptive parents, and take on their physical attributes in the same way they would those of their birth parents. She describes a community in which rates of fosterage are high (up to 25% of minors do not live with their birth parents) but where children are also closely tied to their own natal house. The movement of children is part of a complicated system of kinship in which children are both shared between extended family members and exchanged between houses. Children, Carsten argues, "embody the process of kinship" (1991:425). They are not passive in this process and there is an acknowledgment that children's wishes about where and with whom they should live are important. Parents may wish children to live with certain family members, but many informants told Carsten that there was no reason for the children to be living in a particular place, other than their own desire. Both for the Inupiaq and on Pulau Langkawi, there has, as yet, been no work done of why children might choose to live in one house rather than another. Their own views of their decisions would make for fascinating reading, but so far, and despite the agency shown by the children in these choices, it is only adults who have been asked about children's residence and whom they choose as kin.

Children outside the Family

One recent area of children's experience that anthropologists have begun to study involves children who live outside their parental homes, either on the streets, or in the care of the state. Street children in particular have been of interest because of the ways in which they conceptually challenge the notion that the proper place for the child is in the enclosed family (see Introduction). Taken up as a *cause célèbre* of the nongovernmental movement in the 1980s, street children in South America were denounced as the unacceptable face of economic development and described as children who had either been rejected by their families, or run away from abuse or poverty. This vision has been challenged by, among others, Louis Aptekar (1988), Tobias Hecht (1998), and Catherine Panter-Brick (2002), who found a much more complicated situation. They discovered it was rare for children to cut off ties entirely with their families, and that many children divided their time between the street and their family homes. Hecht, in particular, emphasized the continuing importance that mothers still had in their children's lives and described the many visits home by children, suggesting that the term "street children" is misleading because it misrepresents the relationship between children and their families.

Living and working on the street can be a positive choice for many children to escape the poverty and restrictions of living at home. Children may well choose to live outside and away from their families as much as they might choose the family with whom they want to live. However, it is also important not to overromanticize certain aspects of street children's lives. It is often assumed that children form some sort of family ties on the street, with older children looking after and protecting younger children (in return for certain favors or chores being done for them), and that boys will look after girls. While there is evidence that this happens in some cases, in others the fight for survival means that children do not form bands for protection, or re-create family situations on the street, but are forced to look after themselves first and even to prey on more vulnerable children (Hecht 1998; Ennew and Swart-Kruger 2003).

Anthropologists have also begun to work with children who live in state-run institutions rather than with their families. Roger Goodman (2000) has conducted fieldwork in children's homes in Japan and describes the stigma attached to these places, both in terms of the grim reputation of orphanages in the past, and because of the close linguistic association between the word for children's homes and the word for a home for children with physical or mental disabilities. He also points out that the term "orphanages" is misused as few of the children in these homes have actually lost both parents and they are there instead for reasons of poverty, their family's inability or unwillingness to care for them, or because of abuse or neglect. Goodman's picture of life in some of these institutions is bleak: there is little privacy for the children and professional social services are often lacking. Although the book does not attempt to discuss children's own views of the institutions they live in, it is invaluable because it links contemporary issues in adoption, fostering, and care with wider social issues and looks more generally at the cultural politics of child-hood. Institutional care is still preferred in Japan over fostering because it is cheaper and the government has chosen to spend money on daycare and after-school clubs for the middle classes rather than on social sup-port and protection for the poorest. The children who end up in such institutions come from the most marginalized sections of society who are a low social priority.

The ways in which institutions are run depend on cultural factors about the perceived relationship between parents, state, and children. As discussed earlier, China has been keen to adopt a policy in which the state is not held responsible for the care of the young, the elderly, or the sick, and has therefore pushed through adoption as a means of deflecting responsibil-ities for care back onto families. In other societies the state turns to char-ities or religious institutions to provide care for children, so that the Catholic Church generally runs children's homes in Portugal, which are largely inde-pendent from the government (Aarre 2000). There is little regulation of them and many are run according to the aims of the founder rather than in line with national welfare policies for children. In the children's home studied by Karen Aarre (2000), for example, ideas of poverty and charity were central to its ideology. Children were taught to accept their posi-tion as poor and to believe that liberation came through faith. On a more practical basis they were allowed few personal possessions, little privacy, and were not allowed to exchange mail with their families. Although this ran counter to the government's policy on children, such homes were often left unchecked. Indeed one of the key themes that comes out of anthropological accounts of children's homes is the gap between national and international legislation about the appropriate care for chil-dren away from their families and the autonomy enjoyed by institutions for children which run them according to their own ideologies (Aarre 2000).

This is not the only reason that anthropologists have been wary of insti-tutions and often been critical of them. They have also argued that such institutions may actually undermine family obligations and indigenous kin-ship structures. In 1969 Jack Goody warned that the adoption of Western welfare models for children and young people, such as family courts or children's homes, was inappropriate in African contexts and out of keep-ing with local cultural norms. He believed that African ideas about family responsibility were flexible enough to ensure that all children would be looked after through fosterage, even if their parents could not provide care. Western-style institutional care, or more formalized fostering or adoption policies, he argued, would be disastrous to newly emerging countries which had their own social systems and ways of coping with children. There has been no follow-up to see if fostering systems did indeed break down as countries emerged from colonization, but the fear that institutions may take over from family care is a valid one. More recently, David Tolfree (1995) has argued that orphanages may provide families with an incentive not to care for extended family members and allow them to abdicate responsibility, undermining their sense of obligation to vulnerable, young relatives.

Siblings

Children's relationships are rarely limited only to their parents, and the role of siblings in their lives has been another source of anthropological investigation. Judith Huntsman (1983), for example, has looked in detail at the relationships between siblings in the island societies of Oceania, where life-long relationships and exchange patterns mean that equal numbers of boys and girls are desired in any one family and, in some instances, children are adopted in order to balance the family. The meaning of the term "sibling," like that of parent, needs to be defined in context, and there is a wide variety cross-culturally regarding who is termed a sibling and who is not. Victor Cicirelli sums up some of the many variations:

> In the Marquesas culture of Oceania, only full biological siblings are identified . . . ; in the Pukapuka culture of the Cook Islands in Oceania, siblings include the children of both parents' biological siblings . . . ; in the Kwara'ae culture of the Solomon Islands, siblings include the children of the parent's cross-sex siblings . . . ; in the Malo culture of New Hebrides in Oceania, siblings include cousins of the same sex, the parent's siblings of the same sex, and even grandparents of the same sex . . . ; in the Abaluyia culture of Kenya, siblings include children who were fostered in the same household . . . ; and in the Giriama culture of Kenya, siblings include children of the same village or tribe who are of the same age range. (1994:9)

As siblingship frequently brings with it obligations and duties, who is considered a sibling and who is not has a great impact on children's lives.

As the next chapter will go on to discuss, it is evident that children are often partly socialized by, and through, other children and that the responsibility that children have for each other is immense. Children spend much of their lives in the company of, and under the charge of, their older siblings, who play a central role in their lives (Weisner and Gallimore 1977; Cicirelli 1994). It is taken for granted that older children, especially girls, will take on substantial childcare responsibilities. Open almost any ethnography and there are numerous vignettes and photographs of children looking after younger ones, but why they should be given this responsibility is not always discussed. In many instances it is understood as the work of childhood, especially girls' childhood, or as a way of socializing girls into their future roles as mothers (see chapter 5). It may also be seen as a fallback option in the event of the death of other caregivers (Cicirelli 1994). In other cases sibling caregiving is a way of reinforcing social hierarchies and teaching a child its low social status. Elinor Ochs (1982, 1988), in her study of language socialization in Samoa (see chapter 5), analyzes the role of siblings in childcare not simply as a way of alleviating the mother's burden, but also as a way of emphasizing children's social inferiority. She describes Samoa as a highly stratified society where rank is a central organizing principle. Chiefs are of higher status than untitled people and generation and age also contribute status. A child is therefore of lower status than an adult and a younger child lower than an older one. The two most important aspects of higher status are low physical activity and minimal awareness of, or involvement in, the actions of other people. In terms of sibling caregiving this means that should an infant need care or attention when there is another child in the vicinity, the mother will expect the child to be brought to her by other children; she will try not to move off her mat to deal with the child, nor will she acknowledge that the child is fretting.

> Young caregivers, if present, are relied upon to be mobile. They are primarily the ones to change soiled clothes, wash, and provide food for the child. They also carry young infants to their mothers for breastfeeding and/or cuddling until the infant has learned to ambulate itself and is able to crawl directly to the mother. If a younger caregiver is present, higher status caregivers (e.g. mothers) will also strive not to involve themselves directly with the ongoing interactions among younger persons in the immediate surroundings or with spontaneous actions of a younger child. If, for example, an argument takes place, the higher status caregiver (e.g. mother) will at first leave it to the peers themselves to resolve it, and if it escalates, to an older sibling caregiver to handle. If it is unresolvable through these means, one or other of the children will turn to the higher status caregiver and appeal to her to take some action. Another case of this reluctance to involve

oneself concerns attending to the actions of small children, actions which have not been motivated by some directive from the higher status caregiver. Ideally, if lower status caregivers are present, they will be the ones to watch that a young infant will not fall over the edge of the house or eat stones or touch a burning pot. (Ochs 1982:83)

In Samoa, children are used as caregivers not simply for expediency but also from a belief in the inferior nature of children and the importance of instilling respect for adults. In Tonga, also, ideas about sibling childcare are related to wider ideas about children's inferiority and the need to reinforce an acceptance of social inferiority at an early age. Tongan children are subordinated to their parents and older siblings, and when fostered, it is for adult needs, never their own. Furthermore, Tongan parents will quite openly select a favorite child, who is given less work and spared some of the discipline of his or her siblings and indulged with special treats, thereby emphasizing the inequalities within the households that the child must learn. In Helen Morton's (1996) work on child-rearing practices in Tonga (see chapter 6), the central role that children have in the disciplining of younger siblings is very apparent. It is believed that children need to be molded by those of higher status, such as adults or their older siblings, in order to learn social competence, and that the only way this can happen is through severe physical punishment and discipline. It is often siblings who administer these beatings or who go and fetch the implement with which the younger child will be beaten. The opportunity for siblings to abuse this power and to discipline their siblings too harshly is always present, and the line between abuse and discipline will be discussed in more depth in chapter 6.

While sibling care is a feature of many societies, it need not only be performed by girls. Among the Efe foragers of the Ituri Forest (in the Democratic Republic of Congo), boys and girls are equally involved with the care of one-year-olds, performing many of the same duties, such as playing with them or feeding them and, as they get older, providing more skilled care such as comforting or bathing a child. This care is not dependent on the gender of the caregiver until middle childhood, after the age of six, when boys' and girls' roles diverge and girls stay close to their mothers and continue to care for other children while boys begin to hunt and are away from the camp (Henry et al. 2005). This is an unusual case, however, and generally girls do undertake more childcare than their brothers, making sibling care highly gendered, which has important implications not only for the infant who is being cared for, but also for the carer. Margaret Wolf, for example, comments on the fact that girls in rural Taiwan are disciplined much more harshly than their brothers because of the burdens of responsibility that they have: "Obedience training comes earlier for girls than for boys, less by plan than by the accident of role requirements. A child who must be responsible for a younger child's welfare cannot be allowed to disobey on whim" (1972:79).

Children's own views of providing care for their siblings are rarely canvassed, although many anthropologists note the obvious affection that children express toward their younger charges. Although sibling caregiving, in cases such as Samoa or Tonga, may be a way of reinforcing children's inferiority, in other situations taking on such responsibilities may be a way of showing competence and gaining status. When looking at a person's life over the entire life-cycle, the shift from complete lack of responsibility to liability for those younger is an important one, which changes the ways in which a child interacts with his or her family. While a toddler would not be given care of an infant, a seven- or eight-year-old who is assigned the care of a younger child is being accorded an implicit recognition of his or her agency and ability to cope with responsibility. Taking care of younger siblings or neighbors can be an important way for children to assert a limited authority. Margaret Read (1968), in her study of Malawian Ngoni children, discussed how girls were extremely proud of their skills as guardians and caregivers and protective of their charges. The responsibilities given to children when supervising others are often great, as are the simultaneous, and sometimes opposing, pressures on them, which come both from the children they are looking after, and from the adults around them. In their work among the Kikuyu of Kenya, Herbert and Gloria Leiderman (1973) sum up this tension very well, showing how in sibling caregiving we see children trying to find a balance between independence and irresponsibility and autonomy and dependency.

> The caretaker is usually old enough to know the responsibilities of the household, yet young enough to want to be included in the children's games and activities. In her typical day, she gets up with the mother and helps about the house. She frequently accompanies the mother to collect fuel and water, usually taking responsibility for the infant on these journeys. If needed, she goes with the mother to the fields where she either assists in cultivating and planting, or cares for the child while the mother performs her chores. If the younger girl is left at home to care for the infant, she is solely responsible for his care. She provides food if he is old enough

to take supplemental food, or, if he is still nursing, she carries him to the mother in the fields. Depending on the interest and sense of responsibility of the young caretaker, she might watch the infant extremely carefully, or do so in a more desultory manner, giving in to the temptation of playing with her friends and siblings while overseeing his activities. However, most of the caretakers take their responsibilities very seriously, and many are genuinely interested in and involved with the younger infants in play as well as in caretaking tasks. (quoted in Weisner and Gallimore 1977:174)

Despite this, there may be a certain amount of ambivalence about looking after younger siblings. There are certainly hints that children do not always understand it as a natural part of their childhood and may dislike doing it. Margaret Mead commented that many children find looking after their siblings dull, and further observed how child caregivers could be "small tyrants" who were more interested in a quiet life than socializing children in their care. She wrote: "The little nurses are more interested in peace than in forming the characters of their small charges, and when a child begins to howl, it is simply dragged out of earshot of its elders" (1971[1928]:26–27). Raymond Firth (1936) also suggested that amongst the Tikopia of Polynesia, where children took on much of the day-to-day care of younger ones, they were sometimes quite harsh disciplinarians and beat their siblings when adults would not.

In recent years some children have been forced to become the primary, or sole, caregiver of their siblings. An issue that is likely to become of increasing interest is that of child-headed households in which a child is not only the principal carer for younger siblings but also the main breadwinner. As with female-headed households in the 1960s and 1970s, such families are largely unrecorded and unrecognized in economic statistics, and yet are likely to be among the poorest of all families. Certain emergency situations such as the genocide in Rwanda revealed the existence of large numbers of children whose parents had died and who had been forced to take on primary responsibility for others. What is less well documented is how many children in other circumstances are also running households because of the death or incapacity of their parents. Research on AIDS orphans in sub-Saharan Africa has suggested that the number of child-headed households is likely to rise (Lugalla 2003), but there are, as yet, few detailed studies on how these households manage or how children perform the social or cultural roles of parents. Are child-headed households able to provide bride-wealth payments or dowries? Can brothers or sisters perform necessary initiation rituals, or even know how they should be done? The loss of parents has severe implications for children, not only on an emotional, individual level, but also on a cultural one.

Friends and Peer Groups

Peer relations in children's lives have been most extensively studied by psychologists (see Hartup 1983 for a comprehensive overview), who have examined the great significance of peers in the lives of children. This work, most usually based on children in Western societies, has illustrated the importance of friendships in child development and analyzed the shift away from parental influence to that of the peer group as children get older. Such work has repeatedly emphasized that in adolescence young people are likely to rely on their friends and peer groups as much as, if not more than, on their own families (Steinberg and Silverberg 1986; Bukowski et al. 1996; see also Chen et al. 2006 for a discussion of these issues in cross-cultural contexts). As psychologist Willard Hartup has put it, "In most cultures, the significance of peer relations as a socialization context is rivaled only by the family" (1983:103). Much of this work has looked at how children absorb and negotiate the values of the adult world through interaction with their peers and how forming friendships is a crucial part of a child's social development (Corsaro and Eder 1990). Psychologist Judith Rich Harris has gone even further, claiming that peer groups are a more important factor in socializing children than parents. She writes:

> A child's job is not to learn how to behave like all the other people in his or her society, because all the other people in the society do not behave alike. In every society, acceptable behavior depends on whether you're a child or an adult, a male or a female. Children have to learn to behave like the other people in their own social category. In most cases they do this willingly. Socialization is not something that grown ups do to kids – it is something kids do to themselves . . . Modern children do learn things from their parents; they bring to the group what they learned at home. . . . This makes it look as though the parents are the conveyors of the culture, but they are not: the peer group is. If the peer group's culture differs from the parents', the peer group's always wins. (1998:357–358)

Much of the literature from psychology suggests a universal desire for children to seek out members of their own sex to play with and for a marked division between the sexes to occur in middle childhood. Hartup claims that "children of all ages associate more frequently with members of their own sex and like them better . . . no observer would question the fact that children avoid the opposite sex in middle childhood and adolescence" (1983:110). While this has been well documented in the West however, in other societies, there is no such split. Sara Harkness and Charles Super (1985), for example, have shown that even in a strictly gender-segregated society such as the Kipsigis of rural Kenya, children in middle childhood are not segregated and do not seem to prefer their own sex as playmates. In several hunter-gatherer societies, such as the !Kung or the Efe, groups of children playing only in same-sex or same-age groups have not been observed, and Konner (2005) claims that multi-aged child groups are one of the features of hunter-gatherer life.

In the West, anthropologists have reexamined the idea of universal developmental norms where children inevitably seek out friends of the same age, gender, or ethnic group, and much more attention is now being paid to the cultural context in which these peer cultures are formed (Chen et al. 2006). There is evidence that the segregation of children by gender has been overemphasized and based too extensively on evidence from schools; outside these settings it is less obvious. Marjorie Goodwin (1990), for instance, found little evidence of gender segregation in her ethnography of peer groups of African American children in Philadelphia, with boys and girls being very much part of the same world. Sociologist Barrie Thorne (1993) looked at interactions between nine- and ten-year-olds in an elementary school in America, focusing on the ways that they played and related to each other. She found that inside school, it was very apparent that boys and girls separated along gender lines and played exclusively in single-sex groups, but that outside school, the barriers between boys and girls were not so strong. She further suggested that while segregation in schools might look complete, in fact the barriers between girls and boys were more permeable than first appeared. She uses the term "borderwork" to conceptualize this separation, focusing on the ways in which children formed same-sex friendship and play groups in order to create and strengthen gender boundaries but also to transgress them. She comments on the ambiguity and flexibility of this separation and argues that boys and girls do not necessarily live in different worlds, at all times, but move backward and forward between them. She explains:

> The imagery of "border" may wrongly suggest an unyielding fence that divides social relations into two parts. The image should rather be one of

many short fences that are quickly built and as quickly dismantled. Gender boundaries are episodic and ambiguous, and *the notion of "borderwork" should be coupled with a parallel term – such as "neutralization" – for processes through which girls and boys (and adults who enter into their social relations) neutralize or undermine a sense of gender as division and opposition.* (1993:84, emphasis in the original)

Thus the separation is never entirely complete. Drawing up boundaries also offers scope for these boundaries to be challenged, and while most children did stick to gender-defined groups and behaviors, Thorne describes instances where, usually by virtue of their high status, certain boys and girls have been allowed to engage in "border crossing."

Thorne also links children's same-sex peer groups to ideas about sexuality, and heterosexuality in particular. Thorne notes: "In preschools crossgender friendships are more public, but the risk of heterosexual teasing increases across the years of elementary school, limiting public displays of affiliation between boys and girls" (1993:50). By the time children reach elementary school they are extremely conscious of the differences between boys and girls and sensitive to accusations of "liking" children of an opposite gender. Sociologist Debbie Epstein (1997), who looked at these issues in the UK, found that ideas about heterosexuality are fundamental to constructions of gender among children. She argued that games such as "kiss chase" allow girls to construct an image of themselves as feminine, drawing on ideas about dating and romance, and eventually marriage and motherhood, while boys use them to construct an image of themselves as tough and "manly" and distanced from their feminized playmates.

While sociologists have long recognized the role of adolescent peer cultures, they have also examined friendships among younger children. Sociologist William Corsaro (1985, 2003) has analyzed peer cultures amongst younger children, relying on ethnographic methods and, as far as possible, participant-observation among children. His work has been based in various nursery schools in the USA and Italy and anchored on the premise that young children's peer cultures are as important in socializing them as are their interactions with adults (Corsaro 1985; Corsaro and Eder 1990; Corsaro and Rizzo 1998). He defines peer cultures as "a stable set of activities or routines, artifacts, values, and concerns that children produce and share in interaction with peers" (1992:162). Using this definition, he goes on to show how children themselves reproduce these cultures, which do not always map onto adult ones. Far from simply absorbing and reflecting adult values and knowledge, children are viewed as "discoverers of a world that is endowed with meaning" (1988:2) in which they challenge adult versions of culture. Corsaro stresses that children are active partners in forming peer groups and negotiating meanings within them (Corsaro 1988, 1992; Corsaro et al. 2003).

In Japan the importance of young children's peer groups has also been discussed by Joy Hendry (1986), who notes how teachers often take advantage of the strong peer group pressure that exists, even among young children, and use it for their own ends. Children are strongly encouraged to fit in with others, play, and have fun. If they do not, the teacher encourages other children to ostracize them and refer to them as peculiar and strange. Hendry found that over time very few children refused to join in or have fun, so anxious were they to conform and gain the social approval of their peers. Perhaps more positively, she also shows how children are brought into discussions about group behavior and how the sanction of peers is an important way of punishing those who do wrong. In cases of fights and bullying, for instance, adults will ask children who started the fight and what should be done about it. Several teachers told Hendry that the peer group was much more effective in controlling children than adults were and that children would take much more notice of their peers than of their teachers.

Other anthropologists are starting to look at the importance of peer cultures in both older and younger children's lives, examining how they reproduce certain cultural patterns, and how they differ dramatically from each other cross-culturally. They have analyzed how peer groups have been changed by the introduction of compulsory schooling, television, and the adoption of Western ideas about adolescence (Harkness and Super 1986; see also the discussion of Richard Condon's work in chapter 8). They have also identified ideas about friendship as important ways of understanding children's and young people's worlds (Hardman 1973; James 1993, 1995; Hirschfeld 2002), and much of the recent anthropological literature has focused on how and why young people construct and maintain friendships (Adler and Adler 1998). Helena Wulff (1995) has looked at interracial friendships among girls in London, who emphasized the importance of having someone to trust, listen to music and shop with, as well as having a friend to help them work through issues of ethnic identity and belonging. Allison James (1995) has examined the impact of friendships on children's language structures in a northern British town and found that children were using dialect words which had long passed out of adult speech and which they could have learnt only from each other. There has also been some work considering adult views of young people's friendships and their roles in children's peer cultures, particularly the way they are sometimes perceived as problematic by, or oppositional to, adult society (Kehily 2007). Yet this view of adolescent culture is not universal, and the role of friends in adolescence is not always viewed negatively. Merry White in her comparisons of Japanese and American youth cultures writes: "Allowing for some overstatement . . . Americans support the idea that teenagers should be socially popular, but fear the effects of peer pressure. Japanese support teen friendships and peer associations as a source of social and even hierarchical training for adult life, and only in rare cases, are they concerned with the negative effects of the pressure to conform to teen standards" (1993:22–23).

The impact of peer pressure on the lives of young women college students has been the focus of study for Dorothy Holland and Margaret Eisenhart (1990), who have carried out research on friendships and peer culture on two American campuses, analyzing which social values are seen as most important, and the influence of peers on maintaining or challenging these norms. They found that school adults such as teachers were of very little influence compared with the peer group and that it was the latter that had a major effect on women's choices, both in the present, and about their future careers. Prestige was to be gained through culturally constructed notions of attractiveness and of romance which framed the making of many of these young women's decisions and organized their social worlds. It was through appealing and being attractive to men that women gained status. Female friendships and academic advancement were downplayed and sometimes even seen as a distraction from the more important business of being attractive (see also Eder 1985 for a similar account of younger women's attempts to be popular in US high schools).

Away from schools, and based on fieldwork many decades old, there is a long tradition amongst anthropologists of looking at age-sets. Some of this work may well be out of date now and it is unlikely that some of the youth groups analyzed have survived the political and social changes in the countries in which they were found. Nevertheless, in these older ethnographies we see an acknowledgment of the importance of peers and friends in children's and young people's lives and the ways in which the interactions between young people shape and transform them. There is also the recognition that the study of children and young people is valuable in its own right and that ignoring them means not only that the ethnography is incomplete but also that other wider social issues cannot be fully understood. Philip and Iona Mayer, for example, point to the gaps in ethnography left by leaving out a detailed study of young people's lives and associations.

> It has interested us to reflect that this youth organization, with such important functions as we shall attribute to it, might pass quite unnoticed in a classical structural analysis of a Red Xhosa community. It does not obviously enter into any of the other classical "systems" (of kinship, politics, law, ritual, etc.) although in our view it serves important functions in regard to nearly all of them by inculcating appropriate values and patterns of behaviour. (1970:160)

Age-sets will be discussed again in more detail in chapter 8, but there has also been important work on less formal youth associations in Africa. To give just one example, Philip and Iona Mayer studied the role of peers and friends in the 1950s among the rural Red Xhosa of South Africa. In contrast to the urbanized and more missionized Xhosa of the cities, the young people with whom they worked had kept intact systems of youth groups which transcended families and which provided a structure for young people's lives away from adult society. Although there was considerable overlap between the values of adults and youth groups, these groups had a distinctive identity, not necessarily grounded in kinship ties or based on political affiliations. The Mayers described a situation in which young people, from a relatively early age, formed independent and self-regulating groups that had a greater influence on the members of that group than family members or elders in the community. There were two different groups of youth to belong to, the *intutu*, which consisted of both boys and girls between the ages of around nine and 13 and which was largely located within the neighborhood, and the *mtshotso*, which was joined by older adolescents who had a much greater degree of freedom to travel, and to roam into neighboring communities. The focus of these groups was fighting and sexual activity, although there were strictly controlled limits on both of these. From an early age, Xhosa boys were taught that proper masculinity was bound up with physical prowess, courage, and the ability to fight. Initially, adults in the community would give the boys reeds or small sticks and encourage them to beat each other. By the time they joined the *intutu*, they knew both how to fight and the rules of fighting, so that, for instance, it was unacceptable to hit anyone junior or a girl, and fights had to take place only between age-mates or equals. While boys were members of an *intutu* or *mtshotso*, adults played little part in the fights, which were entirely regulated by peers. It was in these structures that boys fought, either as individuals against each other, or in their own *mtshotso* against other *mtshotso* from other areas (Mayer and Mayer 1970).

Girls were banned from watching these fights, and the Mayers say little about girls' experiences of the *intutu*. In the realm of sexuality, girls played a more prominent role and the group controlled this, as they did the boys' fighting. Sexual experimentation was acknowledged and encouraged as long as it was done in an appropriately open manner where a girl could publicly declare her affection for a boy by presenting him with a decorated stick. He was then acknowledged as her lover. Private love was strongly discouraged and subject to sanctions because it was outside the control of the group and negated the social aspect of courtship. In this way a girl was prevented from seeing more than one lover (a good training for marriage) and the group was able to control the sexual acts a girl performed and the consequences of these acts. Although these views coincided with those held by adults outside the *mtshotso*, it was the young people themselves who policed their members and who imposed their morality on them. Far from being rebellious and anti-authority, these groups of young people upheld and championed the values of their elders.

Conclusion

This chapter has looked at the various meanings of family and the roles that parents, peers, siblings, and friends can play in children's lives. The relationship between child and parents is a much-discussed concept but, as this chapter has shown, it is certainly not straightforward. Children live in many sorts of family and recognize a variety of people as their kin. The idea that biology is the most important factor in understanding kinship does not hold true in cross-cultural contexts, and it is evident that it is social ties and the active claiming of kin, as much as the passive acceptance of biology, that creates families in many circumstances. It is for this reason that a study of adoption and fosterage is so important. Not only does it tell us about children's lives, with whom they live, and whom they claim as kin, but it also helps anthropologists and other outsiders examine ideas about kinship and the relationship between children and adults in any given society. It helps us to understand that ideas about the family and about suitable carers for children change over time and that the nature of parenthood is constantly in flux. Children can be raised by a wide variety of people, of vastly differing ages, both inside and outside their families. Although in many cases parents do provide the main forms of socialization, there are also many formal and informal methods by which children are raised and nurtured. Children themselves take an active part in forming their families – some claim kin, others reject them – and children's experiences of family and nonfamily are multiple and varied. The importance of siblings and peers in many children's lives is great and is essential to understanding their experiences of life, and recent anthropological work is beginning to open up this subject and look more broadly at children's own cultural worlds amongst their peers.

5

TALKING, PLAYING, AND WORKING

Introduction

Although there are many ethno-theories of child development and myriad ways of socializing children, aspects of which have been touched on in previous chapters, there are certain skills that all children learn in their earliest years and which need further examination. Language acquisition, for example, is a universal feature of childhood, and learning to talk, communicate, and understand speech are crucial aspects of childhood learning and development. Anthropological work on children's language socialization has shown not only how children acquire language, but also how social relationships are shaped and negotiated through the processes of language learning. Another aspect of children's lives, which is often seen as the quintessential quality of childhood, is play – meaningless, fun activities that separate the immature from the mature. Yet play is a complex term and studies have shown that play can have multiple meanings and that it cannot be studied without reference to socialization or education. Neither can it be examined without looking at work and an acknowledgement of the economic role of children. This chapter will take these three aspects of children's lives – speech, play, and work – and look at how these have been analyzed and what these studies can say about childhood.

Learning Language

The way in which children learn language is a vast field in its own right, much researched and analyzed by linguists and psychologists. Anthropologists have come to the study of language socialization in children much later, and, in contrast, their work has focused on the interplay between the language that people use and who they are, as well as on the ways in which children's language socialization reflects and shapes wider cultural values. Robert LeVine et al. (1994), for example, analyzed the different ways mothers respond to their babies and the implications this has for understanding ideas about the proper nature of childhood. They compared Gusii mothers in Kenya with middle-class mothers in America and found that while Gusii mothers responded much more quickly than American mothers to sounds of infant distress, they reacted very differently to babbling and other noises made by their babies, which they attempted to check by ignoring them and looking away. LeVine et al. found that Gusii mothers did not coo over babies or kiss them excessively, and that they deliberately tried to dampen down any strong emotion. The ideal state for a Gusii baby was understood as a calm one with the baby neither distressed nor excited, and mothers tried to keep their children tranquil at all times. In contrast, American mothers reacted positively to infant babble, assigning meanings to these sounds, engaging the baby in pretend conversations, and encouraging responsiveness and infant excitement. Both sets of mothers encouraged socially appropriate responses, and it is through how they talked to their children, in the earliest days of their lives, that ideas about childhood and the correct role and response of children become apparent.

Elinor Ochs (1982, 1988) has written extensively on how children learn cultural competencies through language in Western Samoa. She looks at the role of caregivers in young children's lives and suggests how an examination of language can be used to illuminate many assumptions about the nature of childhood, the status and role of children, and the expected behaviors of both child and caregiver. She writes:

> In using language a particular way, caregivers are acting on certain assumptions concerning the capacities of human infants and young children, and concerning the nature of the caregiver role, the behaviors expected of those providing care. It is in the understanding of these assumptions that we can, in turn, understand the process of socialization through

language. A caregiver, in using language a particular way, not only acts upon assumptions, but conveys these assumptions to the child as well. The caregiver provides the child not only with the linguistic input, but with cultural input as well; for example, a set of procedures for interpreting situations, for indicating the appropriate behavior expected of the child and others within and across situations. (1982:79)

Samoa is a highly stratified society where status is based on age and rank, and children are taught this early on. Those of a higher status delegate the chores of child-rearing to those of a lower status, so that children are usually cared for by siblings rather than mothers, and even if the mother is regularly with the child, she is rarely alone (see the previous chapter for a further discussion of sibling caregiving in this context).

One of the features of Samoan life is that higher status persons are not expected to adjust their perspective to that of lower status persons such as children. They would not expect to move physically in order to look after a child, to change their way of behaving, or their register of speech. Baby talk, for instance, is never used, nor are diminutives or simplified forms of words or speech. Furthermore, caregivers in Samoa make little attempt to comprehend or expand children's speech, or to assign the sort of intentionality toward infants that LeVine et al. found in North American mothers. Caregivers make no attempt to decenter themselves or to try to understand the child's perspective, and they do not believe that a babbling child is trying to communicate. The relations of status, expressed through language, mean that Samoan parents do not attempt to interpret a child's sounds. Ochs argues that

infants and very young children are generally not treated (1) as socially responsive beings (cooperative); and (2) as being in control of their actions. The actions and vocalization of infants are treated more as natural reflexes of physiological states (e.g., hunger, discomfort, pleasure) than as intentional, spontaneous acts. The actions and utterances of toddler-age children are often treated as unalterable through social response (resistant). (1982:91–92)

Similar ideas can be found amongst the Kaluli of Papua New Guinea. Ochs and Bambi Schieffelin describes how Kaluli mothers believe that infants have no understanding and claim to look after them because they "feel sorry for them" (Ochs and Schieffelin 1984:289). Mothers rarely leave their children alone, or with other caregivers, and they carry them in netted bags when they are not holding them. Although they address them by name, they rarely address other utterances to them, they do not gaze into their eyes and do not hold them face-to-face when speaking to them. Instead they tend to hold their babies outward so that they can see others in the social group and be seen by them. When older children address the baby, the mother may speak "for" the infant by using a high-pitched nasalized voice, but the words she uses are well formed and likely to be used and understood by an older child. In using language in this way the mother is forming a relationship between the two children, but there is no sense that the baby is initiating this. As Ochs and Schieffelin argue, "in taking this role the mother does for the infant what the infant cannot do for itself, that is, appear to act in a controlled and competent manner, using language" (1984:290).

As children grow, adults will address them more, but usually the speech is made up of one-line instructions telling them to do, or not to do, something. Until the child is 18 months old, adults do not assume that the child can respond and the infant is simply addressed and instructed rather than seen as a partner in linguistic exchange. Once children can say two key words, however, "mother" and "breast," they are assumed to be ready to start learning language, and at this point are actively taught by being provided with a model and being instructed to "say like that" (Ochs and Schieffelin 1984:292). Caregivers try to teach children correct language by example, so encouraging a child to speak by addressing him or her in baby talk is undesirable and unproductive. Furthermore, children have to learn to be assertive and use appropriate forms of speech. While wheedling and begging are seen as coming naturally to children, talking assertively is not, and this way of speaking must also be taught. Children are encouraged to speak assertively because of the Kaluli reluctance to put words into other people's mouths; they say, "one cannot know what another thinks or feels" (Ochs and Schieffelin 1984:290). Clear expression is regarded as being the responsibility of the speaker, and children will be asked to clarify what they have said rather than have adults interpret for them or guess what they are trying to communicate.

Ochs and Schieffelin conclude that "the process of acquiring language and the process of acquiring sociocultural knowledge are intimately tied" (1984:310). Christina Toren (1990, 1993) elaborates this idea in her studies of children's cognition in Fiji and uses the conclusions she derives from these to understand broader ideas about what makes a person. Toren claims that it is necessary to look at both adults' and children's ideas in order to gain a complete understanding of socialization, not simply in childhood, but across the life-cycle. She asserts that "not only are studies of children's cognitive processes essential to understand what adults are doing and saying, but also that to *neglect* to study children is to prejudice analyses of the key features of adult life. By the same token, to study children in the absence of a concurrent study of relations between people in the collectivity at large, can result only in an inadequate analysis" (1993:462, emphasis in original). Toren analyzes children's and adults' concepts of ritual space and the differences between them, arguing that children's cognitive development is a micro-historical process that transforms concepts and practices as well as people. She uses the example of how Fijian children gradually come to change their understanding of the relationship between space and hierarchy. Based on their knowledge and observation of public spaces, children understand that adults have differential positions and that these are linked to their use of space. Children make empirically sound judgments and assign status to those who occupy certain socially important spatial positions. In contrast, Fijian adults suppose the spatial position to be important because a higher status person is there, so that "meanings made by children may be direct inversions of adult meanings" (Toren 1993:462). Toren argues that the children are not wrong in their beliefs and that such assignments are not the result of incomplete socialization, but part of the processes that transform them into adults, when they can deny their earlier knowledge and cognitively construct hierarchical relations in a socially mature way.

The ways in which wider social values are displayed in speech, and the differences between communities in how they deploy language, have also been the focus of work in the USA. One of the classic contributions to this area of study is Shirley Brice Heath's *Way with Words* (1983). She undertook extensive fieldwork in two communities in the rural USA in the 1970s, which she called Roadville and Trackton. Both were situated in the Piedmont Carolinas, but while Roadville was a white working-class community of mill workers, Trackton was a black community of farm workers and others who had grown up living off the land but had begun to work in the mills. Heath looked at how children learnt and used language at home and in the community and found very different styles of talking in Roadville and Trackton, contrasting attitudes to storytelling, and dissimilar values embedded in the language. In Roadville. stories usually involved strong moral messages. Children were told fairy stories, biblical tales, or true stories which emphasized a particular moral message and they were not encouraged to make up their own tales. Indeed stories which were exaggerated or embellished by children were condemned by adults as "lies" and children would be interrupted and corrected if they got their stories wrong or misrepresented facts. Stories that were told tended to be based on true events or conversations with friends and neighbors and often involved the gentle teasing of those present who may have in some ways transgressed local norms by failing to be a "good cook" or a "good Christian." Children were persuaded to tell tales on themselves and to draw out explicit moral messages.

In contrast the children of Trackton were encouraged to be more imaginative and creative in their storytelling. Although some of their stories may have been based on factual episodes, when retelling the story they became more elaborate and fictionalized and children were encouraged to "talk junk," that is, use exaggeration and embellishment. The stories the children heard and learnt to tell were full of simile, metaphor, and humor and the audience was expected to participate. These stories did not contain the moral message that was so highly valued in Roadville, although they often focused on conflict and resolution. From the age of two, children in Trackton were expected to produce their own stories and to "talk junk." If their stories were good enough to hold attention, they were allowed to interrupt adult conversations. Through learning about stories, and the proper language and register to use when talking about events, children in both communities learnt social values and the correct relationships between adults and children and between neighbors. However, the word "story" meant very different things in each community. For children in Trackton a story was a public performance, full of embellished detail, while Roadville children used the word "story" to mean a moral tale, based on the truth and with a satisfactory ending which encoded their community's values. As Heath summarizes: "For Roadville, Trackton's stories would be lies; for Trackton, Roadville's stories would not even count as stories" (1983:189).

A similar concern with storytelling and its links to social organization is found in the work of Marjorie Goodwin. In her book He-Said-She-Said (1990) she analyzes the use of language among peer groups of African American children in a working-class neighborhood in southwest Philadelphia which she calls Maple Street. Focusing on their interactions with each other, she looked at how children used language, how they created their own cultures, and the differences in the ways that same-sex peer groups structured their talk and their play. She examined three aspects of children's language: the use of directives, neighborhood disputes and gossip, and "how the children organized their social life through talk" (1990:19). She found significant differences between how boys and girls played together, so that while boys were more likely to issue commands and directives, such as "give me," girls used phrases such as "let's" or "we gotta." She found no rigid dichotomy, however, between girls playing cooperatively and boys playing competitively, and in some situations, such as when they "played house," girls became more hierarchical and gave orders. There was also a great deal of interaction between girls and boys, and in any verbal disputes girls were not browbeaten by the boys and could hold their own against them. There was no sense of girls and boys having separate cultures, and Goodwin concludes that "gender asymmetry, considered the social-structural principle leading to polar contrasts such as public and private, does not constitute a relevant feature of social organization among Maple Street children" (1990:285). In one aspect of speech, however, there was a significant difference between boys and girls: while boys would engage in direct disputes with other boys, girls were more likely to gossip about other girls who were not there, taking part in "he-said-she-said" discourses in which one girl accused another of talking about her to a third girl. These disputes could go on for over a month, but rather than seeing them simply as childish falling-outs, Goodwin analyzes them as

> a field of negotiated action, complete with its own relevant history, [which] is invoked through the structure of an opening accusation state-ment; a single utterance creates a complex past history of events, providing operative identity relationships for participants, through careful framings of experience and "tactical uses of passion." . . . In investigating stories, girls can call forth feelings of righteous indignation that are relevant to the shaping of a dispute which can last over a month. The interactive frame created by the he-said-she-said event thus links together several speech events – stories, gossip, and argument – within a single process, the management of breaches. (1990:286)

Studying the ways in which children learn language illuminates broader social assumptions and ideas about childhood as well as provid-ing insight into the values of the wider society. Don Kulick (1992), in his work in the village of Gapun in the Sepik region of Papua New Guinea, looks at how language has shifted from Taiap, the traditional language of the area, now spoken fluently by only 89 people, and Tok Pisin, a pidgin language spoken as a lingua franca in Papua New Guinea. Children are crucial to this shift, and through an analysis of language socialization Kulick shows how notions of childhood and maturity are reflected within and between languages. The two languages are associated with more general ideas about the nature of persons and the differences between men and women, adults and children, Europeans and New Guineans, pagans and Christians. People in Gapun believe that children are born stubborn, selfish, uncooperative, and unconcerned with social harmony, a set of personality traits they label as *hed*. As children grow, they begin to learn a sense of social responsibility, generosity, and cooperation, and this is known as *save*. Both aspects are part of the human personality but are linked to age and gender, so that women and children are associated with *hed* and men with *save*. This is manifested in the ways in which men are associated with oratorical speech and women with tantrums, screaming, and the shouting of obscenities. Children's earliest words are assumed to be Taiap insults, but as their speech improves and they become more articulate and sociable, they are seen as entering the world dominated by Tok Pisin, and spoken to accordingly. If a child does not respond to a command in Taiap, his or her parents will repeat it in Tok Pisin, with the consequence that children in the village have grown up speaking very little Taiap. Speaking and understanding Tok Pisin is a sign of maturity and a sign of a child beginning to show *save*, and children are encouraged to use the language, which corresponds to ideas of sense and social competence.

Children and Play

Childhood is the time when all children learn language and acquire the linguistic skills and competencies they need. It is also a time of play when children's activities are consigned to the realms of the meaningless and carefree, bringing fun rather than a serious outcome (Schwartzman 1976; James 1998). From the perspective of cultural studies, Peter Barnes and Mary-Jane Kehily claim that

> play is often regarded as one of the most distinctive features of childhood
> – something that all children have in common, and which makes their world
> strikingly different from that of an adult. Indeed, for many people it is children's capacity for play, their enthusiasm for play and the importance attached
> to being allowed to play that defines what childhood is about. Children
> differ in the games they play of course, not least according to their age
> and gender, but all children play. (2003:4)

There is an implicit dichotomy between the non-economic, non-productive, enjoyable, and less serious world of children, who exist to play, and the serious, important, and productive world of adults. Yet play is also seen as a serious thing, and it has received a great deal of attention, not only from anthropologists but also from psychologists and sociologists, who have challenged the notion of play as meaningless or unimportant. They have claimed that play helps children reach important developmental goals and have referred to play as "the work of childhood."

Anthropology has a long history of analyzing games, adult play, and, indeed, the material culture of play (Schwartzman 1978; Sofaer Derevenski 2000; Rossie 2005). Edward Tylor (1879), for instance, used children's games and ways of playing to promote theories of diffusionism and looked at games in different geographical locations to support his theories about the types and varieties of contact between cultures. At around the same time in the USA, Stewart Culin (1898, 1899) collected descriptions of games from a wide variety of countries and different cultures and argued that games were a feature of all societies. While he disagreed with Tylor's conclusions, he produced extensive descriptions of games, including one monograph devoted to the games played by the children of Brooklyn (Culin 1891). Generally, however, anthropologists have been most interested in those games that had clearly observable rules and structures that could be analyzed and compared with other games (Roberts et al. 1959). There were occasional descriptions of children's play and games in field notes, but anthropologists rarely wrote about it in their published monographs, suggesting that they felt it to be an insignificant area for concern. Others discussed children's play as an incompetent copy of adult activities or, at best, as a way of children learning their future economic roles. Children were described as "playing" house or "play" fighting, depending on gender, thereby dismissing their activities as essentially non-productive and trivial.

In contrast there has been a longer and more continuous tradition of studying children's play activities amongst folklorists, who have published very detailed accounts of children's games, especially those perceived to be on the verge of extinction. Some of the earliest collections of folklore, including Lady Alice Gomme's *The Traditional Games of England, Scotland, and Ireland* (1898), dealt with such apparently endangered games. This work set a precedent for some of the more famous work of the 20th century, including that of Iona and Peter Opie, who proposed that children had a separate culture from adults and that the most obvious manifestations of this culture could be found in children's games (Opie and Opie 1969, 1997, 2001[1959]; Opie 1993; see also chapter 1, under the section on "Children in British Anthropology," for the Opies' view of children's culture, and its links with anthropology). Other folklorists have followed on from this work, looking at children's games and folklore in a wide variety of contexts, including New Zealand (Sutton-Smith 1959) and the USA (Sutton-Smith 1972), and have gone beyond simply listing the rules, or describing how children play games, and have discussed instead ideas about the cultural significance of play and its role in both children's and adults' lives. Brian Sutton-Smith, in particular, has devoted several decades to examining play as a cultural form which is as important as art or music. He has also looked at how and why children and adults play, the links between play in humans and nonhumans, and play as an evolutionary adaptation (Sutton-Smith 1997; see also Avedon and Sutton-Smith 1971; Herron and Sutton-Smith 1971). He describes play as both spontaneous and joyful and stylized and regulated, revealing imbalances of power and social hierarchy, and also as blurring the boundaries of the real and the imaginary (Sutton-Smith and Kelly-Byrne 1983). He has argued: "Play is always a fantasy, but once you get into the frame it is quite real, and everything you do is real. You put acres and acres of real movement and real action and real belief in it" (Sutton-Smith, quoted in Marano 1999).

The metaphor of play has been used by anthropologists to refer to a vast number of activities, including sport, tourism, watching television, and gossip (Sutton-Smith 1997), but its meaning to children has only become the focus of anthropological work in the last 30 years and it is only in this time-frame that children's play has been focused on in its own right rather than as something that can shed light on other areas of social life. In 1976 Helen Schwartzman argued that "research on children's play can and should be evaluated on the basis of what is learned about children's play (not cognition, or social structure, or culture contact)" (1976:290). With this idea as a focal point, children's play became one of the first areas of children's culture to be examined by anthropologists. Indeed, Schwartzman had been a co-founder two years earlier of a specific anthropological group, The Association for the Anthropological Study of Play (TAASP; since 1978, The Association for the Study of Play, TASP), which examined the range of possibilities that the study of play offers to anthropologists and others (see Schwartzman 1976 and 1978 for two excellent and comprehensive guides to the anthropological study of play; see also Stevens 1977; Lancy and Tindall 1977; Roopnarine et al. 1994 for edited collections which look at children's play in a variety of contexts and from varying disciplinary backgrounds).

This focus on children's play has shown that while all children play, there are very distinct differences in how they play and with whom. As David Lancy argues: "Play is a cultural universal. Children are observed playing in every society studied by anthropologists. . . . However, one rarely sees adults playing with children" (2007:274). In contrast to Western developmental psychology, which posits mother–child interaction as an important aspect of child development, mothers in other societies do not play or interact with their children unless there are special circumstances, and fathers play even less. They rarely make toys for their children and, as discussed in chapter 1, ethno-theories of child-rearing, particularly the common notion that "a quiet baby is a healthy one" (Lancy 2007:275), mean that parents are more likely to calm babies, swaddle them, or cradleboard them and keep them in a "benign coma" (Lancy 2007:275) than they are to play with them. In Beatrice Whiting and Carolyn Edwards's cross-cultural study of child-rearing (1988), they found evidence of play and playful interactions between mother and child only in middle-class American society. Lancy (2007) concludes that the idea of the importance of mother–child play is a specific modern phenomenon, not found in over three-quarters of the world's societies.

Play is also an activity that may be used to hide or uncover powerful emotions and social tensions. Jean Briggs (1991), for instance, discusses the ambiguity of play among the Inuit. In a society where people shy away from confrontation and strong emotion, it is through play that tensions are aired. By keeping social problems on a playful level and denying their seriousness, both children and adults manage their feelings and learn appropriate responses to various situations. Children have to learn the difference between what is said or done and what is meant, so that while affection might be expressed aggressively through attack, so is hostility, and children must learn to read the situation and understand the correct response. Briggs describes a situation where

> only in play is it permitted to express feelings with an appearance of intensity – and it is permitted only if the feelings are not really intense. Thus play both breaks and keeps the rule that prohibits the expression of intense emotion.
>
> By breaking the rule, it becomes possible to make explicit and dramatize in play the hidden plots and tangled interrelationships of social life – the

possibilities for conflict and aggression and for physical and emotional loss, the dangers and, also, the delights of being loved and wanted. These games show children what to watch out for, and more than that, they give children powerful reasons to watch. The subject matter of a game often concerns a crisis that the child who is played with is currently experiencing, and the child is the focal actor in the play drama as in the "real life" situation. "Who's your daddy?" will be played with a child who has recently been adopted, and "Why don't you kill your baby brother?" will be played with a child who has just acquired a baby brother. (1991:279)

If children have to guess what adults and other children really mean in some circumstances, in others, it is adults who misinterpret what is going on in children's play. In her work on children's games in Belfast, Donna Lanclos (2003) found that children were relatively unconcerned with religious divisions, despite this being the lens through which the majority of researchers on Northern Ireland attempt to understand their lives. Much more salient for the children she worked with in primary schools were divisions of age and gender and the differences between words which were forbidden and those which were allowed. Lanclos discusses how the games of childhood are not necessarily the polite or innocent cultures presented by the Opies (who refused to include rude games or swearing), but are imbued with taboo words which children use to play with ideas about the forbidden. She discusses at length the children's "rude" repertoire, shown in scatological and sexual jokes and chants which could not be used in front of adults. Religious naming was a minor part of this, with children using words such as pigs and cats (or cows) to refer to Protestants and Catholics, but this was of less importance than drawing distinctions between boys and girls. Girls in particular, while happy to discuss sex in their own same-sex groups, would publicly differentiate themselves from boys by expressing their disgust for boys' dirty jokes. Children remained aware, however, of the broader social issues around them and the impact of Northern Ireland's political situation. Several had fathers in prison, or knew of others who did, and problems such as these were mentioned in rhymes and in play. Children's games in this context reflected the wider social realities of their lives but were also a way of transforming and transcending these realities, so that serious social problems could be spoken about, and come to terms with, through play. Lanclos argues that "play becomes an editorial of sorts, picking up on the generalities and exaggerating them for (especially) comic effect. . . . It is a specific representation of exaggerated tropes, which contain the truths of one-parent homes, domestic abuse, large families, and so on" (2003:86).

Studies of play between older children have also been based on adult-centered ideas of what is happening and have often been regarded as imitative, implying that children merely follow their elders, be they peers or parents, and by copying them learn the cultural norms of their society. Malinowski (1960) observed that children's play was important to study because of its educational value and that it was possible to see in play the acquisition of economic life skills. Thus a child playing with a doll is seen as doing so as a prelude to looking after her younger siblings, and eventually becoming a mother herself, and a boy with a toy bow and arrow is honing the skills he will need later on to be a hunter (Rossie 2005). The problem of seeing children's play as simply imitative, however, is that it does not take into account the ways that children are creative and imaginative. Brian Sutton-Smith (1977) argues that play is best understood as something that "potentiates" rather than socializes children, and Meyer Fortes specifically warned against seeing children's activities as no more than pale imitations of the adult world. He wrote with regard to the Tallensi of northern Ghana:

> Writers on primitive education have often attributed an almost mystical significance to "imitation" as the principal method by which a child learns. The Tallensi themselves declare that children learn by "looking and doing"; but neither "imitation" nor the formula used by the Tallensi help us to understand the actually observable process. Tale children do not automatically copy the actions of older children or adults with whom they happen to be without rhyme or reason and merely for the sake of "imitation." (1970:54)

A description of play among the Mehinaku of Amazonia illustrates this well. Thomas Gregor describes a game called "Women's Sons."

> The game begins as the children pair off as married couples. The husband and wife sculpt a child from a clump of earth, carving arms, legs, features, and even genitals. They cradle the baby in their arms and talk to it. The mother holds the child on her hip and dances with it as she has seen her own mother do with younger siblings. After the parents have played with their child for a while, it sickens and dies. The parents weep and dig a grave for the infant and bury it. All the mothers then form a circle on their knees in traditional fashion and, with their heads down and their arms over each others' shoulders, they keen and wail for the lost offspring.

On the occasions that I have seen ["Women's Sons"] played, the children were enormously amused by the entire enactment. When the time came to bury the "babies," the boys smash them into pieces and the girls interrupted their ritual crying with bursts of giggling and shrieks of laughter. Nevertheless, "Women's Sons" provides a tragic commentary on Mehinaku life – death in infancy and early childhood is all too common in the village. The game helps the children prepare for the time when they may lose a sibling and, later on, an offspring of their own. It also teaches them how to express and cope with grief through the medium of ritual crying. (1977:112–113)

Gregor analyzes this as a "role-playing" game in which children play or act out scenes from real life. Through this they learn emotional skills and socially approved ways of behaving, be they proper gender roles, or the appropriate ways of displaying emotion. Yet this passage illustrates the dissonance between what the children are doing and how they seem to react to it and an adult interpretation. The children themselves see no tragedy in this scene and it is not simply an imitation of adult mourning rituals as there are elements in it, such as the smashing of the baby, that the children have made up and clearly enjoy. Gregor may well have been given a very different account of the game had he asked the children's view of what they were doing. Perhaps it is not surprising that some of those who have been most closely involved in the new anthropology of childhood, such as Laurence Hirschfeld (2002) and Allison James (1998), have also worked on children's games and children's play. They have pointed out the need to ask for children's interpretations of what is going on and rejected the idea that play is simple imitation. As Allison James argues: "Play may be as much about transformation as imitation and as much about social disorder as about order" (1998:105).

Another much quoted example of this is given by William Bascom, who in his work with the Yoruba of southwest Nigeria, noticed a new children's game being played. He wrote:

During my work with their father these three children invented a new game, playing anthropologist. One sat in my chair on my cushion, with paper and pencil in hand. The second sat in their father's chair, acting as "interpreter," while the third sat on a bench as the informant customarily did. The second child turned to the first and said, "You are my master," and then to the third child, saying in Yoruba, "The white man wants you to tell about Odua." The third child replied in Yoruba and the second turned to the first and "interpreted," making a series of meaningless sounds which were supposed to sound like English. The first child scribbled on the paper, and replied with more nonsense syllables and the second child turned to the third with a new question in Yoruba. (1969:58)

There is little in this quote that suggests that playing anthropologist is a preparation for maturity, unless the children are assuming that talking to anthropologists is an intrinsic part of adulthood. Furthermore, they are not simply imitating adults, even when using strange words and pretending to speak different languages. Instead they are both incorporating adult activities into their own world and simultaneously mocking them. They show a complex social understanding of the roles played by various people in the encounter, the power dynamics between researcher, researched, and interpreter, and the multiple perspectives involved.

The importance of power has also become an important aspect of analyses of play, suggesting that the supposed spontaneity and carelessness of play are externally imposed ideas. The games that are played within children's peer cultures reflect ideas about status and power between children and their struggle to impose their will on their peers. Ideas about "cooties," for example, reveal children's categorizations and conceptualizations of the world, and while they are playful, they are also profoundly concerned with hierarchies, exclusion, and pollution. Cooties, in American childhood slang, are a fictional source of contagion that can be spread through contact with other children. Girls in particular are liable to be accused of ritual pollution through cooties or "girl stain," or "the lurgy" in British terms (Opie and Opie 1969), and certain girls are teased as "cootie queens" (Thorne 1993:75). Boys rarely accuse each other of being sources of contagion, and girls tend not to treat boys, or objects associated with them, as polluting in the ways that boys do about them. Thorne writes of cootie beliefs among children:

> Recoiling from physical proximity with another person and their belongings because they are perceived as contaminating is a powerful statement of social distance and claimed superiority. Pollution beliefs and practices draw on the emotion-laden feeling of repugnance that accompanies unwanted touch or smell. . . . When pollution rituals appear, even in play, they frequently express and enact larger patterns of inequality, by gender, by social class and race, and by bodily characteristics like weight and motor coordination. (1993:75)

Gary Fine's (1987) study of Little League baseball is also concerned with how play and power are closely interlinked, especially in the realms of gender, and how through baseball, preadolescent boys learn to negotiate sporting rules and become men. Fine argues that although baseball is a game with formal rules that adults try to teach boys, the boys themselves generate their own meanings, particularly in relation to their public presentations of self and their attempts to be seen as masculine. One of the most significant ways they do this is by disassociating and distancing themselves from younger children and girls (and from homosexuals and nonwhites). This is achieved through devaluing or objectifying all things feminine, making homophobic and racist comments, and picking on those weaker or more vulnerable.

> All this is part of the desire by preadolescent boys to be "men" in the "moral" sense of the term. I do not mean by this that preadolescents will behave as men do, but only that they elect from among the repertoire of behaviors that they perceive that men (particularly media men and other role models) display. They select those behaviors that are congruent with their own needs for independence and separation from the world of girls and younger children. They must show themselves not to be part of these protected classes. (1987:185)

Work or Play?

In the modern Western world, play and work have become conceptually separated – adults work and children play – but this idea is a feature of a particular type of childhood, rooted in specific historical and cultural circumstances (Zelizer 1985; Nieuwenhuys 1996). The view that children should be economically inactive and consumers rather than producers has been extensively critiqued by anthropologists, who have shown the economic importance of children and also unpacked the assumption that work and play are different activities performed by different people depending on their age (James 1998). They have shown that the links between play, socialization, and work are extremely blurred and the categories of work and play do not always correspond to local under-standings (Bloch and Adler 1994). David Lancy's work in Liberia on Kpelle children's play and their cultural routines, for example, shows very different conceptualizations of childhood competencies and of work and play. Lancy (1977, 1996) concentrates on children aged six to 12 and examines the kinds of cultural tasks that Kpelle children must learn in order to be socially competent adults. He divides children's learning into two categories. First he discusses play forms such as make-believe games, songs, or stories which take place in a play space, known as the "mother-ground," away from adults. Second he identifies adult-guided activities, such as apprenticeship or bush schools, which have the explicit intention of preparing children for their roles in life, and which link to the secret societies and ritual knowledge that are an intrinsic part of adult cultural life. Both types of learning are linked to work and it is difficult to draw any sharp distinction between play, work, socialization, and education.

> I didn't find that play has no relationship to work. They are, to use a favourite anthropological term, "integrated" . . . make-believe play seems to be one step in an alternatively collapsing and expanding process. A child of three spends hours observing a blacksmith at work. A child of four brings his stick down on a rock repeatedly and says he is a blacksmith. A child of eight weaves with his friends an elaborate reconstruction of the blacksmith's craft, all in make-believe. The child of ten is a blacksmith's helper in reality; he fetches wood for the forge and no more. At twelve he begins learning the actual skills of smithing, adding a new one every few months or so. At eighteen he is a full-fledged blacksmith with his own forge. Parallel patterns can be observed for virtually every class of work. (Lancy 1977:87)

Play, work, and socialization blend seamlessly into one another. Bram Tucker and Alyson Young (2005), in their discussion of the Mikea hunter-gatherers of Madagascar, argue that children forage for fun and because there is not much else for them to do, rather than for any significant economic or nutritional purposes. Whether this counts as work, play, or socialization, therefore, is difficult to know. Some authors, such as Beatrice Whiting and Carolyn Edwards, have drawn a distinction between "directed" activities such as work and "undirected" activities that include play (Whiting and Edwards 1998; Edwards 2000), while others have used the term "play-work" to refer to the gray area between identifiable economic activity and play or socialization (Bloch and Adler 1994). There are no absolute distinctions, however, and assigning children's activities definitively to any one of these categories is problematic.

Until the late 1970s there was almost no acknowledgment of the economic function of children, their contribution to the household economy, or their ability to free up other members of the household to take on economic work. The idea that work was what adults did to contribute to the household and that socialization was what happened to children to prepare them for their future roles led to the serious underappreciation of children's status as workers. Olga Nieuwenhuys (1996) argues that anthropologists have often ignored the amount of hard and heavy work that children actually do. She claims that they tend to romanticize children's work, as long as it is done in the home or surrounding fields, and does not involve paid labor. This is particularly true in analyses of girls' domestic work and childcare responsibilities, which are either dismissed as "playing" house or viewed as a form of life-training that will enable children to grow up as socially competent and culturally sufficient. Its economic significance is invariably downplayed. As feminist scholars have long noted, there has been a tendency to ignore both women's and children's work and regard it as either housework or education instead of labor (Oakley 1994). While there are many studies of waged, and often exploitative, female child labor (Blanchet 1996; Montgomery 2001a), studies of girls' domestic work are rare and the very real contribution of their labor is frequently unnoticed (although there are notable exceptions such as Ennew 1993; Nieuwenhuys 1994, 1995).

Anthropologists who have looked at children's economic roles and carried out detailed studies of children's time have shown that while children do, in fact, contribute a great deal to households in economic terms, this may not be seen either by themselves or their parents as useful and productive labor. In Java, for example, parents claimed that children did not work, they just tended the ducks, cared for their younger siblings, or collected firewood, even though these activities took up several hours a day (Hull 1975). Adults associated work with the activities done to keep a family together and the responsibilities that came with family life. They looked on the children's work as a form of indulgence, without the pressures and duties that came with adulthood. It was only when the children were involved with waged labor that these parents began to see their children as actively contributing to the household. Housework was specifically discounted, and many parents claimed that children under 15 (i.e., those who did not work as laborers outside the family) were economically unproductive and a drain on household income rather than an addition. It is also worth noting that children themselves will also undervalue their own work. Pamela Reynolds (1991), in her study of child labor in Zimbabwe, watched a 14-year-old girl prepare a breakfast of porridge for herself and her younger brother, wash the plates from the previous night's meal, and collect water twice from a source two kilometers away. Yet when questioned directly about what she had done that morning she replied simply, "Nothing."

Sociologist Sam Punch's studies of children in rural Bolivia (2000, 2001) show a large amount of responsibility falling on children's shoulders in that they are expected to undertake domestic work, agricultural tasks, and animal care from the age of around three. She outlines a detailed age hierarchy in which children gradually take on more and more complex tasks as they get older and become more physically and socially competent. Yet while younger children are expected to help out, they are also expected to combine their duties with play, so that the boundaries between categories of work, play, socialization, and education become indistinct and a child chasing away chickens (as Punch describes) is praised by onlookers and is encouraged to enjoy doing so, at the same time as being useful. In Kenya, sociologists Diane Kayongo-Male and Parveen Walji (1984) discovered that it was not necessarily the heaviest or most tedious jobs that children disliked; rather it was the jobs that restricted their freedom. Often children said that they preferred work such as collecting wood or water because they liked the independence and sense of freedom that such jobs gave them. As Jo Boyden et al. (1998) note, when asked about work, children tend to identify only those things that they dislike doing as work.

One final point when discussing children's work is the role of schooling and education. Anthropologists have tended to use the word "education" to refer to formal, Western-inspired, education in schools and have used terms such as "socialization," or even "initiation" (see chapter 8), to refer to other forms of learning. One of the earliest anthropological books on education, John Middleton's edited collection *From Child to Adult*, examined the impact of Western schooling on various traditional societies and looked at the contrast between formal schooling with a set curriculum and traditional ways of handing down knowledge. Since 1970, when this book was written, schooling has spread to nearly all parts of the world, with the majority of children spending at least some time in school. As Kathryn Anderson-Levitt argues:

> Schooling has partially displaced other socialization patterns, including sibling care, gender segregation, and the learning of local knowledge

through formal or informal apprenticeship to elders. It has brought new kinds of age grading, including micro-age-grading of the early years, and new conceptions of intelligence and maturity. Because of school's sorting function, the performance of young children will determine their future (and perhaps that of their family) – in contrast, for instance, to situations where success depends on events in adolescence or young adulthood, such as making a good match or on starting out one's farm or business well. (2005:999)

In some instances, this has had profoundly negative affects on traditional norms and children's learning. David Lancy, for instance, has discussed how the introduction of Western-style schooling in Liberia has undermined the informal means of learning that sustained Kpelle society and has led to "the abandonment of cultural routines that are essential in transmitting Kpelle culture to the next generation" (1996:198). Children are expected to learn a curriculum that has limited meaning to them and they usually fail to reach a necessary level of skills and consequently drop out. At the same time, the laissez-faire approach to learning that worked so well at a village level is lost and children no longer learn the other skills of "the Kpelle traditional education system[, which] works beautifully without anyone being in charge, without schedules, without parental anxiety" (1996:198). Indeed Lancy goes on to conclude that "the loss of culture can at least be slowed by the elimination of universal primary schooling – one of the worst ideas foisted on the third world by well-meaning but short-sighted bureaucrats from the developed nations" (1996:198).

Other writers have argued that schoolwork is productive, economic work. As Judith Ennew has noted in relation to the role of work in modern Western childhood, "Work refers of course to paid employment. Women's work became housework and children's work was transformed into schooling" (1986:16). Sociologist Jens Quortrup (2001) has gone further, arguing that in the West, where children's employment outside the home has a negligible impact on household economies, schooling is the real work of childhood. It is at school that children transform themselves into the next working generation and the future educated workforce, and therefore their education is a form of production. He argues that if teaching is acknowledged as economically productive work, then the same logic must apply to learning, and that children's learning and socialization is also economically productive work. Such a view may be controversial, but it is useful in pointing out the rather arbitrary distinctions that are sometimes made between work, school, socialization, and education. Often the assumption is made that children who go to school do not work, even though, in reality, many children combine both and may, in fact, spend more hours a day working than they do studying (Boyden et al. 1998; Woodhead 1999; Berlan 2005).

Work on children's own view of schools and schooling has also produced interesting results. John D'Amato (1993) has argued that, all other things being equal, children in North America generally do not want to be in school, on the grounds that it is restrictive and compulsory. They will stay in school only if they perceive there to be either intrinsic or extrinsic benefits. Extrinsically, many white middle-class children, as well as the children of some immigrants, believe that schooling will be the means to a better job, higher pay, and social status, while there may also be intrinsic benefits such as enjoyment in learning, or friendships to be made. These children may well choose to be in school. For others, however, especially low-achieving children, or minority children, schooling does not promise them any such rewards, and some feel that even if they do work hard, external prejudices will count against them and they will not be rewarded for their work (Ogbu 1978). Such children will resist school and leave as soon as they can.

This view of schooling is largely based on studies of Western schools and children within them. Others have argued that while Western social scientists analyze schools as repressive, African or Latin American scholars rarely make such claims (Anderson-Levitt 2005). In many cases schools can be a liberating experience for children and a way of challenging the gender or ethnic discriminations of the outside world. Schooling may also allow children to escape the sometimes heavy demands of physical labor or the risks associated with early marriage and pregnancy (Bledsoe 1992). Kathryn Anderson-Levitt (2005) describes how in the Republic of Guinea she witnessed a schoolboy clinging to the school gates, desperate to be let in, his banishment from school a deeply felt punishment, even though schools in that country were dilapidated, a long distance from home, and allowed corporal punishment. Children in countries such as Guinea have strong extrinsic reasons for wanting to do well in school. Learning a language such as French or English brings status and career benefits, and because schooling is still not open to everyone, children perceive advantages in getting a formal education as a way of improving their own or their family's status.

Conclusion

Studies of language, play, and work illuminate many aspects of children's lives: how they grow up, how they become people, and how they are seen and treated by others in their societies. Through language, children learn about social categories, cultural meanings, and how to make sense of the world. Analyzing the way in which caregivers talk to children and the assumptions inherent in their interactions with children clearly shows how infants and children are viewed in society and their social roles. Studies of play also illuminate aspects of children's lives and how childhood is conceptualized and understood. They also show the ways in which children are absorbing, creating, and changing their own cultures. A girl playing with a goat or a calf can have various, complementary and overlapping, meanings: she may be "simply" playing, having fun, enjoying the moment; she may also be creating her own meanings or subverting those of adults, she might be learning future roles by beginning to understand the necessity of responsibility, or be directly contributing to the family economy by caring for its livestock. She is also learning her appropriate gender role, and the duties, behaviors, and ideologies of womanhood, and how to construct herself as properly feminine. Just as work and play cannot be separated from each other, so they cannot be disassociated from socialization, or education in its broadest sense. Childhood is a time of learning; it is also a time of contestation. Through studies of work, play, and language, we can see these negotiations very clearly.

6

DISCIPLINE, PUNISHMENT, AND ABUSE

Introduction

Discipline is a particular area of socialization that has attracted the attention of many anthropologists, and it is often when discipline is being described that children have been most visible in ethnography. This chapter will examine how different views of children affect the ways in which they are punished and will show how understandings about the nature of childhood are revealed in disciplinary methods. It will discuss the instances where children are seen as having no sense, so that discipline is pointless because they do not understand. In some societies, children are seen as naturally good and therefore rarely punished or disciplined, while in others, especially in more punitive Christian traditions, children are seen as being born wicked and sinful and in need of punishment, not in response to their actions, but as a matter of course. As the physical punishment of children becomes less common in the West, descriptions of beatings elsewhere stand out, and the approval of them which many anthropologists have shown can shock contemporary readers. Child abuse has become a particular concern for Western societies, and many of the punishments described in this chapter can appear abusive. The line between acceptable and unacceptable treatment of children is always a fine one, however, and one which shifts over time. The final part of the chapter will analyze how anthropologists have dealt with this and distinguished abuse from discipline.

Discipline and Punishment in the Western Tradition

Before turning to ethnographic accounts of punishment and discipline it is important to situate these in historical and cultural context, not least because so many anthropologists have brought their own, often unspoken, assumptions about the correct methods of child-rearing to their work and have implicitly privileged the importance of physical discipline. It is only with the emergence of a child rights perspective that physical punishment has begun to be questioned by anthropologists and the line between abuse and discipline discussed. Otherwise, as will be shown, a common feature of much ethnography is the assumption that physical discipline is a normal, and indeed necessary, part of child-rearing which elicits little or no comment.

Smacking, spanking, whipping, and caning have a long history and deep cultural roots in the Anglo-American world (for an overview of corporal punishment in the USA see Hyman and McDowell 1979; Ryan 1994; Donnelly 2005). Historian Lloyd de Mause has gone as far as claiming that "the history of childhood is a nightmare from which we have only recently begun to awaken. The further back in history one goes, the lower the level of child care, the more likely children are to be killed, abandoned, beaten, terrorized, and sexually abused" (1974:1). Although de Mause's rhetoric may be provocative, there is strong evidence that physical punishment has long been an accepted form of socialization in both homes and schools. Lawrence Stone has claimed that "severe flogging was a normal and daily occurrence in the . . . grammar school" and "whipping was the normal method of discipline in a sixteenth- or seventeenth-century home" (quoted in Donnelly 2005:46). Fellow historian J. H. Plumb concurred with this, arguing that before the 18th century "harsh discipline was the child's lot, and they were often terrorized deliberately" (1975:66). Theories about discipline and punishment were closely tied to wider worldviews about the relationship between parents and children, God and man, and the necessity of protecting the child from sin. Puritan teaching, especially in New England, linked the harsh physical punishment of children to the concept of original sin. It was believed that as children were born in a state of sin, they had to be taught obedience and brought to God through physical punishment. In the words of Cotton Mather, writing in the late 17th/early 18th century, "Better whipt, than Damned" (quoted in Ryan 1994:72).

It is, of course, very easy to pick and choose certain statements and represent them as typical of a period. Certainly, history, like anthropology, should caution against making universal generalizations about how children were treated at certain periods in history (Pollock 1983). It is equally easy to point to conflicting views about childhood, such as those espoused by Jean-Jacques Rousseau and his followers, who championed the view that children should be treasured for what they were, left alone to play, and be protected as far as possible from the adult world (Jenks 1996; Montgomery 2003). There have always been those who counseled gentle and non-physical treatment of children and who disliked the harshness of beatings and whippings (Ryan 1994). Nevertheless the belief in the necessity and correctness of physical punishment has left a legacy. While some of the harshest forms of discipline, such as sustained whippings and beatings, may be declining, the USA and the UK continue to allow parents to punish their children physically, in contrast to Scandinavian countries such as Sweden, which banned all forms of physical punishment of children in 1979. Murray Straus and Michael Donnelly have claimed that

> whatever the ambiguities in how we think and talk about corporal punishment, the overwhelming majority of adult Americans approve of it. Many regard corporal punishment positively as a customary and necessary technique of child rearing, and almost everyone believes that it may be necessary at least as a punishment of last resort. Close to 100 per cent of parents use corporal punishment on toddlers. Just over half of all American children are still being hit by their parents in adolescence, and for about a quarter hitting continues until they physically leave the family home. (2005:4)

Others, looking at lay theories of corporal punishment, have concurred with this, arguing that the majority of US parents believe that corporal punishment works as a disciplinary technique and pointing to a split between child psychologists, who tend to view the physical punishment as counterproductive, and even morally wrong, and those, such as teachers, who see it as necessary and effective (Furnham 2005).

The advent of children's rights has had important impacts on the physical punishment of children. Imagining children as rights-bearing citizens means allowing them the same rights of protection as adults, as well as acknowledging their special vulnerabilities. If hitting adults cannot be tolerated, then hitting children, for whatever reason, is increasingly seen as problematic and is being challenged in the courts. In 1998 the European

Court of Human Rights ruled that the United Kingdom violated Article 3 of the European Convention on Human Rights, which prohibits torture and inhuman or degrading treatment, when it failed to protect a nine-year-old boy from being beaten by his stepfather. The increasing willingness of the legal system to side with children against parents means that there have been changes in the ways that parents treat their children, as well as shifts in understanding about the nature of childhood, and the changing duties and responsibilities that adults and children have toward each other. To analyze child punishment and discipline in a contemporary context means doing so through this lens of children's rights and modern understandings of child abuse. Yet, as will be shown from the ethnographies discussed in this chapter, ideas about the correct treatment of children have changed dramatically, both in terms of the societies discussed, and in the assumptions of the anthropologists writing about them. Only recently have children's own perspectives entered this analysis, and understanding children's own experiences of discipline puts a very different slant on previous ethnographies.

Physical Punishment

The physical punishment of children is well documented in anthropological monographs and there have been attempts to collect together these descriptions and look for wider cross-cultural patterns in the use of corporal punishment. Some of the most relevant of these have drawn on the Human Relations Area Files, which have shown that while the physical punishment of children is common, it is not universal. In his study of violence in 90 small-scale, peasant societies, David Levinson (1989) found that in 16 out of 90 societies, physical discipline was rare or non-existent. In societies where it was more common, he found correlations with other forms of violence, so that societies which allowed the corporal punishment of children also showed higher levels of wife abuse and sibling aggression, suggesting that the physical punishment of children is part of larger patterns of familial violence. Using some of the same data, Carol and Melvin Embler conclude that corporal punishment is strongly related to the presence of money and social inequality in a society, suggesting that "perhaps parents think, consciously or unconsciously, that corporal punishment is a dramatic way to convey the discrepancy in power between themselves and their children, and that the perception of this discrepancy by the child will generalize to an acceptance of power inequalities later on when the child grows up" (2005:615).

When anthropologists have looked directly at why children are hit, they have received a variety of answers. Jonina Einarsdóttir (2000), for example, asked Papel mothers in Guinea-Bissau why they smacked their children and was told that physical punishment was necessary to teach children and that those who were not beaten would grow up lazy and discontented. One mother described the results of her dislike of physical punishment and the problems that her refusal to beat her children was now creating:

> Children are the product of their upbringing. To have success in life children have to be prepared not to become lazy and deceitful, you understand? Because I do not have the heart to beat my children they never help me. My children never help me. Because I don't beat them, I have to do all the work myself. (Einarsdóttir 2000:104)

Physical punishment may also be seen as inherently necessary for children in order for them to learn about pain and learn to control their reactions to it. In Amazonia, Yanamamö boys are taught from an early age to be "fierce"; they are encouraged to hit their parents and siblings and to learn how to control their own reactions to pain (Chagnon 1968). In central Brazil, Akwẽ-Shavante children are also encouraged to hit back when anyone hits them but are discouraged from crying with pain. While crying in anger is acceptable and the severe tantrums of thwarted children are met with indifference or amusement, the Akwẽ-Shavante find it shameful if a child cries in pain and will physically discipline a child for this (Maybury-Lewis 1974:69). Nisa, the !Kung woman interviewed by Marjorie Shostak, gives a long account of her upbringing on the edge of the Kalahari desert in Botswana, claiming that, as well as being hit for disobedience, children were beaten regularly for not sharing food, for fussing or complaining about being weaned, or for showing jealousy to a younger sibling who had supplanted them on their mother's breast. Nisa remembers constant beatings as a child, although they had little effect on her: "People failed at bringing me up. I was too difficult for them" (1983:63). There is also an implicit acknowledgment in some ethnographies that children are disciplined because their parents have lost their temper and cannot help themselves. Marjorie Wolf (1972:70) describes Taiwanese children being hit when they are disobedient but links this not only to the child's behavior, but also to the inevitable frustrations felt by mothers when the *khi*, or steam, rises in them and has to be released if it is not to cause mental or physical illness.

The severity of the discipline handed out to children has been linked to ideas about a child's developmental stage. According to Otto Raum, at the time he conducted fieldwork in East Africa, the Chaga had "a well-thought-out pedagogics of punishment" (1940:228), adapted to the child's age. They recognized that an infant was small and vulnerable and should not be beaten, that a toddler could be both naughty and willful and may deserve a beating, and that older children could be beaten more severely but less often. Helen Morton (1996) also makes the point that children in Tonga are smacked most often when they are between the ages of three and five, when they are assumed to be at their most willful and problematic. Others use different developmental markers as the point at which a child may, and possibly should, be disciplined. Margaret Read (1968) mentions the emergence of the second set of teeth as a key developmental stage among the Ngoni of Malawi. When children have only their first teeth, they are rarely disciplined, but once the second set is through, they can be disciplined by estrangement and social ridicule. In other cases, it is the developmental markers themselves that will bring on a physical punishment. The West African Beng will spank a child if it is precocious in its motor development and starts to walk too early. They believe that it is taboo for children to walk before the age of one year and therefore they keep careful account of children's ages and will smack them if they try to walk before that age (Gottlieb 2004).

All these examples suggest that physical discipline is not simply a method of punishment but is tied to wider philosophies of socialization and ideas about the correct relationship between people. Caroline Bledsoe (1990b) in her study of child-rearing in Sierra Leone views physical punishment as a way of teaching children their subordinate place in the social order. She looked at situations when children are fostered out to distant relatives and patrons, where they are sometimes treated very severely and subjected to harsh physical regimes. Complaints to their parents are rarely upheld and their families are very reluctant to step in and remove the child, believing that such treatment is ultimately beneficial for him or her (see also chapter 4). It is believed that through physical discipline, children learn that life is a struggle, in which they must earn, rather than learn, knowledge (Bledsoe 1990b). The belief in the importance of corporal punishment as a generalized threat to keep all children in their place, rather than the ultimate sanction against a particular individual, is also evident. According to Marjorie Wolf's description of rural Taiwan, parents told her: "Children ought to be hit. It does them no harm" (1972:69). Indeed, it is part of a fundamental philosophy of child-rearing:

> The basic philosophy of socialization among farmers seems to be that if you wish to train a child, the child must fear you. The only way to encourage *desired* behavior is to punish *undesired* behavior severely. As one mother said, "Do you think that they will listen to you when you scold them? What good does that do? All you can do is grab one and really hit him hard. Then the others will be good too." (1972:68, emphasis in original)

Based on fieldwork conducted some years later, Charles Stafford (1995) concurs with this, and found that in the Taiwanese fishing village in which he worked, children were sometimes punished physically for no reason other than to show them that life could be harsh and that they must learn to bear pain without complaint.

The role and importance of punishment as an integral part of child socialization has been analyzed in great depth by Helen Morton, previously writing as Helen Kavapalu, in her studies of child-rearing in Tonga (Kavapalu 1993; Morton 1996). Her work on Tonga has examined why children are beaten with such frequency, what its effects are, and how it is related to indigenous ideas about power, status, and correct social behavior. She describes a society in which children are regularly beaten by adults and other children and where siblings a year or two older than the offending child are expected to inform on the child, collect an implement for beating their sibling with, and even to inflict this punishment themselves. Punishments can be severe and children are beaten from a young age, yet this is not random violence or cruelty but linked to wider ideas about the nature of childhood and the necessity of shaping children in a particular way. As Morton argues: "The ideology and practice of child punishment is embedded within a more general theory of personhood and development" (Kavapalu 1993:317). As discussed in chapter 2, children in Tonga are seen as lacking social competence. Key components of this include respect, obedience, and, importantly, an understanding of social hierarchies and status relationships. Physical punishment is explicitly talked about as a way of teaching a child about these hierarchies and as a reflection of wider Tongan society, where violence is always directed

from high-status people to low-status ones. Beatings are a way of enforcing the power relationships between adults and children, and between
older and younger siblings (Kavapalu 1993).

Punishment in the Tongan context is also concerned with teaching
children emotional and behavioral self-control and ensuring they conform
to social ideals of respect and obedience. Children are expected to endure
punishment without crying or moving too much and to apologize in a
quiet, monotonous voice. Beatings are designed to inflict both physical
and emotional pain on a child and to ensure that children are aware not
only of their foolishness, but also of their subordination. This is emphasized further by the response of those beating the child, or witnessing
the beating, which is to laugh. While this may be a way of diffusing the
tension of the situation, Morton claims it can also be very cruel and humili-
ating to the child. Yet there is also an ambivalence in this laughter, which
she sees as mirroring the ambivalence felt more generally toward hierarchical relationships.

> Ambivalence toward punishment is also part of a broader ambivalence
> toward hierarchical relations. In simple terms, higher status persons are
> protectors and providers as well as punishers and wielders of power. Since
> punishment is positively valued as a form of teaching and an expression
> of love and concern, the distinction between protecting/providing and hurt
> ing is somewhat blurred, and the ambivalence that results is deep-seated
> and complex. (Kavapalu 1993:321)

Few anthropologists have looked as directly as Helen Morton at indigenous theories of punishment and child socialization. Instead accounts
of physical punishment occur regularly in ethnographic accounts of
children's lives, often implying that such incidents have the full approval
both of the society under discussion, and of the anthropologist. Several
have assumed that smacking or beating children is a universal method
of discipline and, as such, it is mentioned with little comment. Isaac
Schapera, for instance, described the elaborate and quite painful punishments meted out to Kgatla children in the Bechuanaland Protectorate (now
in South Africa). He wrote:

> The domestic training in conduct and character is not carried out in
> any set manner, but through the exhortation or reprimand, as well as
> chastisement, as the occasion arises. Mistakes are corrected, ignorance is

dispelled, good behaviour is applauded and insolence or disobedience is immediately followed by punishment. This generally consists of a scolding or whipping. Small children are slapped with the bare hands or lightly beaten on the buttocks with a wooden switch or reed broom. Adolescent girls are generally beaten with switches on the body or shoulders. Adolescent boys are made to lie face downwards at full length, and are whipped on the bare back with a cane. (1971[1940]:227)

Of course, language, context, and relativity are extremely important in interpreting these passages, as will be discussed in more detail in the final section of the chapter, but what is clear is that Schapera regarded whippings, spankings, or a sound slapping as a normal part of parental discipline. It is only when he noted that some parents seemed to beat their children "mercilessly" that he became uneasy (1971[1940]:227).

Individual ethnographers' prejudices often become very evident when discussing punishment, so that it is not uncommon for anthropologists to use pejorative terms such as "spoilt" or "indulged" when describing children subject to nonpunitive regimes. David Maybury-Lewis, for example, referred to children as "small tyrants . . . exceedingly spoilt by our standards" (1974:68), because of the perceived lack of parental discipline. In a similar vein, Theodore Hernandez wrote with disapproval that "the aborigines of the Drysdale River [of western Australia] do their best to spoil little children with an over-indulgent love, and, needless to say, they succeed admirably" (1941:129). It is very rare that ethnographers question the use of physical punishment in children's lives. Hortense Powdermaker, in her account of the Lesu of Melanesia, wrote that discipline was not severe in early childhood, but then mentioned in the same paragraph that children were spanked until they cried (1933:84). Colin Turnbull's ethnography of the Congo Mbuti describes them as peaceful, happy-go-lucky, and relaxed in their attitude to their children, and he states that they rarely use corporal punishment. Yet his description of their idyllic lives contains the surprising comment: "For children, life is one long frolic interspersed with a healthy sprinkle of spankings and slappings. Sometimes these seem unduly severe, but it is all part of their training" (1961:129). It is difficult to know how to interpret these two contradictory statements – that corporal punishment is not much used but that children are regularly smacked – other than to suggest a certain blindness on the part of anthropologists about their own prejudices and views of how children should be dealt with.

Another example of this is shown in Charles Wagley's account of the lives of the Tapirapé of Brazil. He claims that he "seldom saw a Tapirapé parent use corporal punishment, except in extreme irritation" (1977:148), but immediately goes on to claim:

> More than once I saw a Tapirapé father shoot an older son, a mischievous, slightly older [boy] (about nine to ten years old), with a blunt arrow tipped with beeswax. On one occasion a father who was irritated with his son took aim from about twenty yards away without rising from his hammock; he hit the boy on the thigh. The boy cried and it raised a lump. The whole affair was highly amusing to the whole village, and villagers teased the small boy because of his "wound". (1977:149)

It is unclear whether Wagley views this as a form of corporal punishment or not, or simply an amusing story, but it underlines the point that physical punishment is often regarded as a normal, universal method of discipline by Western observers.

Western children's response to punishment and abuse has been the subject of some attention from psychologists, but there is, as yet, surprisingly little anthropological material on children's own feelings and reactions to disciplinary measures. Marjorie Shostak (1983) comments on the frequency with which the !Kung talked about the beatings they experienced when children and the life-long feelings of anger these produced, but she was talking to adults looking back on their lives. She also raised doubts as to the accuracy of these memories, writing that she herself never saw the sorts of beatings that her informant Nisa described. Taiwanese respondents in David Wu's (1981) survey remembered the humiliation of having to kneel by the door facing the street so that passers-by could see them, and remembered this, rather than beatings, as causing most pain. An exception to this tendency not to ask children themselves is Helen Morton (1996), who asked children specifically about their feelings on being punished. She found an ambivalence toward being disciplined amongst the children, who tended to give socially acceptable answers such as "I feel sad" or "I feel guilty," but also reported negative personal feelings of shame and anger. Adults also would talk with pain and upset about the beatings they were given as children (1996:198–200). Morton quotes one 13-year-old girl who articulated these contrary feelings well: "When they punish me I honestly feel angry and hateful at first but after a while I understand them and see what they want from me. This makes me love them more" (Kavapalu 1993:321).

Alternatives to Physical Punishment

Through studying methods of discipline it is possible to draw out ideas about childhood, adult/child relations, and issues such as whether or not children possess sense, whether they are social people, and their role and status in society. Despite the widespread use of physical chastisement as a way of controlling and disciplining children, its use is not universal, and there are instances where it is believed that it is unnecessary. In the case of young children in particular, there is often a view that they have no sense and therefore no idea what they have done wrong or why they are being disciplined. Carol Delaney points out that adults in rural Turkey "generally try to give them [children] what they ask for because it is sinful and greedy to withhold something from a child. Since they lack reason, children cannot be held responsible for unreasonable demands" (2000:139). In other accounts from Taiwan (Wolf 1972), Nepal (Hardman 2000), and Micronesia (Le 2000), parents consistently say that until children learn social competence (however that is defined), there is no point in disciplining them. Others see in young children a weakness and vulnerability that means that parents should never be harsh with them, regardless of circumstances. In Bali, children are treated with extreme calm and care, soothed at the first sign of crying, and have their faces covered to prevent them from seeing anything unpleasant (Diener 2000). Their life-force is understood to be fragile and all steps are taken to protect them. Physical punishment, no matter how mild, would threaten a child's well-being and is never used. The Amazonian Yanamamö, too, although they encourage fierceness among their children, rush to soothe infants when they cry, believing them to be susceptible to spirits who wish to take their souls, which are not yet firmly established in their bodies and which leave through their open mouths. When babies cry, they are quickly comforted (Chagnon 1968).

Other ethnographers have noted that parents can seem relatively unconcerned about their children's upbringing, even to the point of danger. Barry Hewlett (1991) writes that even though the children of the Central African Aka pygmies are treated with considerable leniency, their society is not child-centered and adults will put a small baby down on the floor of the forest to chase game if the need arises. The core values of Aka society consist of autonomy and respect for the individual, which means that parents rarely attempt to impose discipline on a child. If a child disobeys a request to fetch something, the parents simply do it themselves. Similarly Annette Hamilton's (1981) monograph on Aboriginal child-rearing mentions that adults never interfere with a child's activities unless the latter are in distress, and David Maybury-Lewis (1974) notes, with some surprise, Akwē-Shavante parents' reluctance to interfere in their children's affairs. When his wife smacked their son for misbehaving and taking advantage of Akwē-Shavante children, the villagers were shocked and gave his son a stick to retaliate against his mother. Children, he reported, might be scolded, but no parent ever made a child do something that he or she did not want to.

This sense that a child cannot be forced to do something is articulated most clearly by Briggs (1991) in her work on child-rearing among the Inuit. Children lack consciousness and rational thought (*isuma*), and the acquisition of this occurs as the child becomes older. Parents do not attempt to teach a child they believe is not ready to learn.

> *Isuma* is thought to grow naturally as children grow and to provide both the ability and the wish to learn. What one needs to do in order to educate a child is to provide the *isuma* with the necessary information, and sooner or later the child will remember. Thus, one Inuit catechist, in baptising a baby, reminded the parents: "Don't scold her, teach her." There is no point trying to force children to learn something before they are ready to remember, and there is no need to win every battle, because when children are ready to remember, they will do so. (1991:267–268)

To attempt to force a child into doing something is seen as unseemly, and while parents do attempt to get children to do what they want, to get angry would demean the adult by reducing him or her to the child's level. Too much scolding, or beating a child, is seen as counterproductive and likely to make the child angry, rebellious, or hostile toward his or her parents. Inuit children are left to grow up at their own pace and to become socialized when they are ready (Briggs 1970:112). Unusually, Briggs also discusses how children's childishness is actively celebrated. There is often the implication that nonpunitive methods of child-rearing can lead to children being "spoiled" or "indulged," and yet Briggs has written of the enjoyment that adults take in the antics of young children, without any of the negative connotations of "showing off" that these might evoke elsewhere.

Ignoring children may be a positive choice and a way of ensuring discipline instead of, or alongside, physical punishment. Therefore children who cry are not always comforted and ignoring them is seen as a way of teaching them to control their emotions. Marjorie Wolf (1972) noted that Taiwanese parents did not always comfort a child as some felt that crying was a positive form of infant exercise and necessary for growth. Other parents may withhold praise from their children, fearing it will make them immodest and uncontrollable and make it harder for children to accept their inferior status (Poffenberger 1981; Hendry 1986). One of the mothers in Wolf's study said: "I praise her but not to her face. You cannot let children know that you approve of them. If they know that you praise them, they won't try to improve" (1972:68). In West Africa, Fulani parents likewise avoid praise, arguing that it would be unbecoming and would undermine culturally prized qualities of restraint and modesty. Fulani parents will insult their children, saying, "I am older than you and I have seen all of the foolish things you have done" (Johnson 2000:193), thereby teaching them their proper place in a society where age hierarchies, as well as decorum, are extremely important. Yet in other contexts, children's anger or crying may be taken much more seriously and parents will attempt to reason with small children. Philippe Descola (1996) describes an incident among the Jivaro (an Amazonian group located on the border of Peru and Ecuador) when a small girl was sulking about something of which no one knew, or had long forgotten, the cause. The adults made great attempts to find out the reason for her distress because they took all forms of anger and resentment seriously, whatever the age of the person showing them, and deemed it important to root out the cause of the anger to prevent lasting resentments.

Some communities use shame and social disapproval rather than physical punishment as the most effective way of disciplining children. Raymond Firth wrote that the Tikopia of Polynesia would often threaten children, but very rarely used force on them, and if they did, it was mild and done to shame rather than hurt them, "the result being that the spirit rather than the body is bruised. . . . It is the affront to self-esteem which is the greatest wound" (Firth 1936:154). The idea that people would think badly of them if they misbehaved was instilled into Tikopia children at an early age so that physical force became unnecessary. Ian Hogbin (1970a) described a similar scenario among the Wogeo of New Guinea, who threatened to withhold pork from their children next time a pig was killed, or to send them out into the forest, but who never carried out these threats, so that the children learnt not to be scared of them. Beating a child was only ever done in the heat of the moment when parents lost control, and even then, only within certain limits. Parents claimed a pedagogic purpose, "We hit the children only to teach them" (1970a:161), but despite this recourse to physical punishment, Hogbin argued, like Firth regarding the Tikopia, that it was the affront to a child's personal dignity that was the worst punishment and the one which children felt most acutely. Joy Hendry (1986), too, discusses the humiliation and ridicule that children are sometimes faced with and its effectiveness as a sanction in Japan. Children are so concerned about conforming that an ultimate insult is to be dubbed peculiar or strange. As children get older and their sense of shame increases, physical punishment needs to be used much less than previously and ridicule becomes far more effective.

Finally, a common method of keeping children disciplined is by the use of threats of the supernatural, nonhuman beings that will come to take them away if they misbehave. These might be either the authority of the ancestors (Firth 1936) or spirits that specifically prey on naughty children. These bogeymen range from rather vague threats to elaborate charades. There are reports of children being frightened by a leaf being waved in front of them and an allusion to ghosts (Lesu children, Powdermaker 1933), of threats of ghosts or demons coming to eat them (Japan, Hendry 1986), of being put out and left for the hyenas (Gusii children, LeVine and LeVine 1981), or of a mother herself imitating the cry of a hyena in order to scare her child (Chaga, Raum 1970). How successful these ruses are is not always stated, although Hogbin (1970a) commented that threats of Karibua, the spirit said to steal Wogeo children who would not go to sleep, were widely ignored in a community that did not believe that spirits have an interest in the affairs of mortals. Probably more effective are the elaborate methods of frightening children into obedience which involve making the child believe a spirit is coming to take them away. An Ifaluk mother in Micronesia might, if a child misbehaves, ask another woman of the household to go away and come back dressed up as a spirit and approach the child as if she is going to eat it (Le 2000). A Chaga mother, too, might adopt this pretence:

> "Listen!" says its mother suddenly. "Do you hear the hyena howling? Shut up, or it will come to eat you! At once!" If this is of no avail, she puts the child down and, going outside, imitates the howl of the hyena: "Ng'uu, ng'uu, ng'uu." But raising her voice then, she replies: "Hilo, hilo, hilo! Oh, oh, oh! Sir, I beg of you, don't eat my little one!" She returns to the hut.

"Did you hear him?" she queries. "He won't come back now, because
I asked him for your sake. But don't you cry anymore, for he might return."
(Raum 1940:132–133)

Who Can Punish Children?

Raymond Firth (1936) makes the point that for Tikopia children there were
no strangers and that every member of a community would be known
and probably related by kin to that child. Children traveled freely between
houses and, when older, visited kin in other villages for several days. Yet
discipline and child-rearing were still primarily the responsibility of the
child's parents, and the parents of a child that made a nuisance of him-
or herself at a public gathering were admonished for not having raised
the child properly. Although other members of the community looked
after small children when necessary, it was rare for anyone other than
the parents to discipline the child. For an adult other than a parent to
punish a child was seen as shameful and an implicit criticism of another
person's child-rearing skills and social values. This sense of shame and
criticism has been shown in many different contexts. Isaac Schapera
found that parents tended to resent anyone other than themselves beating their child. He found that in the past all adults had a right to beat
children, and still did in the 1930s when he was undertaking his fieldwork,
if they caught a child stealing directly from them. He noted that attitudes
were changing and it was felt that if an adult had a grievance against
a child, they should tell the parents and let parents exercise their rights
to beat a child rather than doing it themselves. In more recent work
this idea can still be found. In Guinea-Bissau, a Papel mother told
Jonina Einarsdóttir:

> You should never beat a child that is not yours, or one you are not respons-
> ible for. It is a humiliation when other people hit your child – that way
> they say that you have not brought them up properly. It is your obliga-
> tion to educate a child. If it does not behave well you have to beat it, but
> you should only beat your own child, you understand? If another person
> beats your child, you feel insulted. (2000:104)

Marjorie Wolf (1972) claimed that in rural Taiwan, mothers were
particularly concerned about curing their children of aggression and

unruliness. Not only did a naughty or difficult child reflect badly on her as a mother, but also such a child affected her relationships with other women, women she had to rely upon for loans, advice, and sympathy. As an outsider in her husband's household, she had to form alliances with others in the village, and these would be jeopardized if her children were problematic. She could expect little sympathy from others if her children misbehaved. Children themselves played on this fear, and if they sought justice for some injury, they were unlikely to go to their own mothers, who would scold them for getting into trouble in the first place, but would more likely go to the culprit's mother, who they knew would punish her child as a way of keeping on good terms with her neighbors. On the other hand, despite this emphasis on the inviolability of the natal family, neighbors did intervene if a mother hit her child too much or lost her temper too frequently. "Ordinarily, outsiders would not dare interfere in a 'family' affair, but anyone, even a stranger, is expected to interfere when a mother clearly has lost control of her temper while beating a child. If this was not an accepted custom, there would be many more severely battered children in the villages than there are" (Wolf 1972:71). Even older siblings of the child, who in normal circumstances would be severely punished if they interfered in adult activity, were expected to pull a younger child away from such beatings.

Generally, therefore, it is parents who physically discipline their children and the role of relatives is one of intervention if punishments get out of hand. However, there may be differences between parents when it comes to punishment, and mothers and fathers may well have very different agendas. Napoleon Chagnon (1968) has described how Yanamamö mothers actively goaded their sons into attacking their fathers, even providing them with sticks to do so, thereby provoking possible reprisals from the father. Mothers may not be gentler with their children or more reluctant to beat them than fathers. David Maybury-Lewis has described how, among the Akwẽ-Shavante, it is women who are far stricter with their children than their fathers, who never smack them. Among the Aka, physical punishment is almost never used and is grounds for divorce if one parent accuses the other of hitting a small child (Hewlett 1991). Lesu parents might also take against each other if the child was smacked, even if there was acknowledgment that the child was in the wrong (Powdermaker 1933). Furthermore, a Lesu mother would react very strongly if someone else disciplined her child. Hortense Powdermaker gave the following example:

One day a child of about seven was struck by one of his clan relatives because he would not give him betel nut when requested. The mother was absent when the incident occurred. She and her sister returned and found the child crying, and learning the cause of the tears, the two women each took a branch of a small tree and fought the man who had struck the child. The other members of the hamlet thought that the man got what he deserved. (1933:82–83)

Child Abuse

The growth of interest in children's rights has inevitably meant that discussions of discipline are now tied to considerations of abuse. From an anthropological perspective, this has made analyzing the physical punishment of children problematic. Studies of childhood, warns Nancy Scheper-Hughes, have a tendency "to reconsider the nature of parenting in traditional and non-western societies in light of the child abuse and child survival preoccupations of our times" (1987:7), thereby failing to take account of indigenous theories of socialization and accepted methods of discipline. At the same time, others have questioned this stance of cultural relativity, arguing that emphasizing local ethno-theories of punishment prevents anthropologists from seeing anything they do not want to, including the abusive treatment of children. Helen Morton argues: "In their study of non-Western societies, anthropologists have often tended to ignore, trivialise, exoticise, or even defend aspects of child care and socialisation that are negatively valued in 'the West'" (Kavapalu 1993:314). It has been supposed that child abuse is largely a Western phenomenon and more or less unknown in other societies, whose small-scale nature, more communal attitude toward child-rearing, and different cultural attitudes toward children make it more unlikely (Fraser and Kilbride 1980). Nelson Graburn (1987), for example, discusses child abuse among the Inuit, but is at great pains to state that it is extremely rare, very idiosyncratic, and universally condemned. Alternative explanations given for the perceived lack of child abuse in societies such as Japan suggest that with abortion, infanticide, or abandonment as recognized and acceptable methods of disposing of unwanted children, parents are more likely to abandon or kill children than keep and abuse them (Wagatsuma 1981).

Those who have focused directly on abuse have had to find a balance between their own personal beliefs and the social and cultural context in which they have worked. Helen Morton's accounts of disciplinary practices in Tonga can make for painful reading, and it is obvious that, despite her understanding of the rationale behind beating, and its place in the Tongan worldview, it was difficult for her to watch the constant physical chastisement of young children (Kavapalu 1993; Morton 1996). She writes of the Tongans having 30 different terms for hitting children and of adults finding the physical punishment of children amusing, even when the children are clearly in distress (Kavapalu 1993). She has highlighted how anthropologists have, in the past, trivialized the harsh treatment of children and quotes the discrepancies apparent in earlier studies of Tonga carried out by Pearl and Ernest Beagleholes, who, in their field notes, spoke of the sadism of the beatings carried out by parents and the agony of the children. In their diaries they give an account of a mother "beating her child with thwarted fury that seems nine parts pure sadism and one-quarter part altruistic-disciplinary. To us, as we watch the scene, these child beatings seem to exceed all that is reasonable and just" (quoted in Kavapalu 1993:313). In the Beagleholes' published work, however, this shock at the severity of the beatings and their view that this was abusive is transformed into the bland statement: "The child who disobeys or who is thought to be lazy in carrying out a command is generally severely beaten by the mother. The beatings . . . appear to be village-practice in enforcing discipline" (quoted in Kavapalu 1993:313). In her own analysis of the role of child punishment in Tonga, Morton does not shy away from the severity of the beatings imposed on children, or her own reactions to it. However, by recognizing the role of harsh punishment in Tongan society and relating it to other power differentials between people of low and high status, she is able to argue that, within their own context, severe beatings by parents are not abusive. Physical punishment is a statement of power, status, and hierarchy, and it is only when this punishment is applied in an inappropriate context, or by someone who does not have the authority to do so, that it is liable to be seen as abusive.

Jill Korbin (1981) provides a much-needed framework when discussing child abuse, differentiating between three types of practices which need to be untangled in discussions of discipline and abuse. The first category she examines is that of cultural practices such as initiation or beatings, which may seem harsh, unnecessary, and even abusive to outsiders, but which are deemed culturally necessary and have the full approval of the community. The second category is the idiosyncratic or individual maltreatment of a child, carried out against cultural norms. Finally, the third type of abuse she identifies is the social or structural abuse of children, where children as a group are targeted or when they suffer distinctive consequences as a result of poverty, ill-health, or social neglect. It is worth discussing each of these in more detail, in order to recognize the different forms of abuse.

The first type of practice Korbin identifies is that which is condemned in one culture but not in another. Previous examples have discussed the many child-rearing practices which, while they might be unpleasant or wrong in the eyes of outsiders, are seen positively within their own contexts. It is not difficult to find numerous examples from ethnographic accounts of what appear to be extremely painful, and physically and mentally harmful, practices carried out on children. Otto Raum, for example, in his study of East African Chaga children wrote of children being punished by being tied up in uncomfortable positions or imprisoned and then being severely beaten and having fat or nettles rubbed into their wounds in order to make them hurt more, or of being suspended over fires while their parents continued to pinch, slap, or even throttle them until they urinated or defecated with fear (1940:225–6). There are descriptions of the Amazonian Jivaro punishing their children by beating them with nettles, giving them strong hallucinogenic drugs that put them into a trance, and placing them over burning peppers on a hot fire until they become unconscious (Harner 1969). Also in Amazonia, Mehinaku children are scraped with dogfish teeth to make them strong and to teach them to bear pain without flinching (Gregor 1977).

Inflicting pain on children is not limited to punishment. Many body modifications can also be painful and scarring to children. The most emotive example of this is female circumcision (called by some female genital mutilation as a way of emphasizing its abusive nature). Often carried out on very young girls, it is immensely painful and, it is claimed, can affect a woman's later sexual health (for a graphic, first-person account of the process, see El Saadawi 1980). Other examples include elongating babies' heads, scarification, neck stretching, foot binding, tattooing, or ear piercing. Yet, although painful and sometimes having life-long effects, it is hard to argue that these are abusive practices *per se* rather than part of socially and culturally approved initiation rituals (see chapter 8). L. L. Langness, in his review of child abuse in New Guinea, argues that while some practices, such as mourning rituals when the first joint of a young girl's little finger is cut off with a stone axe, might be extremely painful and horrific to outsiders, children, "although painfully treated in the context of initiations or other institutionalized situations, are welcomed, indulged to an extreme, highly valued, and virtually never abused in the Western sense of that term" (1981:25).

Although such practices may be controversial, and some might argue that condoning female circumcision or finger removal is taking cultural relativism too far, by understanding this practice in context, it is possible to differentiate between aberrant, abusive behavior, on the one hand, and culturally accepted practice, on the other. As Korbin argues:

> While we cannot take the extreme relativist position that any cultural practice is acceptable by worldwide standards, we must avoid imposing our own standards and expectations in our quest for an internationally acceptable definition of child abuse. . . . While the mutilation of a small girl's hand may be difficult for us to understand, and while we do not have to condone the practice, we surely must separate this from the aberrant mutilation of a child in cultures that provide no context for the behavior. (1977:10–11)

Furthermore, as she goes on to point out, abuse is relative, and there are some Western child-rearing practices that might be regarded as equally distressing to outsiders.

> The parent who "protects" his or her child from a painful, but culturally required, initiation rite would be denying the child a place as an adult in that culture. That parent, in the eyes of his cultural peers, would be abusive or neglectful for compromising the development of his child.
>
> It is equally sobering to look at Western child-rearing techniques and practices through the eyes of these same non-Western cultures. Non-Western peoples often conclude that anthropologists, missionaries, or other Euro-Americans with whom they come into contact do not love their children or simply do not know how to care for them properly. Practices such as isolating infants and small children in rooms or beds of their own at night, making them wait for readily available food until a schedule dictates that they can satisfy their hunger, or allowing them to cry without immediately attending to their needs or desires would be at odds with the child-rearing philosophies of most . . . cultures. (Korbin 1981:4)

The final issue to comment on when looking at the cultural relativity of child treatment and mistreatment relates back to chapter 2 and the question, "what is a child?" In the section on children who were seen as nonhuman, there were accounts of child witches and child sorcerers who were subjected to the most horrific punishments and who were tortured, killed, and dismembered. Again it is debatable as to whether seeing such actions in their context is taking cultural relativism too far, but conceptually there is a difference between the sadistic torture of a child who is recognized as human and part of the community and that same violence directed toward something considered the embodiment of evil, which must be destroyed to protect the community.

The second set of practices discussed by Korbin in her consideration of abuse concerns behaviors that are outside the range of acceptable practices within cultures. Abuse, in this second category, is carried out on an individual and idiosyncratic basis and is likely to cause a child serious harm (Johnson 1981). Therefore, while cutting off a part of a small girl's little finger may be appropriate in certain instances, such as during mourning ceremonies, to make the same mutilation outside of this context, or as a form of punishment, would be unacceptable (Langness 1981). The Samia of Kenya believe in the existence of the "evil eye" and claim that certain women, such as those who are barren, or jealous co-wives, might set out deliberately to harm another woman's child through witchcraft; such acts are considered forms of child abuse and are always denounced (Fraser and Kilbride 1980). Other cultures that tolerate physical punishments of children still have limits on beatings and recognize the point at which punishment becomes abuse. The Ilahita Arapesh of Papua New Guinea admit that beatings can get out of hand and that through temper, or malice, adults may beat their children too severely (Langness 1981). In this instance others in the community should step in to calm the parent down and to protect the child. The Beng of West Africa similarly recognize the difference between a disciplinary slap and abuse, which occurs when a mother hits a child too hard or repeatedly (Gottlieb 2004). Among the Papel of Guinea-Bissau there is discussion about whether or not it is right to beat children at all. Nevertheless, beatings are common and usually carried out by parents. Again, however, there are instances when the beatings are too harsh, prolonged, or otherwise severe and people talk with unease about the parent, claiming that he or she must be sick in the head to beat their child in that way (Einarsdóttir 2000). In all these cases, parents have gone beyond what is acceptable practice and are prevented from further abusing their children by social opprobrium. All these communities recognize a distinction between discipline and abuse and will intervene to protect a child who they feel is being maltreated. The severity of the punishment is, however, of less importance than the deviation from the cultural norm (Korbin 1977:12).

One final instance of recognized abuse must also be discussed: abuse as the non-performance of certain practices – what parents do not do, rather than what they do. David Wu discusses the idea that it is a lack of discipline, rather than too much, which is seen as abusive toward the child: "Chinese parents are faced with a dilemma regarding disciplinary beating of their children; the choice is between unwillingly inflicting pain on the child and allowing the child to become a delinquent by not punishing him. As a father said, 'We know that beating too heavily or too frequently is not right, but a most "abusive" parent is one who does not discipline his or her child, hence "drowning the child with love" ' " (1981:154). Morton also argues that while punishments and beatings are harsh and painful in Tonga, they are also talked of as a form of affection, with some children claiming that their parents "punish me with their love" (1996:196).

The third kind of abuse in Korbin's typology is that caused by social or structural factors rather than by individuals. This is the social and economic form of child abuse, typified by poverty, hunger, social inequality, poor health, war, and governmental policy. It is rarely referred to as child abuse, and in affluent Western countries there is a much greater emphasis on the behavior of individual parents or, more sensationally, on the dangers posed by strangers and outsiders, than there is on the collective responsibility that the wealthy in society have to others (Best 1990). Many studies point to the disproportionate effects that poverty or violence has on children and the special vulnerabilities of children in the face of adversity. Others have discussed the particular impacts on children of social problems such as racism (Bourgois 1998), violent neighborhoods (Garbarino 1999), environmental pollution or nuclear testing (Stephens 1995b), or institutional or communal violence (Scheper-Hughes 1995; Bernat 1999). Other important edited collections have focused on child abandonment (Panter-Brick and Smith 2000) and child survival (Scheper-Hughes 1987), all acknowledging that while individual pathology plays a part in the mistreatment and abuse of children, it is wider social forces which may well have the more devastating impact on children's lives. Scheper-Hughes and Stein have argued very powerfully:

> The "choice" of child abuse as a master social problem of our times, also includes a strong "choice" for only certain forms of child abuse – battering

and sexual abuse – and a *selective inattention* to other forms – specifically poverty-related neglect. This selective inattention is a consequence of the need to deny the role of our punitive public policies in contributing to the "feminization of poverty," and to the problem of childhood mortality in our inner-city, minority neighborhoods. (1987:353, emphasis in original)

Indeed it is often the forces beyond parental control that may overwhelm children and negate their parents' best efforts on their behalf. Allan Holmberg, writing of the Siriono of eastern Bolivia, notes that parents seem particularly loving and gentle to their children at periods of most intense hunger in the community. He writes that "among the Siriono, love appears frequently to serve as a compensation for hunger" (1969:256). The hunger of these children would rarely be called abuse, but parental love and care is easily overwhelmed by a lack of basic necessities. It is this point that is taken up by Nancy Scheper-Hughes (1992) in her study of the *favelas* of Brazil. Although she paints a picture of benign neglect and of mothers investing little emotional energy in children until they are likely to survive, the mothers themselves are well aware that it is poverty that is killing their children.

Ideas about abuse are subject to change. Roger Goodman (2000) describes the situation in Japan when national child abuse hotlines were first introduced. Rather than receiving calls from children wanting advice, or from friends and neighbors reporting child abuse, the calls were mostly from mothers wanting to know if the ways in which they disciplined their children were still acceptable or whether they were liable to be seen as abusive. In Tonga, recent understandings of abuse, heralded in by the UNCRC, clash with traditional views of punishment but are beginning to affect the ways that children are treated (Morton 1996). More problematic are those cases where parents move to different countries with different understandings about acceptable and non-acceptable treatment of children. In these situations, appeals to cultural relativity are more difficult to uphold. Korbin recounts a case of scarification undertaken by a Yoruba woman living in London in 1974. Although the process was dying out in her native Nigeria, the woman slashed her sons' faces and rubbed ash into them. She was prosecuted, found guilty of actual bodily harm, but was not punished as the court accepted her defense that she was asserting her cultural identity. Korbin (1979) further discusses the misdiagnoses of abuse among Vietnamese children in the USA who came to see pediatricians with large, unexplained bruises on their bodies, which were caused by "coin rubbing" – the pushing of a coin with considerable force onto a child's body to protect the child from fever and chills. Similarly, Mexican parents in the USA have been accused of child abuse because some would treat listlessness, vomiting, and diarrhea in their children by shaking them, holding them upside down, or putting the child's head in water, all practices which caused retinal bleeding and other "classic" symptoms of child abuse (Korbin 1979). It is in instances like these that cultural relativism comes into conflict with the policies of nation-states, and also with understandings of universal children's rights. It would be impossible to set different standards for childcare depending on ethnic background, so that, for example, cutting a child's face would be acceptable as long as that child was of Yoruba descent. Without an understanding of different cultural backgrounds, however, misdiagnoses and injustices against parents who are already often marginalized in their host countries are inevitable. It is also important not to romanticize non-Western childcare or to assume that abuse is unknown outside Western contexts. The many examples already discussed in this chapter have shown that most societies do have a strong notion of what constitutes abuse and do acknowledge that individuals may be guilty of it, however it is defined.

Conclusion

Discipline and punishment are only two aspects of child-rearing and socialization, but looking at them in detail points, once more, to the heterogeneous nature of children's childhood and the impossibility of understanding childhood as a social phenomenon without reference to context or to cultural background. How children are treated, disciplined, and punished is directly related to ideas about their nature, the expectations placed on them, and their role in the community. The idea that children have rights, especially in relation to protection from their parents, is a relatively recent one, but one which has changed the way that anthropologists have understood punishment and discipline. It is impossible nowadays to look at the punishment of children without also looking at ideas about abuse. Many anthropologists have felt uneasy witnessing the harsh treatment of children in the societies they study, and it is an area where some have struggled to maintain a stance of cultural relativity, and, indeed, questioned whether such a stance is desirable. Abuse is not a single or unchanging phenomenon, and the forms and understandings of it depend on social context, but all societies acknowledge and recognize that some ways of treating children are abusive and cause serious harm. Abuse, as the title of one of Helen Morton's articles suggests, is the "dark side in the ethnography of childhood" (Kavapalu 1993).

7

CHILDREN AND SEXUALITY

Introduction

The image of the sexually innocent child lies at the heart of Western constructions of childhood. While there may be debates about whether children need to be kept ignorant about sex or whether they simply have no sexual feelings, the notion of childhood as a protected space leaves little room for discussions of children's sexuality. Although puberty is generally acknowledged to bring with it an upsurge of sexual feelings and experimentation, this, too, causes great anxieties and attempts at adult control. Children's sexuality is one of the great concerns of early 21st-century Western societies and lies at the heart of discussions about personal and social identity. It is not a topic that has been studied in great depth by anthropologists, for reasons that the next section of this chapter will go on to discuss, but what is apparent from a cross-cultural comparison is that what are seen as universal, biological drives from a Western perspective seem very different elsewhere and that the cherished characterization of the child as a sexual innocent is not ubiquitous. Acknowledging the sensitivities of the issues surrounding this subject, this chapter will examine what is known about children's experiences of sex, and how they and their communities understand sexuality. It will look at the difficulties involved in studying the subject and the influence of Freud on Western thinking, before turning to the few ethnographies that have shown the variations in children's sexual cultures.

Anthropology, Sexuality, and Childhood

Different, and sometimes "exotic," sexual practices have been a long-discussed theme in anthropology, from Bronislaw Malinowski's provocatively entitled *The Sexual Lives of Savages in North-Western Melanesia* (1929), to more recent, reflective anthropological work that has looked at how anthropologists' own sexuality and sexual behavior have informed understandings of identity, community relations, methodology, and kinship (Wade 1993; Kulick and Willson 1995; Markowitz and Ashkenazi 1999). Anthropologists have reclaimed sexuality from biology, rejecting the idea of sexuality as a universal, natural impulse. Indeed, the more anthropologists have examined sexual practices and ideas about sexualities, the more it has become clear that sexual acts and behavior do not carry the same meanings cross-culturally, that the idea of a universal "sex drive" is false, and that rather than culture being the "added extra" which might explain the odd variation in sexual practice, it lies at the heart of understanding different sexualities (Caplan 1987; Rubin 1989; Vance 1991). In Carol Vance's analysis, "a sexual act does not carry with it a universal social meaning, [therefore] it follows that the relationship between sexual acts and sexual meanings is not fixed, and it is projected from the observer's time and place at great peril" (1991:878).

Despite a few ethnographies which have celebrated different sexual cultures and talked in explicit terms about sexual practices (Gregor 1985; Parker 1991; Crocker and Crocker 1994; Fordham 1995, 1998), detailed analyses of sexual behavior have been largely absent from ethnographic accounts. Cora Du Bois's 1944 study of the Alor in Java is one of the few books in which an anthropologist has asked very directly and explicitly about exactly which sexual acts are performed and enjoyed within a community. Generally, however, studying sexuality has proved problematic for anthropologists, and to date there is still a certain squeamishness about prying too intimately into matters that are often viewed as private. Furthermore, anthropologists must rely solely on what they observe (which can be awkward when studying sexual behavior) and what they are told, while knowing that there is usually a big difference between what people do and what they say they do, or between what they think they should do and their actual behavior, a situation succinctly summed up by Parker et al.:

> The description of sexual culture, in turn, involves a set of basic distinctions between cultural ideals vs. actual practice, public vs. private conduct,

and prescribed vs. voluntary behavior. While the stated norms of a society may ideally require one mode of behavior, in reality a wide range of different behaviors may actually be found in any given community. What people say and do in public with regard to sexuality may differ greatly from and even contradict their private sexual behavior. The forms of sexual behavior that are prescribed in different situations may contrast sharply with the ways in which individuals may behave voluntarily. (1991:79–80)

Sexual behavior is also a difficult area to explore because of the instability and uncertainties surrounding the various definitions of sexuality and the multiple meanings around the same acts. Sexuality in some instances may be seen as being synonymous with reproduction or, conversely, as a social problem demanding intervention to prohibit fertility (the concern about teenage sexuality in the UK and the USA, for example, consists largely of how to instruct young people *not* to get pregnant). It comes with a variety of connotations, covering not only sexual acts such as intercourse or masturbation but also sexual knowledge or unactualized sexual feelings, and, in a Western context, sexuality suggests enjoyment and appreciation of sexual experience, as well as being closely tied to personal identity. However, whether these ideas, especially about the inherent pleasurability of sex, are universal or fundamentally Western is highly debatable, and not all communities necessarily equate sex and pleasure, or indeed sexual activity and social or personal identity.

In terms of children's sexuality and sexual behavior, these problems can be particularly difficult, and the unease that many feel when talking to children about their sexual behavior has meant that even anthropologists who specialize in children have largely shied away from discussions of children and sex. As attitudes in the West toward homosexuality or premarital sex have become more tolerant, and such acts carry less stigma, those toward child sex have hardened. Although children in Europe and North America are having sex earlier than before, and their experience and knowledge of sex may be greater than that of children in previous generations, children's sexual behavior, especially if it involves any sort of age imbalance between partners, remains very difficult to discuss without accusations of prurience or even perversion. In contemporary Western societies, adult/child sex causes particular repugnance and is seen as inherently abusive. Outside the West, however, this is not universally understood or applicable and there are ethnographic cases in which children and teenagers are encouraged, and expected, to have sex with those very much older than themselves. Discussing these is problematic and, given the acute sensitivities around the subject, it is not surprising that little work done by anthropologists concerns children's enjoyment of sex, or their own sexual cultures, or that studies have tended to focus on abuse rather than enjoyment. Yet even the work done on sexual abuse has often remained theoretical; there are few anthropologists who wish to accuse the people who have hosted them, and whom they wish to understand, of abusing their children. Moreover, sexual abuse, by its very nature, is secretive, transgressive, and difficult to observe or discuss.

In the contemporary West it is axiomatic that sexual experience and sexual identity are intertwined and that the type of sexual experience defines a large part of identity, so that labels such as homosexual or heterosexual have become intrinsic parts of both social and private identity. As social historian Jeffrey Weeks asks of the West: "how is it that in our society sex is seen not just as a means of biological reproduction nor a source of harmless pleasure, but, on the contrary, has come to be seen as the central part of our being, the privileged site in which the truth of ourselves is to be found?" (1981:6). From an anthropological perspective, however, this identification may not always be the case. In Thailand, for example, the rise of a specific gay identity is a very recent phenomenon, first identified in the late 1980s when the arrival of HIV/AIDS led to a backlash against the previous tolerance of homosexual acts (Jackson 1989). Until that point it was acknowledged that men could commit sexual acts with other men, and even enjoy them, but that this should not preclude marriage and children, which were the primary focus of a person's identity. In terms of understanding children's sexuality, this conflation of identity and experience is particularly important. The "wrong" sort of sexual experience in childhood is thought to damage children so fundamentally that they can never recover, yet ethnographic studies of children's lives suggest that this need not be the case in contexts where sexuality is differently perceived. The ethnographies that will be discussed later in the chapter complicate any easy identification of certain types of early sexual experience with later adult dysfunction.

Children and Sex: The Influence of Freud

It is impossible to talk about children's sexuality without reference to Sigmund Freud, who popularized the notion of the innately sexual child and who understood sexuality as part of the natural developmental process.

His influence on anthropology, and indeed on more general understandings of sexuality, cannot be overestimated, and even those who disagree with him are compelled to engage with his ideas. Furthermore, his influence is such that many of the concepts he first identified, such as the Oedipus complex, the death wish, or penis envy, have become well known, even by those who have not read him. Freud's great contribution to the study of children's sexuality was to argue that, far from being a time of asexual innocence, early childhood was a time of sexual conflict, repression, and tension. Freud claimed that childhood activities such as thumb sucking or genital manipulation had to be seen as part of a child's growing sexual nature which the adult world aimed to bring under control and repress. That unresolved sexual conflicts in childhood could cause psychological problems in adulthood was also central to Freud's thesis, a point which many anthropologists have built upon in their own studies of sexuality and sexual repression (see chapter 8 for a discussion of initiation as a way of overcoming those psychological traumas which originated in childhood repression).

In 1905 Freud published *Three Essays on the Theory of Sexuality*, which looked broadly at issues of sexuality and which sought to show the links between early childhood experiences and adult behavior and personality. In the second essay, "Infantile Sexuality," he argued that sexual feelings were present in the child from the moment of birth and rejected the idea held by his contemporaries that sexual experiences and sexual feelings began only at puberty. He claimed:

> One feature of the popular view of the sexual instinct is that it is absent in childhood and only awakens in the period of life described as puberty. This, however, is not merely a simple error but one that has had grave consequences, for it is mainly to this idea that we owe our present ignorance of the fundamental conditions of sexual life. . . . So far as I know, not a single author has clearly recognized the regular existence of a sexual instinct in childhood; and in writings that have become so numerous on the development of children, the chapter on "Sexual Development" is as a rule omitted. (1953a[1905]:173)

In this essay, Freud went on to argue that everyone, from birth onward, was driven by sexual or bodily pleasure and this pleasure was derived from the release of mental and physical tension. However, the instinctual efforts of infants and young children to gain pleasure were frequently punished and thwarted by parental and social control. Children therefore experienced their childhoods as a series of conflicts that had to be dealt with and overcome in order to turn them into healthy, normal adults. In other work, Freud argued that for some adults, unresolved conflicts in various stages of their development could lead to conditions such as mental illness, hysteria, or homosexuality in adult life (Freud 1953b[1913]).

Freud labeled the earliest stage of infant development the oral one, in which the infant sought release, and obtained his or her pleasure, through sucking. The anal stage followed on from this, during which pleasure was linked to release through defecation. Afterward the young child developed an interest in his or her genitals and acknowledged them as a source of pleasure, understood by Freud as the phallic stage of development. Furthermore, he claimed that during the phallic stage of development (occurring around the age of five), male children went through a particular phase of psychosexual development characterized by the Oedipal conflict. This occurred when the boy began to be jealous of his father as his mother's sexual partner, feeling desire for the exclusive love of his mother and an unconscious wish for his father's death. This, however, aroused the father's anger and the boy became afraid that the outcome of his desire would be castration by his father; a fear Freud labeled the castration anxiety. Around the age of five, the Oedipus complex was usually resolved by the repression of both attraction for the opposite-sex parent and hatred of the same-sex parent. A normal child at this point internalized his father's rules, understanding that he could not sexually possess his mother and should turn his attention toward other objects of desire. He then entered a "latency" period when sexual motivations became less obvious and which did not become as significant again until puberty, when bodily development and genital changes occurred.

Freud's views were controversial when first published and have been continuously debated ever since, especially by writers who argue that Freud ignored evidence of actual child sexual abuse because he would not, and could not, believe in it (Masson 1984). There is also still unease about whether children really are sexual beings from such a young age, or, if they do act in ways that adults might interpret as sexual, whether they are aware of this, or understand it as such. Freud's work raised important questions about children's sexuality which have yet to be definitively answered, such as whether children are sexually active and aware, but adults ignore or repress their sexuality, or whether they are sexually innocent, in the sense that they know nothing about sex. Is sexual experience a natural part of a child's development or an aberration? These are all issues that those looking at children's sexuality have to deal with, but because of their sensitivity and the difficulties inherent in this subject, such questions have remained largely unanswered by anthropologists.

Incest and Abuse

From the earliest days of the discipline, anthropologists have noted, and analyzed, the universality of the incest taboo and the abomination of having sex with, or marrying, close relatives. Freud (1953b[1913]) himself used the work of Sir James Frazer, who collected accounts of aboriginal customs and who discussed the concept of taboo, to draw his own conclusions about the complete abhorrence of incest in all societies. Although, of course, the idea of what constitutes a close relative is culturally defined, and there is no single set of prohibitions that apply everywhere, all societies have marriage laws about who can marry whom, and who is forbidden to marry. One of the major concerns of anthropologists has been to deconstruct different ideas about incest and use them to discuss wider ideas of kinship and marriage (Fox 1983).

Although much of this work might seem tangential to children's sexual lives, it contains some of the few hints that exist from the ethnographic record about children's experiences of sex. Robert Fox, for instance, quotes Melford Spiro, who studied sexual attraction and sexual behavior among children on Israeli kibbutzes and described how children around the age of two showed signs of "heterosexual behavior," including "stroking or caressing, kissing and touching of genitals" (quoted in Fox 1983:30). While this may be true, such statements need to be interpreted with care, and the labeling of this behavior as heterosexual says as much about the adult beholder as it does about the child. Jean La Fontaine cautions against seeing such play by children as necessarily sexual, arguing that "before puberty children may engage in what is usually termed 'sexual play' with one another. This is how adults interpret it, in the same way that adults understand much childish behaviour: by reference to their own understanding" (1990:159). She further makes the point that much of what we know about children's sexuality is based on supposition. There is little evidence about how much young brothers and sisters actually do play sexually with each other (although it is frequently assumed that they do). Nor is it clear if the curiosity that children may feel about the genitals of other children is an exploration of gender and bodily difference or the stirrings of sexuality.

The most serious problem with discussing incest and children's sexual behavior, however, concerns the fact that, until recently, anthropologists have tended to assume that taboos against, for example, father/daughter incest meant that sex between these people did not occur (La Fontaine 1988). It was not until the 1980s that social anthropologists began to look at why sexual abuse occurred even when there were strong taboos against it, and at the links between incest, sexual abuse, and wider socioeconomic and political issues. Three books in particular, Jill Korbin's *Child Abuse and Neglect* (1981), Judith Ennew's *The Sexual Exploitation of Children* (1986), and Jean La Fontaine's *Child Sexual Abuse* (1990), have been very influential in this respect because they have located child's sexuality within familial power structures and analyzed the abuse of children as being the result of an imbalance in power relationships, and as a betrayal of trust between adult and child, rather than as an extension of sexuality.

Despite Freudian claims about innate childhood sexuality, the Western ideal of childhood as a time of sexual innocence remains strong and is increasingly promoted as a global ideal. Many of the "modern panics" of recent times have focused on threats to this sacred, sexual innocence (Best 1990; La Fontaine 1998). The debate now focuses on whether children have always been sexually abused, and it has only recently been talked about, or whether this is a newer problem, exacerbated in the West by the breakdown of the nuclear family. What is indisputable, however, is that child sexual abuse is now considered a serious social problem, and that concern about protecting children's sexual innocence has grown exponentially. In 1975 an American psychiatric textbook estimated the number of children sexually abused to be one in a million (La Fontaine 1990:39), a figure that today seems absurdly small. There is also a strong belief that any threat to children's sexual innocence will damage a child so fundamentally that recovery may not be possible. As sexual identity and sexual experience are seen as synonymous, sexual abuse is understood as being so psychologically damaging as to distort the whole of a child's personality.

From an anthropological perspective, the recent interest in child sexual abuse has provided parallels with other long-standing concerns. Jean La Fontaine (1992) has drawn explicit links between the figure of the pedophile in Western cultures and that of the witch in other contexts, and the fears over Satanic and ritual abuse can clearly be seen to fit into sociologist Stanley Cohen's paradigm of moral panics (Cohen 1973; La Fontaine 1998). Despite the majority of sexual abuse cases occurring within the family, the overwhelming concern is focused on "stranger danger" or the monstrous abuse of children by Satanic practitioners. The lack of evidence for the latter and the relative infrequency of the former seem to have little impact on the fear that child sexual abuse generates. As with many concerns of the West, there is now evidence that these fears have been exported and are becoming global. While small, isolated communities may still practice very different sexual behaviors and have radically different understandings of sexuality, the idea of an asexual, enclosed childhood is becoming the norm (Boyden 1997) and anthropologists have found evidence of a rise in concern about sexual abuse outside in the West. Roger Goodman (2002) has looked at the discovery of sexual abuse in Japan, where, unlike in the West, the physical abuse of children has been of as much concern as the sexual. In Thailand and the Philippines, meanwhile, fears of child sexual abuse have been linked to mass tourism and the figure of the child-sex tourist (Black 1994; Montgomery 2001a).

In India, child marriage is sometimes analyzed by nongovernmental activists as a form of child sexual abuse. Similarly, when concern about child prostitution was at its height in the 1990s, Indian *devadasi* cults came under scrutiny as possible covers for sexual abuse. These cults are centered on certain temples in which girls are dedicated to local deities. The girls are sponsored and initiated by local men and may be expected to have sex with them in return for their protection. *Devadasi* are variously claimed to be dancers, sacred concubines, or prostitutes. Although some anthropologists, such as Frédérique Marglin (1985), claim that girls do not dance or take lovers until after puberty, there have been claims in the media that much younger girls are used as child prostitutes under the guise of being *devadasi*. The reality may lie somewhere between these two extremes. Treena Orchard's recent study of *devadasi* girls (2004) in rural Karnataka in India has suggested a more complex picture where young women and girls do appear to practice some form of religiously sanctioned prostitution. While acknowledging that there were exchanges of sex for money, mediated through claims of sacred sacrifice, Orchard's work focuses more holistically on the entire sexual culture of the *devadasi*'s lives, in which they experience sex differently in different types of relationships. Although seen by nongovernmental and medical organizations as social problems, vectors of diseases, and as the practitioners of a debased tradition, the *devadasi* themselves see their sexual lives very differently and are able to distinguish between acceptable and nonacceptable sexual behaviors and between their own sense of personal identity and the sexual acts they perform.

Ethnographies of Children and Sexuality

The number of ethnographies that focus directly on children and sexuality has been very limited and descriptions of children's sexual experiences have often been given as part of broader discussions of children's and young people's lives. Malinowski, for instance, discussed Trobriand children's sexual games and sexual behaviors claiming that "at an early age children are initiated by each other, or sometimes by a slightly older companion, into the practices of sex. Naturally at this stage they are unable to carry out the act properly, but they content themselves with all sorts of games in which they are left quite at liberty by their elders, and thus they can satisfy their curiosity and their sensuality directly and without disguise" (1927:55). Adults noted this without concern and would refer to it as "copulation amusement" (1927:56). Other anthropologists have also noted that certain forms of sexual behavior are common amongst young children, even if they are disapproved of or denied by the adults in the community, and there is an awareness that young people do have sex, even if it is not talked about. Melvin Konner (2005), writing about the !Kung of northwestern Botswana, takes it as self-evident that sexual experimentation went on amongst young people and that although it was disapproved of by adults, they also admitted it was a normal and inevitable part of development.

Margaret Mead, in her pioneering work on children's lives in Samoa, looked at adolescent girls' sexuality as part of a larger analysis which aimed to challenge the prevailing idea that the "storm and stress" of adolescence, first identified by psychologist G. Stanley Hall in 1904, was biological in origin (see chapter 1). *Coming of Age in Samoa* (1971[1928]) was Mead's attempt to refute Hall's argument that this was a universal, biologically driven stage and she argued that it was culture, as much as biology, which affected young people's lives in adolescence. This book contains some of the earliest work on children's and young people's sexuality, and while sexual behavior was not the primary focus of her work, her descriptions challenged ideas about the universality of sexuality. In the book Mead analyzed the daily lives of Samoan girls from infancy through early childhood until adolescence, aiming to make explicit comparisons between the USA and Samoa by looking at how adolescence, and the effects of puberty and sexuality, were managed differently in the two societies, thereby emphasizing the importance of culture. According to Mead, the girls whose lives she studied started to take a series of lovers just after puberty. Usually a girl's lover would be much older than herself and, before her marriage, she would expect to have many lovers or casual sexual partners. Sexuality was identified as a source of pleasure, rather than tension, and the flexibility of adolescent girls' sexual behavior gave them freedom from many of the problems suffered by their counterparts in the USA. In Samoa, stress and strain were not an inevitable part of adolescence, and Mead concluded:

> Adolescence represented no period of crisis or stress, but was instead an orderly developing of a set of slowly maturing interests and activities. The girls' minds were perplexed by no conflicts, troubled by no philosophical queries, beset by no remote ambitions. To live as a girl with many lovers as long as possible and then to marry in one's own village, near one's own relatives, and to have many children, these were uniform and satisfying ambitions. (1971[1928]:129)

Mead identified several cultural reasons why growing up in Samoa was less stressful to both individual and society than it was in the USA, and sexual freedom was one of them. Young people in Samoa also had very limited choices which revolved around staying in their villages with their families, marrying and having children in due course, and remaining within their communities until they died. In contrast, North American adolescents were bombarded with choices and options which made their lives more difficult as they had to decide what they wanted from life.

Mead's work has generated much debate, and a certain amount of hostility, ever since. Most publicly she was criticized by Derek Freeman (1983, 1999), who claimed not only that she overlooked many of the sources of tension in Samoa and played down the strict control that elders had over girls' sexuality, but also that Mead's informants hoaxed her, telling her what she wanted to hear rather than giving her accounts of their actual behavior and beliefs, which were in fact very different. Based on his own fieldwork and interviews with surviving informants, Freeman maintained that the young women of Samoa had lied to Mead, claiming that they indulged in casual and premarital sex, when in fact virginity was a highly prized cultural ideal. It has proved hard to either confirm or refute these accusations. By the time they were interviewed by Freeman, Mead's informants were elderly women, many of whom had converted to Christianity after years of missionary activity and who may well have played down their experiences as girls and were now expressing changed cultural ideas of chastity. They may also have been more comfortable talking about their sexual experiences with another woman of a similar age than they would with a much younger man many decades later. Whatever the criticisms of Mead, however, her work retains valuable insights into adolescent sexuality that deserve to be emphasized. Although sexuality was not the only focus of her work in Samoa, she drew an important conceptual distinction between the study of sexuality and that of marriage or child-bearing. She was also one of the first anthropologists to take children's experiences of sex seriously and to write about them without negative comparison to Western ideals. In showing that the "problems" of adolescence were as much cultural as biological, she also showed that sexuality had to be discussed within its cultural context, that sexual morality was not universal, and that children's experiences, and enjoyment, of sex depended very much on cultural expectations. These insights have all been supported by others who have focused more directly on children's sexual behavior.

In many societies, young children are very knowledgeable about sex and it is part of their daily lives. In communities where privacy is not valued, children are likely to grow up hearing adults talking about sex, seeing, and even watching, their parents and other adults having sex, and its mechanics are no great mystery to them. Cora Du Bois (1944) claimed that in her study among the Alor of Java, young boys openly masturbated in public and that sexual knowledge was freely available to children. She assumed that by the age of five, young children knew the terminology and meanings of words concerned with intercourse and birth. Thomas Gregor, who has written extensively about the sexual behavior and sexuality of an Amerindian group living in central Brazil called the Mehinaku, claims that parents openly attribute sexual motivation to very young children, joking about it and viewing it with amusement: "As toddlers play and tussle in a promiscuous huddle on the floor, parents make broad jokes about their sexual relations: 'Look! Glipe is having sex with Pairuma's daughter'" (1985:29). In this environment, an eight-year-old boy told Gregor "I haven't had sex yet, but in a few years I will" (1985:29).

Sexual knowledge, and the open acknowledgment of sexuality by children, is not uncommon. However, this does not mean that children's sexuality is always viewed as unproblematic or that Mehinaku society does not distinguish between acceptable and unacceptable behaviors. While little attention is paid to children's sexual experimentation, children are expected to do this discreetly away from the community. If children are caught, they are teased and taught that public displays of sexuality are not welcomed. The situation also changes as children get older, and boys in particular are subject to strictures once they reach the age of 12 or 13. The Mehinaku believe that boys do not mature and grow into men naturally and that this process must be brought on through medicine and through sexual abstinence. Around the age of 12, therefore, boys are secluded at one end of the communal house behind a palm wood barrier. Here a boy must take medicine, follow certain dietary rules, speak softly, and above all avoid any sexual contact with women and girls, who, once they reach puberty, become dangerous to boys, and whose menstrual blood and vaginal secretions can cause sickness.

The important point here is that sexual contact must be appropriate and that appropriateness is culturally defined. It is also noticeable that, in this case, sexual contact is limited to young people of roughly comparable ages, and while there might be a debate about how far children see this as sexual, it is harder to argue that it is abusive. Evidence from other ethnographic sources stretches understandings of cultural relativity much further. The Canela, another Amerindian group living in Brazil, have no taboos on premarital sex, and children are encouraged to have frequent and early sexual experiences. Amongst the Canela, it is considered necessary and desirable for both boys and girls to begin experimenting sexually from a young age (around six) both before their marriage, which takes place for girls between the ages of approximately 11 and 13, and after (Crocker and Crocker 1994). Sexual generosity is important in this community and is viewed as an ancestral custom. Girls are expected to take part in "sequential sex" where they take on multiple partners at once, and girls who show any reluctance to do this are described as "stingy" and scolded by their female relatives.

Children up to 6 or 7 grow up watching and hearing adults being open about extramarital trysts and sequential sex and learn how their role models enjoy these activities. Extramarital sex thus becomes a valued expectation of these young people. Experiences continue to enhance this expectation for both sexes into adolescence, when young people become thoroughly involved in extramarital sex themselves. The general atmosphere of joy and fun surrounding extramarital sex may be the principal factor which influences young people to accept and enjoy sequential sex. (Crocker and Crocker 1994:166)

This is not simply a society where girls experience great sexual freedom or where they are able to control their sexuality, but is a society with very different ideas about the body and the nature of sex. The Canela, like other Amerindian groups such as the Huaorani (Rival 1998), believe that once a woman becomes pregnant, any further semen she receives from other men becomes a biological part of the growing baby. Therefore children have several fathers, known as co-fathers or contributing fathers. Sexual intercourse with many men is desirable and necessary for women for the formation of their child. To outsiders these practices may seem bizarre and even repugnant, yet William and Jean Crocker point out that there are strictly observed rules about who can have sex with whom and that child abuse, as it is understood in the West, is very infrequent in this society.

> Our concept of child abuse includes the destruction of the child's trust in kin and others who are supposed to be her or his protectors. We also think of such abuse as involving pain and physical damage to the sexually immature child. . . . The experience of pain in first sex is not a part of Canela sexual lore. Although girls had some anxiety before their first sequential sex, I never heard any discussion of painful experiences. Here again, cultural expectations heavily influence the physical experience. (1994:166–167)

These examples point to the complexities of studying children's sexuality and the impossibility of doing so without linking discussions to much wider issues of gender roles, reproduction, marriage rules, and even cosmology. In other instances this becomes even more complicated when sexual acts carry very different meanings cross-culturally. The clearest example here is Papua New Guinea, where certain communities practice a form of "ritualized homosexuality." In his work with the Sambia, Gilbert Herdt has shown how, from the age of seven, boys are gradually initiated into manhood by a series of rituals in six stages that involve fellating or being fellated by other men of the tribe. Herdt explains:

> Sambia practice secret homosexual fellation, which is taught and instituted in first-stage initiation. Boys learn to ingest semen from older youths through oral sexual contacts. First- and second-stage initiates may only serve as fellators; they are forbidden to reverse erotic roles with older partners. Third-stage pubescent bachelors and older youths thus act as fellateds, inseminating prepubescent boys. All males pass through both erotic stages,

being first fellators, then fellateds: there are no exceptions since all Sambia males are initiated and pressured to engage in homosexual fellatio. (1993:173)

On reading this passage it is difficult to see anything other than sexual activity, and possibly sexual abuse, going on. Yet it is arguable whether these rituals have anything to do with sex at all. To understand what is happening here involves looking at gender roles in Sambian culture and the cultural meanings placed on semen. Sambian society is rigidly split into male and female, with women being seen as inferior to men. In order to turn boys into men, they must be taken away from their mothers, whose milk they have drunk in their early years, and turned into men through the ingestion of semen. Semen is the essence of manhood and it cannot be produced by boys alone. Younger boys therefore have to take semen into their bodies from older partners, and once they have reached a certain stage of maturity they will then pass semen onto others in turn. Herdt claims that initially boys are reluctant to take part in these rituals but come to enjoy them later on. As they become older, boys become betrothed to a preadolescent girl and enter a bisexual phase. When the girl is mature, her husband will give up the homosexual rituals of his youth and become exclusively heterosexual.

The case of the Sambia is an important one because it directs attention away from girls' sexuality, which is often given much greater prominence than boys', and also because it calls into question the nature of sexual activity. In this instance what is seen as a sexual practice in Western terms becomes something very different when looked at from a Sambian perspective. The expectations on boys to perform fellatio and the cultural meanings given to semen mean that boys cannot become men without being initiated and initiating others in turn. Therefore it is debatable whether these initiation practices have anything to do with sexuality or even if they are sexual acts. Yet Herdt (1999) writes that after an initial reluctance, the boys come to enjoy these activities, and there does seem to be some element of sexual gratification in them, complicating understandings and raising questions about sexuality and sexual pleasure. Whether or not such initiations still occur is harder to know, and Herdt has argued that modernization, globalization, and the advent of Christianity (among other things) have led to a rapid decline in ritualized homosexuality and that as a custom it is now rare. Bruce Knauft (2003), who worked on ritualized homosexuality in another part of Papua New Guinea, recalled the shocked and horrified reactions of contemporary young men when he described the practice to them; they voiced disbelief that their fathers had ever done such a thing. That such practices did occur in the past is not disputed, even though there is some unease about the fact that they were labeled ritualized homosexuality, when perhaps the term "boy insemination" would have proved more useful and less open to accusations of imposing false, Western labels.

Child Prostitution

Many of the same difficulties of discussing children and sex turn up in studies of child prostitution, especially when it occurs in non-Western contexts. Prostitution is viewed very strongly as the "wrong" sort of sexual experience for children, violating not only their bodies but also socially constructed ideals of the child who is innocent of sex, work, and money. Child prostitution has been a major concern of the international children's rights movement in recent years and has attracted much media attention. It has often been based on the assumption that the psychological trauma inflicted on children by prostitution is so great that they will never recover. The small amount of anthropological work on children's own understandings of what they do, and how they view sex within this context, however, has given a very different picture (Muecke 1992; Montgomery 2001a; see also, from a sociological perspective, O'Connell-Davidson 2005). As previously discussed, definitions of prostitution can depend very much on perspective. The *devadasi* studied by Orchard were called prostitutes by outsiders and those campaigning to end the practice but the girls themselves rejected this label.

I have previously conducted fieldwork among young prostitutes aged between six and 15 in a small tourist destination in Thailand (Montgomery 2001a). Both boys and girls worked as prostitutes here, and unlike the majority of young prostitutes in Thailand, their clients were exclusively Western, male tourists. The focus of my work was the kinship ties between these children and their families and their own understandings of sexuality, their bodies, and the extent to which they understood prostitution as a form of abuse. The children with whom I worked lived with their families, and one of my main conclusions was the importance of understanding kinship obligations and filial duty in any analysis of the children's justifications for working as prostitutes. It was because of the duties that kin felt toward one another that the children were able to rationalize and condone what they did. Children were seen a parental investment with an anticipated return and were expected to work for the family as soon as they were able. Owing to the lack of well-paid jobs in the neighborhood, prostitution was a known source of income that children turned to after they had tried a series of low-paid and dangerous jobs such as begging or scavenging on local garbage tips. The concepts of gratitude and obedience toward parents were taken seriously and the duties that a child had to his or her mother were especially important. The mother/child relationship was viewed as the most important one of the child's life and the one which carried the heaviest burden of obligation and reciprocity.

This emphasis on filial duty has been a constant theme in ethnographic and other studies of prostitution in Thailand. Economist Pasuk Phongpaichit (1982) has shown that daughters who left their rural homes to work as prostitutes were not running away, or discarding the principles of support and repayment, but were fulfilling them as best they could in a changed environment, by earning money elsewhere and sending home the remittances. Marjorie Muecke (1992) makes the same point, arguing that while their mothers' generation would have earned money to fulfill their filial obligations through market trading, contemporary young women were likely to earn money through prostitution. Although there has been increasing political and social condemnation of both child and adult prostitutes, and their parents, the one section of society most tolerant of prostitution, at least in its refusal to condemn it, is the Buddhist clergy. With the focus in Thai Buddhism on the intention rather than the act, and on making merit through good deeds, the sale of sex can be understood somewhat differently. Muecke interviewed monks about this, claiming that while "some monks denied that merit could be made through prostitution, most opined that the karmic outcome depended upon the prostitute's 'intention' in prostituting herself. If she did so solely to help others or to make merit and not for pleasure, they found it plausible (but not likely) that her merit would be sufficiently great to counterbalance the demerit of prostituting herself" (1992:894). Other anthropologists have been even more explicit in linking prostitution with the low social role that women occupy in institutional Buddhism (Thitsa 1980; Kirsch 1982, 1985), looking at how the most important source of merit-making open to a man, joining the monkhood, is closed to women. Women are seen as pollutants to monks and the temple and as spiritually inferior to men (Kirsch 1982; Tanabe 1991). This inferiority, combined with the promotion of female sacrifice as an ideal, helps explain some of the motivation that a dutiful daughter has in becoming a prostitute to help her family. Khin Thitsa writes that "with the low value attached to the female body and the female spirit by Buddhism, they [women] have been sufficiently degraded already to enter prostitution-service" (1980:20).

When I asked the children whom I was working with about prostitution, these ideas were often referred to and I was always told that prostitution was a means to an end, a way of fulfilling the filial obligations that they felt were demanded of them by their families. Although they did not engage with the philosophy, they claimed to be Buddhists and continually made references to what they understood as Buddhist views of filial duty and sacrifice for their families. Despite the known stigma against prostitution, a powerful mitigating circumstance for many of them was the financial support they provided for their mothers. This is not to argue that child prostitution is an intrinsic part of Thai culture or that it is not abusive, but it does emphasize that the children's view of prostitution should be understood through the cultural reference points of duty and obligation. From the interviews carried out, and the observations made of these children, it was clear that they had profoundly different understandings of sex to those seen as fundamental and non-negotiable by Western observers. For these children, neither prostitution nor sexuality was the focus of their identity, which was based instead on being a dutiful son or daughter, belonging to a society, and fulfilling obligations to their family and community.

The children had strategies for rationalizing prostitution and for coming to terms with it. They had found an ethical system whereby the public selling of their bodies did not affect their private sense of humanity and identity. When I asked one 13-year-old about selling her body, she replied "it's only my body," but when I asked her about the difference between adultery and prostitution, she told me that adultery was very wrong. In her eyes, adultery was a betrayal of a private relationship whereas prostitution was simply done for money. She could make a clear conceptual difference between her body and what happened to it and what she perceived to be her innermost "self." She, like the other children interviewed, could delineate clear boundaries between what happened to her body and what affected her personal sense of identity and morality. Betraying family members, failing to provide for parents, or cheating on spouses or boyfriends was roundly condemned, but exchanging sex for money, especially when that money was used for moral ends, was not blameworthy and violated no ethical codes. Ideas about sexual abuse played limited parts in these children's understandings of what they did.

My study also showed very different understandings about both the short- and long-term effects of sex on these children. In Western psychological terms such acts would be seen as causing life-long damage, but they were seen very differently in this context. When asked about whether or not she was worried because her eight-year-old son was a prostitute, one mother replied, "It's just for one hour. What harm can happen to him in one hour?" Even though a child's body is too small for penetration by an adult and some of the harm done by these men was evident in the bleeding and tearing that occurred during these encounters, this aspect tended to be ignored. It would be easy to condemn the mothers of the children – such physical evidence of abuse must surely have suggested that these encounters were unbearably exploitative and abusive – and yet even this comment must be interpreted with caution as my own personal value judgment. Mothers would condemn such acts and do whatever they could to help their children overcome the pain of such encounters, but the understanding of the effects of such abuse was very different. Mothers did not see it as fundamentally harmful in the long term to their children or as damaging to their mental health. Such occurrences were viewed entirely in physical, rather than psychological, terms, and there was no belief that long-term damage could be inflicted on a child in "just one hour." Such viewpoints challenge once again the limits of how far cultural relativism can be pushed and whether it is enough to simply take what informants say at face value. Anthropologists have been criticized in the past for ignoring the abuse of children which took place before them (see chapter 6), but even owning my own feelings of revulsion and condemnation at this, it was clear that the children and their parents had a radically different understanding of sexuality and their bodies from my own.

During the time I worked in this community, there were observable changes in the ways in which children talked about sex and there were signs that governmental and social pressure was changing the way that people behaved, even if there was less evidence that it changed what they believed. Children stopped talking so openly about prostitution, and sometimes referred to it as an "ugly" thing. Both children and their parents became aware of the penalties that allowing prostitution would incur, such as the children being placed in rehabilitation homes and the parents put in prison, with the loss of all parental rights. More importantly, HIV/AIDS started to take its toll and many people left the community, afraid of disease. Globalization, in the form of pressure from nongovernmental organizations, also began to have an impact on these children's lives, showing that, as ever, ideas about childhood, and appropriate experiences for children, be they sexual, physical, or emotional, change and are influenced by wider social and political forces. However, this study illuminates that even those issues that to modern Western sensibilities are most important – the inviolable body of the child and the sexual innocence that is seen as the right of all children – are not natural, unshakable, universal facts, or even unquestionable human rights. They are challenged and contested in other places by peoples who have a very different understanding of children, their bodies, their sexualities, and indeed their families and societies.

Conclusion

This chapter has looked at the little amount of literature that has analyzed children's sexuality. It has identified several themes and several bodies of work which have looked at children's sexuality from a variety of angles and which have shown that children's sexual experience, and their understandings of it, cannot be divorced from its cultural context. Children's sexuality has very rarely been the focus of anthropological research; ethnographers have looked at it extremely obliquely, and in order to find what is there, we have to look in studies of incest, religion, and, more recently, abuse. The biggest gap in the literature remains children's own understandings of their sexual experience and, in particular, an examination of their own ideas about what is sexual. Modern Western concerns about child sexual abuse have made it particularly hard for adult ethnographers to question children about their sexual experiences, and the degree of sensitivity around the subject is such that it is not surprising that many people are disinclined to make it their focus of study or are discouraged from doing so. It remains a subject that is central to modern understandings of children and childhood, however, and it would be a shame if such sensitivities prevented anthropologists from looking at such an important area of child research in the depth it deserves.

8

ADOLESCENCE AND INITIATION

Introduction

This final chapter will turn to the question of when childhood ends, looking at ideas about adolescence and initiation. As with childhood, there has been a great deal of anthropological work on aspects of adolescence, such as how it is defined, what its characteristics are, what impact it has on the transition from childhood to adulthood, and how it shapes children's understandings and experiences of gender. Anthropologists have been interested in adolescence both as a transitional stage and as a time of life that is worth studying in its own right. They have also argued that adolescence is a time not only when children are learning and changing their social role and looking forward to adulthood, but also when they are unlearning much of the dependency, irresponsibility, and asexuality of childhood (Schlegel and Barry 1991). This chapter will start with a discussion of how adolescence is defined, whether it is, indeed, a universal stage of psychological and biological development, and the implications that different definitions of adolescence have for the lives of children moving toward adulthood. It will then turn to the substantial body of work on rites of passage, particularly initiation rites and puberty rites. In order to keep focus, this chapter will concentrate on the theoretical background of initiation studies as they relate to understanding childhood, rather than on how initiation rites can illuminate studies of religion, ritual, or cosmology.

What is Adolescence?

Discussions of adolescence have come up several times before in this book, particularly in the study of peer groups and also in the analyses of anthropological accounts of sexuality (chapters 4 and 7, respectively). It has previously been suggested that adolescence is largely a Western construction, characterized by psychologists such as G. Stanley Hall (1904) as a time when physiological changes have an overwhelming impact on the growing child and when the biological alterations occurring at puberty lead to extremes of behavior and stress for both the individual and the society. For Hall, adolescence was associated with particular behaviors such as mood swings, increased interest in the opposite sex, and the turning away from parents toward peers. The "discovery" of adolescence as a distinct, transitional phase of life has been an important area of interest for both sociology and psychology (see Kehily 2007 for a summary of this work) as well as, to a lesser extent, for history (Demos and Demos 1969).

Within anthropology, John and Beatrice Whiting have defined adolescence as "the transitional period between the end of childhood and the attainment of adult social status" (1987:xvii). There remains some debate, however, about whether or not this stage exists universally. In their study of adolescence, based on large-scale, cross-cultural comparisons, Alice Schlegel and Herbert Barry start with the hypothesis that "a universal or nearly universal stage of social adolescence exists between childhood and full adulthood, characterized by differences from the preceding and following stages in the ways that adolescents behave and are treated" (Schlegel and Barry 1991:12), but end up modifying this, to conclude that while adolescence may be universal for boys, it is not always so for girls. Others have argued that adolescence is a feature only of complex societies and is unknown elsewhere. Sociologist Edgar Friedenberg claims that adolescence is only necessary in societies which are "so complicated and differentiated that each individual's social role and function takes years to define and learn" (1973:110), while in non-industrial cultures outside the West, "one is either a child or an adult and adolescence is absent" (1973:110). Richard Condon claims that "the degree of variation concerning the social recognition or nonrecognition of adolescence as a distinct life stage is perhaps more pronounced than for any other stage of the human life cycle" (1987:7). Although there are some cases where a distinct phase of adolescence does not appear to exist, there is strong ethnographic evidence that a transitional phase between childhood and adulthood is recognized in many societies, even though the expectations and roles of young people in this stage may differ greatly across cultures, it may be given very different names, and be associated with very different behaviors.

Adolescence is a cultural concept that can only be understood contextually. Like childhood, it is related to biological change and human development, but it is important to establish a distinction between biological and social puberty, or, as John and Beatrice Whiting have argued, "while the physiological changes that occur at adolescence are universal to all human populations, the social and cultural reactions to these physical manifestations are not" (1987:xvi). Clearly the social stage of adolescence coincides approximately with physical puberty, but there are no definitive markers as to when puberty starts or ends. While first menarche may be taken as a sign of the start of puberty for girls, it is more difficult to nominate one for boys, although Peter Rigby (1967) suggested first nocturnal emissions. By looking at what constitutes adolescence in its own particular context, and viewing it as a transitional phase between childhood and adulthood, rather than as a time of physiological changes caused by raging hormones, anthropologists have challenged the assumption that adolescence is characterized by the same features wherever it occurs. Western psychologists have emphasized that adolescence is a time when young people are forming their own identities, which involves separation and autonomy from the natal family and a rise in the importance of the peer group (Erikson 1963, 1968). This process is seen as a time of conflict when young people are prone to antisocial behavior and deviancy and it is a time which must be controlled by adult society, leading to further conflict. There are some ethnographic examples which might appear at first to fit closely to this model of separation and conflict, but there are also important differences which warn against using Western notions of adolescence elsewhere.

Some of the other best-documented accounts of a formal, transitional state are found in analyses of the East African Maasai and Samburu category of *moran*, which, for boys at least, signifies the beginning of the end of childhood. Both the Maasai and Samburu have a gerontocratic political system, meaning that power accrues with age and that the elders marry much younger women. Both societies are highly age-regulated and organized by age-sets, which are replicated every 12 years or so (Spencer 1965). Age-set members have particular responsibilities toward each other, and an age-set is characterized by the equality of its members.

Members of each age-set pass through three stages of life: boyhood, moranhood, and elderhood. Moranhood is a period of life between the ages of around 15 to 30 into which boys are initiated through circumcision and other rituals, and during this period they live as part of an age-set away from the main community while they try to prove their prowess by rustling cattle and seducing the wives of the elders. There is no comparable state for girls, who are formally classified as either girls or women and who are married as soon as possible after circumcision (Llewelyn-Davies 1981).

The moran exist in a socially and politically marginal state; they have few responsibilities, cannot marry and build up their herds, and are excluded from political decision-making. They are also assumed to be impulsive, unpredictable, and irresponsible (Spencer 1965). It is a state described by Paul Spencer as "a period of considerable frustration for the moran . . . a state of social suspension" (1965:162). Despite this, moranhood is viewed positively and is central to the ways in which people think about themselves as Maasai. Elders look back on their own moranhood with pride and "moranhood is understood by everyone to be a period of health, vitality, close fellowship, freedom and fearlessness, and the elders admire the moran as much as anyone else. It is the prime of life before the cares of building up a family and a herd take their toll of a man's health" (Spencer 1965:143). Even though the elders express a dislike of aspects of moran behavior such as the seducing of their wives, the damage they cause, or the fights they get into, they do not want to see the system discontinued. Maasai women, too, look upon the moran with admiration and an appreciation of their glamor.

Although the period of life of moranhood may generally appear to coincide with puberty, becoming a moran is dependent on age-set rather than age. Chronological age or biological development are not deciding factors in when a boy will be initiated into moranhood. Although the stated ideal is that a boy should be circumcised at the first available opportunity for his age-set, other practical considerations are also important and a father may decide to wait until the next initiation, which may be several years away, before circumcising his son. Initiating a boy earlier will enable him to have a longer period of moranhood and thus a longer chance to gain respect and become prominent, but can also bring disadvantages for his family. If a father has several boys in an age-set, then there may be too many boys being circumcised at one time who will also then be reaching elderhood and wanting to marry at the same time, which may prove prohibitively expensive. The elders may collectively decide that certain age-sets are too small or large and delay circumcision until later, depending on how many adult men are needed or wanted within a family or community. The decision about who will be initiated, and when, is dependent on social and economic factors as much as on biology or age.

More recently other anthropologists have challenged the assumption that adolescence is necessarily a time of social conflict and individual turmoil. In their study of Moroccan youth in a town known as Zawiya, Susan and Douglas Davis (1989) looked at the changing roles of young people and the impact that recently adopted ideas about adolescence were having on the town. They describe a community undergoing a rapid period of social change in which education had become freely available, career choices for young people had increased, marriages were being delayed, and the importance of the peer group, including the possibility of forming cross-sex friendships, had increased substantially. This had significant impacts on family relationships and young people were attempting to cope with rapid change and the conflicting values to which they were exposed. Girls, who would previously have married at puberty, were now in school and making friends with their male peers, thus risking their modesty and family shame. Young people were leaving school and studying for professional qualifications but were still expected to show honor and respect to their parents, who were illiterate and uneducated. Despite all this, however, Davis and Davis did not find the conflict between generations that characterizes European and American concepts of adolescence. Young people still trusted their parents more than their peers and still believed in the religion and values of their parents, which enabled them to adapt to these changing circumstances. Davis and Davis conclude: "We have repeatedly noted that the young people of Zawiya do not seem to be in rebellion, and we have suggested that being part of familial, cultural, and religious value systems that still command respect is an important source of strength" (1989:182).

Another aspect of adolescent behavior, assumed to be universal because it is based on biological change, is an interest in sex. As the previous chapter suggested, ideas about sex are extremely complicated and what are considered appropriate expressions of sexuality, and at what ages, are very different depending on their context. Yet the control of adolescent sexuality, or, more importantly, reproductive ability, is an important feature of anthropological accounts of adolescence from Margaret Mead onward, and while sexuality and reproduction are managed very differently cross-culturally, they are major themes in discussions of both adolescence and initiation. The links between sexuality, marriage, and reproductive capacity are central to discussions of girls' adolescence, and these issues also appear to be the ones most likely to change in the face of modernization. In her work on the Aboriginal community known as Mangrove, Victoria Burbank (1988) describes a new stage of "maidenhood" in the life of Aboriginal girls which corresponds to the period between puberty and marriage. Until missionization and white colonial rule, Aboriginal girls had been promised by their mothers to suitable young men as young children and were married before first menarche. In contemporary Mangrove society this now rarely happens and girls are neither promised nor married before puberty. Furthermore, few girls marry in accordance with their parents' wishes and they now place much greater emphasis on their own personal choice and the self-selection of a marriage partner. Some even refuse to marry at all. Control over a girl's sexuality has thus shifted away from parents and onto the adolescents themselves, creating and sustaining the new category of maidenhood, which has no precedent. Adolescence here is a time when there is struggle for control over a young woman's sexuality and her fertility, but the balance of power has shifted away from the community and onto the individual.

The final salient feature of adolescence which is apparent in anthropological accounts is the great difference between the adolescences of boys and girls. Just as several ethnographies have commented that the length of children's childhoods depends on gender (see page 53), so the same is also true of adolescence. Girls' adolescence tends to be between two and four years shorter than boys' and the transition between childhood and adulthood is more continuous. Schlegel and Barry (1991) suggest that this is caused by patterns of subordination: while children are subordinate to adults, and women to men, girls have less to readjust to than boys at adolescence, and although their status changes at adolescence, they are still subordinated. On the other hand, boys' roles and status change more dramatically and they have to unlearn more than their sisters at this time. For both boys and girls, however, the biological changes at puberty, and the ways in which they are socially interpreted, combine to affect how they are treated, how they see themselves and others, and how they negotiate the transitions from girlhood to womanhood and from boyhood to manhood. Schlegel and Barry conclude:

> Social adolescence, then, is a response to the disjuncture between sexual reproductivity and full social maturity. It appears to be universal for boys;

for girls, in the majority of societies, at least a short period of social adolescence intervenes between puberty and the full assumption of adult roles,
usually at marriage. (Schlegel and Barry 1991:19)

Adolescence and Globalization

As the two examples of the Aboriginal girls and Moroccan adolescents
discussed previously have shown, concepts of adolescence outside the
West are new, evolving, and subject to external influences. Inevitably, as
anthropologists look at adolescence in the contemporary world, they are
doing so at a time of change. Many of the major stages and transitions
in young people's lives are now constrained by bureaucratic forces and
by globalization. Schooling in particular increasingly forces children into
age-graded classes that accentuate the importance of particular cohorts
that might not take on the same significance outside school. Global consumerism means that young people in almost all countries are exposed
to the same advertising and music, although their responses to this are in
no way uniform or easy to predict. International legislation also imposes
chronological boundaries on childhood, although the UNCRC, which
defines a child as anyone under 18, makes no mention of adolescence,
even though there are legal differences between children and adolescents.
The move from childhood to adulthood is marked by the growing accu-
mulation of legal rights (and responsibilities), so that, for instance, young
people in the UK can consent to sex at 16, learn to drive at 17, and attain
full voting rights at 18. They also acquire more legal responsibilities as
they get older. Under the age of ten, young people cannot be prosecuted
for a crime in England, whereas once they have reached this age, they
are deemed responsible for their actions. In the USA such decisions are
made federally, so that a young person attains different stages of adulthood depending on geography. These legal rights are accrued cumulat-
ively and passively because of a young person's age and have nothing to
do with an individual's biological development or social competence. There
is no social agreement on when adolescence begins or when it ends, and,
without the rites of passage discussed later in the chapter, this transitionary
period is more likely to be defined bureaucratically than by any other means.
Richard Condon has argued that in the USA, "the adolescent life stage is
extremely long, lasting anywhere from ten to 15 years or more. Social
maturation is a gradual process with no clear-cut transitions or initiations

to mark an individual's entry to adulthood. If anything, there is only a series of rather ambiguous transitions that do not necessarily imply culturally significant status or role changes" (1990:268).

Even more blurred are the social and economic transitions that occur as children grow into adolescents in the West. While adolescence was analyzed by psychologists and sociologists, the "teenager" was discovered by marketers and advertisers, who were aware of the vast purchasing power of young people in the post-1945 era. Becoming an adolescent in the West means making economic transitions as well as social and psychological ones, reaching toward financial independence, having the ability to control resources and attaining markers such as holding down a job or leaving home to set up independently. In contemporary Western societies, however, it is these economic transitions that may be hardest to effect and the sphere in which young people find it most difficult to "grow up." Adolescence has become longer as fewer young people are able to become economically independent; their money is rarely enough to live on by themselves, and many young people, especially those who stay on in further education, have to rely on the resources of their parents until well into their twenties. The sociologist Paul Willis once claimed that "the wage packet is the provider of freedom, and independence" (1977:150), but this is now only partially true, and even when young people make the transition from education to work, they are now likely to find that a pay packet does not give them the independence and the adulthood they had hoped for. They are likely to remain adolescents for much longer than previous generations.

One ethnographic example of this is shown in the work done by Tom Hall (2003) on homeless adolescents in the UK. He examines the difficulties that young people have in navigating the transition from childhood to adulthood when they are socially and economically excluded. Although they live independently, they are denied the civil, political, and consumer power of their peers. They exist in a sort of limbo where they are afforded few of the privileges of adolescence, such as legal protection, and none of the sympathy usually shown to children, and they are unable to effect a complete transition to adulthood. They cannot contribute economically as either consumers or producers and they are multiply marginalized and likely to become delinquent and alienated as the trappings of childhood, adolescence, and adulthood are all denied to them.

Globalization, and the impact of television and marketing, have been of particular concern in recent anthropological studies of adolescence.

Merry White (1993), in her comparative work on adolescents in Japan and America, has examined the relationship between adolescence and the consumption of music, fashion, and technology. She concludes that there are indeed certain commonalities between young people in America and Japan, such as the paradoxical desire to both conform and be different, the importance of the peer group, and the search for an identity. However, although young people in both countries may wear the same clothes, listen to the same music, and be targeted by manufactures and advertisers keen to tap into the same "youth market," there are also very different ideas about adolescence in the two societies that suggest that the effects of economic globalization may well not be as strong, or as uniform, as is sometimes assumed. White argues that

> the cassette player doesn't make your fifteen-year-old Japanese, and the chocolate-chip cookie-dough ice cream doesn't produce a culture-change operation on a Japanese child. The similarities of our material worlds only throw into relief the different meanings attached to consumerism and popular culture, as well as the relationship of these with our goals for teenagers. (1993:13)

She describes the experiences of adolescents in Japan as being fundamentally different to those in the USA and based on very different understandings of the role of adolescence in the life-cycle. While in America adolescence is seen as "a dangerous limbo period in which adolescents are at risk to themselves and others" (1993:10), in Japan, adolescence is "the most critical, most fully mobilized time of life . . . [one's] teens are key to one's future prospects" (1993:10). White argues that the Japanese may have adopted the word "teenager" (or *cheenayja*), but they have not adopted the same expectations of bad behavior or the idea that adolescents are driven by biological urges and uncontrollable hormones. Japanese adolescents therefore do not seek autonomy from their parents, confrontations between adult and child are rare, and, in her analysis of their diaries, White finds evidence of Japanese young people expressing respect for their parents' opinions and views on their futures. Rebellion is not a key feature of adolescence, and those young people who do rebel or indulge in antisocial behavior, particularly those who use drink or drugs, are seen as the exception rather than the rule. Schooling is a time when future career paths are decided and when a young person's friends are viewed as positive reinforcements rather than a source of negative peer pressure. As White puts it: "Being a teen in America today, according to popular belief, means being at risk: in Japan it means, most people imagine, being at promise" (1993:21–22).

Against this background, adolescent sexuality is not seen as the same problem in Japan that it is in America. American adolescents are given mixed messages about sex: on the one hand, they are told that it is dangerous and forbidden and, on the other, that being an adult means becoming sexually active. There is no such pressure in Japan and adults are generally more concerned with the appropriateness of sexual expression than with pathologizing young people's sexuality. Although Japanese young people are often sexually active, this is not seen as a moral problem and the understanding of sex in Japan is that it needs to be compartmentalized, kept in its proper place, and should not interfere with a person's social obligations. This attitude is reinforced by Japanese ideas about situationally appropriate behavior. What in America is usually condemned as hypocrisy, acting one way in one situation and differently in another, is seen as the epitome of socially responsible behavior in Japan. White argues that Japanese adolescents are generally more concerned about school work and getting into a good university than they are about romance or sex, so that even while they may be having more sex than their American counterparts, it is not so preoccupying to them (1993:194).

The impact of Westernization in the form of television and schooling on how expectations of adolescence have changed is a central theme of Richard Condon's work on Inuit communities in Canada (1987, 1990). He describes how the previous stage of transition, called *inuhaaq*, is now glossed as teenager, but was previously used to describe the point, usually between the ages of ten and 13, when a child was thought to begin the transformation into adulthood. For boys, this might be when they first trapped small game, while for girls it happened when they started performing household chores, or started to produce their own sewing. At this stage, gender became increasingly significant, and while children were not referred to previously as either boys or girls, they now became differentiated by gender so that boys became *inuuhuktug* and girls *arnaruhiq*. Girls would have traditionally been married at, or just prior to, first menarche but boys would not marry until they had proved themselves as hunters. In the contemporary society studied by Condon, significant changes had occurred in ideas about adolescence and the expectations placed on young people. Firstly, Inuit languages had died out, so that English, and its concepts of "kids," "babies," or "teenagers," had become dominant. The introduction of television in 1980 had also caused noticeable changes to adolescent life in the community and brought with it new aspirations, as well as new ideas about relationships, and the role of cooperation and competition. Traditional Inuit games, which had been based around ideals of cooperation and communality, had been eclipsed in popularity by ice hockey, with its emphasis on competitiveness and even aggression. Condon (1995) found the young people were demonstrably more boisterous and competitive in the years after television was introduced. The changing physical aspects of Inuit life had also changed relationships between parents and children and between children and their peers. The population had become concentrated in settlements rather than in nomadic family groups, schooling had been introduced, and, rather than relying on their families, Inuit adolescents had turned to school friends (Condon and Stern 1993). Consequently both boys and girls were marrying much later and experiencing a longer transition between leaving childhood and attaining full adult status.

The adolescents studied by Condon were not simply in the process of transition from childhood to adulthood but they were also coming of age at a time of great cultural, economic, and linguistic change. Delayed marriage, the difficulties of getting jobs within the community, the rise in opportunities for leisure activities, as well as the influence of drugs and alcohol, had all meant that adolescence had become more problematic for both the adolescents and their society. While education and technology had, in theory, increased the choices for these young people, they also made life more difficult for them, especially for young men. While girls could continue to live at home, or earn money from sewing, the opportunities for young men to prove themselves as hunters and providers were more limited and Condon describes a category of young men who, despite being in their twenties, were described by older people as adolescents because they did not have the responsibilities of maintaining a household.

Once again, however, despite being heavily influenced by American and Canadian ideas, adolescence retained some distinctly Inuit features and was not simply an importation of an alien North American concept. The autonomy and rebellion seen as defining characteristics of adolescence were largely absent from Inuit conceptualizations of young people, as were the overt stresses and strains of American adolescence, which were avoided through Inuit belief in emotional restraint. In a society which valued autonomy, practiced non-interventionist child-rearing, and where parents did not seek to control their children, there was less pressure to rebel and break away from families. Responsibility and autonomy were not seen as dependent on each other, so that Inuit children were allowed a great deal of personal autonomy long before they took on significant responsibilities. Condon describes how "Inuit teenagers and parents seem almost to drift past one another and engage in minimal interaction through the course of a normal day" (1987:101). Nevertheless, Inuit teenagers remained intimate with their parents and kept close emotional bonds with them, even though this affection and support were rarely displayed overtly.

Initiation

Having discussed different ideas about adolescence, and the impact of change on young people's lives, this part of the chapter will turn to previous anthropological work on transitions and, in particular, initiation. Initiation has been approached by anthropologists in numerous ways: as a means of studying ritual more generally, as an example of the fruitful overlap between anthropology and psychology, as a way of analyzing cross-cultural ideas about pain, or in terms of gender and the shaping of men and women into given social roles. Initiation rituals have also been given particular prominence in cross-cultural comparative surveys, which attempt to uncover universal patterns (Burton and White 1987). All these understandings have produced large bodies of material and generated their own controversies about the role, meaning, and function of initiation in the lives of young people. Rarely, however, do children themselves talk about initiation, either their fears, or indeed excitement, before it, or their transformation afterward (although Heald 1982 does quote one young person talking about his experience). The few first-hand accounts that exist – for example, Nelson Mandela's account of his initiation ceremony, or the account given in the autobiography of Maasai Tepilit Ole Saitoti – tend to be populist accounts written many years after the event with little reflection on the experience as a child participant (Saitoti 1986; Mandela 1994). In the case of female circumcision, accounts are most often written to show the brutality of the practice (El Saadawi 1980; Dirie and Miller 1999). Despite the absence of children's own accounts, however, there is a wealth of anthropological material that can provide insight into the ways in which initiation transforms children.

It is impossible to start any discussion of initiation without reference to Arnold van Gennep and his tripartite system for analyzing rites of passage. His book *Les Rites de Passage* was first published in French in 1909 and translated into English in 1960. According to van Gennep, rites of passage are "rites which accompany every change of place, state, social position, and age" (quoted in Turner 1969:94). They occur at key times of crisis in an individual's life, such as birth, initiation, marriage, and death. Van Gennep claimed that all social and individual life could be understood as the process of crossing a series of ritual thresholds. In his words, "For groups, as well as for individuals, life itself means to separate and to be reunited, to change form and condition, to die and to be reborn. It is to act and to cease, to wait and rest, and then to begin acting again, but in a different way" (1960[1909]:189). In van Gennep's thesis, individuals continually change states throughout their lives; they move from one role to another, and this transition is manifested by a series of rituals of separation and reincorporation into the social body. The transition from one stage of life to another is, he argued, marked symbolically and publicly, and all true rites of passage occur in three stages, and have separate components:

1   separating from the familiar and leaving it behind (rites of separation);
2   a liminal or in-between stage, which occurs during the transition from the old to the new one (marginal or liminal rites);
3   return and reintegration into the original social structure (rites of aggregation).

He argued that each stage in the rite of passage is distinctive. The first one, separation, involves initiates undergoing rituals designed to separate them from their previous social statuses and to strip them of their former identities. This might involve head-shaving, changing clothes, discarding ornaments, or changing the normal place of residence so that former selves can be symbolically discarded. During the separation period, initiates might be expected to undergo ordeals or trials, to give their new social status legitimacy. Bodily modification, be it circumcision, tattooing, or scarification, is common during this period. The next part of a rite of passage, according to van Gennep, is the liminal or marginal period during which the initiate is in limbo between two states, and often thought to be particularly vulnerable and also potentially dangerous. The final stage of a rite of passage is when the initiate emerges with a new social identity and social role and is formally reintegrated into society with a changed (and usually enhanced) social status.

Although each rite of passage has to contain these key elements of separation, liminality, and aggregation, in different rites each of these has a different significance or is given more prominence than in others. Thus the element of separation is more important in funerary or mortuary rites, while aggregation is more important in marriage rites. In many initiation rites, the stage of liminality is especially important, particularly when it involves the participants in many months, and sometimes years, of separation and isolation from their normal societies. Van Gennep believed that rites of passage were necessary for the continual renewal of society and were a way of maintaining social stability. He saw them as a way of reducing the harmful effects of change, such as death or aging, and of allowing the next generation to take their place as full members of society.

The distinction between biological and social change is critical to understanding van Gennep and has had a profound influence on anthropologists ever since. Van Gennep argued that while many initiation rites occur around puberty and are concerned with the distinction between childhood and adulthood, physical puberty itself is not particularly important and it is social maturity that is of primary concern during rites of passage. As Ruth Benedict argued: "In order to understand puberty institutions . . . [we need to know] what is identified in different cultures with the beginning of adulthood" (1934:25). She stated categorically that what is important is "not biological puberty, but what adulthood means" (1934:25). Indeed physical puberty is not a prerequisite for initiation, and those who are initiated may or may not have reached puberty. Commenting on van Gennep, Max Gluckman (1962) argued that biological puberty was much less important than social transformation and that initiation rites were concerned with social change and the transition in a child's life from childhood to adulthood. He saw them as a way of undoing the status of childhood and investing a person instead with the status and expectations of public, political adulthood.

Many anthropologists have found van Gennep's tripartite scheme to be a useful way of analyzing initiation and other rites of passage, but, inevitably, there have also been criticisms and modifications and others have sought to expand or refute his theories (Turner 1967, 1969).

Gluckman (1962) defended van Gennep from the criticism that, at base, all he was claiming was that rituals have a beginning, middle, and end, arguing that this way of looking at ritual allowed anthropologists to look at how social roles changed over a person's lifetime. Jean La Fontaine argues that van Gennep's "success lies in having related symbolic meaning to wider social significance, a feat which few before or since have emulated" (1986b:26). However, criticism remains of van Gennep's work, in particular his failure to discuss why rites of passage might be performed, and La Fontaine sees his argument as essentially circular – rites are performed because they are necessary, but why they are necessary is less satisfactorily answered. Van Gennep argues that rites of passage reduce the harmful effects brought about by changes in the life-cycle, but does not give details about why change might be harmful or why rites of passage are necessary to mediate this change. Nevertheless, his influence remains profound, and in studies of the Maasai or the Samburu, for example, his tripartite analysis of initiation remains very relevant.

Initiation: A Psychological Approach

While van Gennep looked to sociology to provide an understanding of rites of passage, others have turned to psychology. Some of the fiercest debates over initiation rites have focused on their supposed psychological meanings and the correlations, for example, between the severity of the initiation rites and the child-rearing practices of the community under discussion. Psychological analyses, especially concerning children and the long-term effects of child-rearing practices on both the individual and the community, have been abiding concerns for American anthropologists, and in discussion of initiation rites these have been particularly prominent (Paige and Paige 1981). Much of the work on initiation, and on circumcision, in particular, has had a pronounced Freudian emphasis. It was Freud's hypothesis that circumcision is a symbolic substitute for castration and he analyzed the circumcision rituals that he had read about in other societies as proof of this. He wrote:

> We have conjectured that, in the early days of the human family, castration really was performed on the growing boy by the jealous and cruel father, and that circumcision, which is so frequently an element in puberty rites, is an easily recognizable trace of it. (1964[1933]:114)

Freud's theories have come under attack from a number of sources, both within psychology and from anthropology. In *Symbolic Wounds* (1955), Bruno Bettelheim challenged Freud's original thesis, claiming that circumcision was a way for men to link symbolically with the feminine and for them to attain the female privilege of shedding blood. Men, he claimed, were envious of women's reproductive and menstrual functions, and certain male circumcision rituals, such as splitting the male urethra, were performed to make the penis look like the vulva. He rejected the negative and inhibitive aspects of Freud's theories of castration and saw instead a more positive "vagina envy" where men wished to replicate the reproductive functions, particularly those of child-bearing, of their mothers, although he also emphasized the ambivalence that many men felt about this. Furthermore, he claimed that circumcising boys meant that the glans on the end of the penis was permanently exposed, making the penis look erect at all times. In doing this, the child was transformed from a nonsexual being into a sexual one, from an innocent child to a sexual adult. More importantly, the boy was separated from women and was marked out symbolically as a male. He underwent a symbolic rebirth, this time being born from men rather than women. This rite therefore reinforced male superiority in two ways: by allowing the boy to shed blood and by giving the child the appearance of a fully mature, sexual man (Bettelheim 1955).

Theories about initiation, especially circumcision, have gradually been transformed by post-Freudian psychoanalytical theories. It was suggested in chapter 1 that feminist writers such as Nancy Chodorow (1978) replaced the emphasis on the father–son relationship with that of mother–child bonds and, in doing so, undermined traditional Freudian views of both male and female identification. Freud (1953b[1913]) had argued that the primary identification of a boy was with his father and that he was born with a masculine identity and a heterosexual relationship with his mother. Post-Freudian psychoanalysts argued that both boys' and girls' primary identification was with their mother and that growing up presented different problems for boys and girls in their attempts to establish their identities. As children grow and become self-aware, part of this awareness is a recognition that they are either a man or a woman, that they must behave in certain ways and be socially recognized as either male or female. For boys, this is particularly problematic. After a long period of close identification and unity with their mothers, they have to break away from them in order to establish themselves as a separate, masculine person, differentiated from their mothers. For girls, this problem is less acute as they never break away fully from their mothers, and their own sense of self and femininity is reinforced in their relationship with their mother (Chodorow 1978). As David Gilmore puts it, a boy

> must break the chain to his mother. He must renounce the bond to her and seek his own way in the world. His masculinity thus represents his separation from his mother and his entry into a new and independent social status recognized as distinct and opposite from hers. In this view the main threat to the boys' growth is not only, or even primarily, castration anxiety. The principal danger to the boy is not a unidimensional fear of the punishing father but a more ambivalent fantasy-fear about the mother. The ineradicable fantasy is to return to the primal maternal symbiosis. The inseparable fear is that restoring the oneness with the mother will overwhelm one's independent selfhood. (1990:28)

The move away from classical Freudian interpretations of initiation can be seen in the work of John Whiting, who argued that initiation rites had to be understood as a way of resolving the social and psychological conflicts engendered in infancy by particular child-rearing practices (Whiting and Child 1953). He suggested that key to these was the "conflict of sex identity" suffered by children, which was based on status envy and the competition for control of resources such as food as well as love, comfort, or nurture (Burton and Whiting 1961; Whiting 1961). He traced these issues with identification back to the child's sleeping patterns in early infancy, a time when a child may not have been given the resources he or she needed and which therefore set up future conflicts within that child. He focused in particular on children's sleeping patterns. In societies where a girl slept with both parents, Whiting believed that she would grow up identifying with the adult male, while in those societies where a girl slept primarily with her mother, it was thought that she would suffer from a crisis of sex identity when this pattern was terminated and she entered a world in which men had greater control over resources. Boys, too, would suffer if they slept primarily with their mothers in infancy and would have a heightened conflict of sex identity. The solution to these tensions, Whiting argued, lay in initiation rites. Furthermore, he suggested that in cases where the conflict of sex identity was particularly acute, the greater the need would be to resolve it through severe initiation ordeals.

Whiting's methods and theories were adopted by others, who attempted to show, through the use of secondary data, correlations between various social structures or practices and initiation rites. One such attempt was Judith Brown's (1963) analysis of girls' initiation, based on data sets from 75 societies. She argued that psychoanalytical views of girls' initiation had focused too much on genital cutting, which was comparatively rare, and had not looked at wider social institutions. She concurred with Whiting's views on the relationship between the intensity of the sex identity conflict and the need for harsh initiation rites and extended this to girls. Her primary focus, however, was the connection between female initiation and matrilocal residence. She argued that in societies where a girl lived with her maternal family after marriage, there would be a problem with her perceived status. Having been known within that community as a child, an initiation rite was necessary to prove symbolically and socially that she was now an adult woman, with adult responsibilities. In a patrilocal society where a girl would move away after marriage, initiation rites were unnecessary, as the girl would enter her husband's community as a socially recognized adult woman. No one would have known her as a child and there would be no conflict with her identity. Such research, based on cross-cultural studies and the Human Relations Area Files, immediately came in for criticism by those such as Harold Driver (1969, 1971) who questioned both Brown's methodology and conclusions and claimed there was no such correlation. Although such studies were useful in moving away from classical Freudian theory and looking at other patterns of infant attachment and child development, they did not fully answer the questions that they themselves had raised, especially the dilemma that if initiation rites were born out of universal, psychological human needs, then why did some societies not feel it necessary to initiate children at all, and why did some initiate only boys, while others initiated both boys and girls?

Post-Freudian theorists might argue that boys are initiated more often than girls because maleness is often perceived as more problematic than femaleness. David Gilmore (1990) argues that manhood, in contrast to womanhood, is a state that needs to be continually confirmed through feats and trials. Femininity, he claims, involves "essentially cosmetic behaviors that enhance, rather than create, an inherent quality of character. An authentic femininity rarely involves test or proof of action. . . . Rather than a critical threshold passed by traumatic testing, an either/or condition, femininity is more often construed as a biological given that is culturally refined or augmented" (1990:11–12). This argument has been disputed, however, and, as will be shown by the discussion below of Pharaonic circumcision practiced on Sudanese girls, femininity and biological femaleness may well be equally problematic. Nevertheless Gilmore argues that maleness is something that has to be both attained and sustained:

> There is a constantly recurring notion that real manhood is different from simple anatomical maleness, that it is not a natural condition that comes about spontaneously through biological maturation but rather is a precarious or artificial state that boys must win against powerful odds. This recurrent notion that manhood is problematic, a critical threshold that boys must pass through testing, is found at all levels of sociocultural development regardless of what other alternative roles are recognised. (1990:11)

Gilmore challenges orthodox Freudian theory that states that it is fear of castration that causes universal male anxiety over masculinity and which makes men contest and reaffirm their masculinity. Instead he argues that it is the initiation ordeals that prefigure manhood which serve to break boys away from their mothers and to prevent them from remaining in the comforts of childishness.

The instability and fragility of manhood and the ways it must be shored up and tested through ritual and initiation are themes running through Gilbert Herdt's (1981) analysis of the Sambia in Papua New Guinea. In the previous chapter his work on initiation was discussed in terms of sexuality and sexual abuse. It was argued that initiation rituals among the Sambia should be seen not in sexual terms but as a way of making men and separating them from women. Herdt describes a situation in which boys spend almost all of their early lives with their mothers, drinking their breast milk, and being socialized by them. Femininity, however, is devalued and boys are seen as being at risk from these feminine influences, both psychologically and in terms of their physical growth. Boys must thus be socialized away from their mothers and toward the socially approved paths of manhood. This involves a series of rituals, not just fellatio and the ingestion of semen, but also nose-bleeding, which is done to purge the boys of feminine contaminants, such as breast milk, which they have ingested.

Among the Sambia, it is men, not women, who are made, and it is men who are subject to initiation in order to transform them. Maleness is not assigned at birth; it must be striven for in opposition to all that is female and it is masculinity that has to be culturally constructed, while femininity is more naturally achieved. Herdt argues that "nature provides male genitals, it is true, but nature alone does not bestow the vital spark biologically necessary for stimulating masculine growth" (1999:94). It is initiation that does this, and these initiations take place over many years and in many different stages. The Sambia themselves are explicit on this point:

> [Sambian] men are adamant: the sexes have quite different "problems" in attaining adult reproductive competence. For women, biology and behavioral development are fused; feminine behavior and female reproductive capacity are natural outcomes of a female's anatomy and training. Men are different: anatomy and behavior are split up; neither biology nor early learning experiences ensure the development of masculinity or the capacity to act as reproductively competent men. (Herdt 1981: 314–315)

Masculinity in this case is seen as weak and under continual threat from women. Guarding against feminine contamination is a life-long problem and men will go on bleeding their noses in private throughout their lives as a way of removing the contaminants to which intercourse with their wives exposes them.

Initiation is not simply a time when people pass from one social state to another; it is also a time of profound psychological change. Suzette Heald's study of a circumcision ceremony, known as *imbalu*, performed by the Gisu in eastern Uganda exemplifies this (Heald 1982). Circumcision is a physically gruelling and painful operation that involves cutting the foreskin and then removing the subcutaneous fat from around the *glans penis*. It is acknowledged as an excruciatingly painful experience and is performed only on boys who are thought to have the strength to go through it, which usually means that boys have to be between 18 and 25 in order to withstand the pain. Overcoming fear is an important part of the ritual, as is a belief in the importance of choosing to undergo it. The Gisu believe that violent emotion or *lirima* builds up in a boy until he himself demands to undergo circumcision. Interestingly it is one of the few accounts which directly quotes a young man discussing his own initiation and his feelings about it, particularly his subjective experiences of overcoming fear, and his insistence that his initiation was a matter of personal choice (although as Heald points out, there is enormous social pressure on young men to take part in the initiation and both they and their families are shamed if they do not).

> No one has asked us to do it. No one is forcing us. We ourselves have overcome our fear. Now it is my heart itself which wants it. No one is forcing me. Father has not ordered me. It comes from my heart alone. Let me explain it in this way, even though I am here talking with my friends I feel like a spirit-shadow (*cisimu*) and don't know what I am doing.
>
> It is as they tell you. It comes from your heart itself. You don't sleep but think only of *imbalu* and that if it means that I will die then I must die. You cannot say, well just let me try. For it is in your heart. It is the heart itself. It is my heart which is speaking now. Every time I hear the sound of the other boys' bells I want to run and see them and my stomach trembles like that of a circumciser. (Heald 1982:19)

Heald argues that in order to understand *imbalu* fully, anthropologists must look not just at the external process of transformation, as a boy is being turned into a socially recognized man, but also at the internal process, and the change in individual psychology. *Lirima*, or the violent emotion that boys need to face circumcision, is a way of preparing a boy for the ordeal ahead, but it is also the aim of the ritual, to turn a boy into a man with the capacity to feel *lirima*. By understanding and emphasizing what Heald refers to as "vernacular psychology," she is able to sidestep some of the problems of using Western psychoanalytical models to explain initiation. As she writes: "The contribution of the communicative aspects of ritual symbols, then, is not to carry largely hidden messages about social relations but to directly structure the psychological field in which the individual is prepared and made capable of acting" (1982:32).

Initiation and Education

Initiation has been described as "the only formal education received by the primitive child" (quoted in Richards 1956:125), and, indeed, many early ethnographers saw initiation, particularly that of girls, as having primarily an instructive function. Girls were taught by their mothers or other elder women in the tribe what was expected of them as wives and mothers; initiation in this analysis was far less concerned with the spiritual or transformative than with the practical. One of the most obvious examples of this is Otto Raum's description of girls' initiation rites among the Chaga of East Africa. Although a detailed and highly readable study, it is uninterested in the ritual meaning of the ceremonies and initiation and its preparations are presented as a way of passing on the knowledge that girls will need to make them into wives and mothers. As Audrey Richards remarks: "I confess to a mental picture of the girls sitting in the initiation hut and listening to talks from an old woman on what might be called in modern idiom 'marriage guidance'" (1956:126). Raum (1939) describes the ceremony as beginning with singing before novices are sent off to look for various things in the wilderness such as grasshoppers, tadpoles, twinfruit, and nettles. Such objects seem to be chosen for their practical significance and because of the physical resemblance to parts of the body or the processes of conception and childbirth.

> Now the teacher begins to explain the meaning of the various objects. Apparently the frogs or tadpoles are used in a lesson describing "quickening" in pregnancy. They are placed on the girl's abdomen and their movements explained as similar to those of the embryo's. With regard to the narrow leaf of the *lelema* plant the novice is told that when she is giving birth to the child she will see a thin string like this coming away from the child's umbilicus. She is warned that if she does not respect the old women the midwives will cut the cord badly and the child will die on the spot. The meaning of the twinfruits is explained as representing the scrotum of the heir whom every Chaga women hopes to bear in her first confinement. The little tuber stands for the foetus itself. The *lelema* leaf is tied round it suggesting the appearance of the child after birth. The novice is shown how to cut the cord, and told to pay attention that the midwife does not maliciously sever it in a wrong manner. The nettles do not form an object of teaching. If the novice has a bad reputation she is stung with them and not allowed to utter a sound. (1939:558)

Throughout his description, Raum stresses that initiation is primarily a form of education which can tell ethnographers limited amounts about either the sacred world or social organization. He concludes: "Probably the most significant conclusion from our study is that the traditional over-emphasis on ceremony and ritual has led to a regrettable neglect of the educational factor which really forms the fundamental motive of initiation" (1939:565). Such a view immediately presents problems, however, which Raum does not address. If the function of initiation is educative, then why bother with elaborate ceremonies and obscure references to past events? Why not simply teach the girls what they need to know in another context without initiation? Raum makes clear that the girls are previously taught the answers to questions about what the tadpoles refer to, or what the tubers represent, so that the lessons that initiation supposedly teaches them are already known.

This view of initiation is specifically rejected by Audrey Richards (1956) in her study of girls' initiation ceremonies, known as *chisungu*, among the Bemba of Zambia. In the ceremonies she studied, although women used the same term, *ukufunda*, when they spoke of both education in schools and the knowledge passed on at initiation, in reality, initiation taught girls little new practical knowledge or information. Most of the duties of a wife and mother were well known to Bemba girls; they had been working at home, tending babies, cooking, and collecting mushrooms since they were little girls, and to claim that an initiation ceremony taught them how to be women and perform these duties was absurd. Even sex was not necessarily a mystery to them: some of the girls had been betrothed since before puberty, and sexual experimentation, if not full intercourse, had already taken place (Richards 1956). Several of the Bemba women Richards interviewed acknowledged that the girls carried out exactly the same duties before and after initiation but that afterward they fulfilled them with a different spirit and with a new manner. "[Senior Bemba women] explain that, when young, a girl can idle in the gardens if she likes and her mother will shrug her shoulders and say 'She is not grown up'; but when she is married, she cannot refuse her duties or it will be a cause of divorce, husbands will scold a lazy wife and this will bring shame on her family. As one woman put it: 'Before, if they were called to work they could go slowly. Now they have to run'" (1956:128).

Chisungu represented a transformation in the individual child, as well as in her social status, and was a public demonstration of the duties and responsibilities expected of her. It was designed to protect her during the changes she would undergo at puberty and to acknowledge the difficulties and rewards of this transformation. *Chisungu* was concerned with growth rather than education, with managing and celebrating transitions and change on both a social and a spiritual level. Richards sums up: "[The women performing *chisungu*] were changing an alarming condition to a safe one, and securing the transition from a calm but unproductive girlhood to a potentially dangerous but fertile womanhood. They were making the girls grow as well as teaching them" (1956:125). On a wider level, Richards also saw *chisungu* rituals as a way of securing matrilineal claims to the girl's offspring; in the absence of inducements to keep the girl's husband in her own village and under matrilineal authority, there was always the temptation for him to remove his wife and children. *Chisungu* was a way of dramatizing the girl's descent and publicly claiming her future children.

Initiation and Gender

One of the major threads running through studies of initiation has been the difference between the initiations of boys and girls and the relative lack of attention given to girls' initiations. As feminist anthropologists have pointed out, there has been a male bias, both in terms of what was studied, and in the ways in which female initiation rites were understood as pale imitations of their male counterparts (Lutkehaus 1995). This has been particularly emphasized when looking at initiation as a form of socialization, because it perpetuated the idea that while boys had to be culturally manipulated into becoming men, girls became women more "naturally" and their transition to adulthood was less socially important. As Marilyn Strathern argues in the case of the Papua New Guinean Highlands, if "we regard initiation ritual as having a socializing function, then we are faced with the fact that Highland boys need to be socialized where girls do not, or at the least that what takes place for girls is of a very different order" (quoted in Roscoe 1995:222). More recent scholarship has emphasized the importance of girls' initiations in many societies and the important links between culturally sanctioned sexual behavior, fertility, and the transformation of girls into women.

Initiation often does mark the beginning of sexual maturity and can be seen as the start of the process of turning an asexual child into a sexual one. The symbolism of many initiation rituals is often closely tied to sexual maturity and adult sexuality; there are many examples of overt references to sexuality and sexual practices during initiation. Among the Amazonian Barasana, for example, it is initiation rather than marriage that is the "passage from the asexual world of childhood to the sexual world of adults" (Hugh-Jones 1979:110). Others have seen the bodily modifications sometimes associated with initiation as the symbolic stripping away of the sexual characteristics of the opposite sex in order to make that person more fully masculinized or feminized. Van Gennep (1960[1909]), for instance, argued that clitoridectomy removes from the female the parts of the genitalia that most resemble the penis and Gluckman (1962), commenting on this, remarks that the reverse is also true: circumcision removes from a boy the features that most resemble labia. "Circumcision and clitoridectomy may thus be seen as intensifying masculinity and femininity by removing those anatomical features of each sex which resemble those of the opposite. They also create distinctions between mature and immature individuals of each sex, so that social and physical differences coincide" (La Fontaine 1986b:113). Janice Boddy (1989) takes up this point in her work on female circumcision rituals in Sudan. Although female circumcision happens here at an early age, between the ages of five and ten, it is a way of imposing gender on children's bodies and of creating the appropriate female body. In the community in which she worked, children were identified as male or female by their genitals at birth, but this identification was considered ambiguous and inadequate. Circumcision, carried out when children began to show self-awareness and understanding of Allah's laws, was a way of socially aligning a child's gender with her or her sex: "It completes and purifies a child's natural sexual identity by removing physical traits deemed appropriate to his or her opposite: the clitoris and other external genitalia in the case of females, the prepuce or covering of the penis in the case of males" (1989:58).

Appropriate, socially sanctioned fertility and sexual reproduction are constant themes in discussions of circumcision and clitoridectomy. Jean La Fontaine (1986b) has written about the Pokot of Ghana, where clitoridectomies were performed as part of initiation ceremonies that lasted several months. A girl was expected to show bravery during the operation but, as importantly, clitoridectomy represented a symbolic break with the past. Before initiation a girl could have sex without serious social implications, but after initiation sex had to take place as a prelude to procreation – the privilege of adult men and women. This point is emphasized by Boddy's (1989) analysis of female circumcision in northern Sudan as a way of channeling fertility into socially approved forms. While it has often been analyzed by Western feminists as a way of men controlling and suppressing women's pleasure, or as a way of ensuring virginity, looked at within its own context, it has, in fact, little to do with sexuality. Circumcision is not carried out to prevent promiscuity among women or to increase sexual pleasure for men. It is done to enhance women's femininity, which involves deemphasizing sexuality and highlighting the important role of women as the mothers of men. Without circumcision, a girl cannot marry and have children, and therefore will not gain a position of respect when she is older. As Boddy argues: "In insisting upon circumcision for their daughters, women assert their social indispensability, an importance which is not as the sexual partners of their husbands, nor – in this highly segregated, overtly male-authoritative society – as their servants, sexual or otherwise, but as the mother of men. The ultimate social goal of a woman is to become, with her husband, the cofounder of a lineage section" (1989:55). The radical circumcision carried out in this area of Sudan, in which all the external genitalia are removed, is a symbolic way of asserting moral purity and appropriate sexuality. Through the smoothing and purifying of the outer entrance of the womb, the girl's body is symbolically representing the ideal social space "enclosed, impervious, virtually impenetrable" (1989:74), which also serves as a metaphor for the resilience of the village when faced by hostile external influences. After circumcision the entrance of the vagina is sewn up, and has to be opened by a husband on first intercourse. This happens several times throughout a woman's life, and women undergo a series of reinfibulations after giving birth, or before remarriage, in which the entrance that has been opened in order to allow the child to be born is sewn up. After each birth, a woman is re-presented to her husband as a bride and given jewelry and presents. She is returned symbolically to her virginal state. Boddy concludes that while there is a very high social value placed on virginity, it is "a social construct, not a physical condition. And it has less to do with sexual innocence than a woman's dormant fertility" (1989:55). Virgins are therefore made and the loss of virginity is, in part, reversible.

One of the most important differences in emphasis between girls' and boys' initiation has been the link to puberty. As discussed earlier, this has partly been because it is easier to date a girl's first menstruation and it is a more obvious marker of puberty than nocturnal emissions for boys. However, the assumption that girls' initiations are based on puberty, and biological change, is one that is increasingly questioned. Sherry Ortner (1974) famously based her women/nature and men/culture dichotomy on the belief that women were always associated with nature, and that it was less highly valued than culture. She also argued that male superiority was shown in its adoption of, then triumph over, women's natural functions, so that the natural would be replaced by the cultural, the biological by the man-made. This view, although heavily critiqued, has been evident in the way that many initiation rituals have been previously described. Either girls' initiations have been downplayed as private puberty rituals rather than public, group initiations, or they have been understood in terms of a girl learning that her body and its secretions were shameful. Menstrual huts, seclusions, and the idea that women became unclean at puberty were features of this approach, in various contexts including Amazonia (Fock 1963; Gregor 1985), Melanesia (Herdt 1982a), and Africa (Buckley and Gottlieb 1988). A girl's initiation was seen as reinforcing her biological destiny, while a boy's initiation was concerned with overcoming his.

There has also been an assumption that male initiatory rites, especially those which involve blood, are designed to parallel menstruation; showing that men have mastery over the natural processes of women and that men, through culture, can control biology. Margaret Mead claimed that "the initiatory cult of New Guinea is a structure which assumes that men can become men only by men's ritualizing birth and taking over – as a collective group – the functions that women perform naturally" (1949:98). In some instances informants make this connection and explicitly link ritual bloodletting and menstruation (Hogbin 1970b; Hugh-Jones 1979). However, this is not always the case and the links between male symbolic bloodletting and female menstruation may not be clear-cut. Gilbert Herdt, who has written extensively about induced nose-bleeding among the Sambia of Papua New Guinea, places it in a much broader context of gender antagonisms, the symbolic meanings of bodily fluids, and the cultural construction of male and female persons. Menstrual blood is one type of bodily fluid harmful to the Sambian male, and one whose effects he has to counteract through the ingestion of semen. Rather than seeing nose-bleeding as a form of symbolic menstruation, Herdt argues that it is more accurate to see it as a way that men get rid of the pollution that they take in when they sleep with women or as a way of becoming men through purging themselves of their early feminized state (Herdt 1982b). Gilbert Lewis (1980) also warns against drawing explicit parallels between bloodletting and menstruation. His own informants in another part of Melanesia told him that they did not believe that the two were in any way similar and used different terminology to describe them.

Marilyn Strathern (1988) argues that Western understandings of male and female do not always help in analyses of Melanesian societies and that identity in Melanesia is based on the concept of the "multiple person," made up through relationships with others. As Lutkehaus argues, "Rather than a biological given, an individual's kinship identity is considered to be the result of numerous individuals' contributions to a person's physical growth. Thus, a person's identity is an aggregate of social relations, the links he or she has to other individuals" (1995:14). Such insights have important ramifications for the study of initiation as they imply that social personhood is conferred not only by initiation, but also through intangible relationships with others. Initiation rituals are part of these relationships but they are not the conferrers of social personhood in themselves. Strathern elaborates on this, and her analysis of child socialization in Melanesia starts with the understanding that a child is an androgynous or cross-sex being, made up of both female and male elements. In order for this child to reproduce, this identity must be deconstructed or dismantled and the androgynous male/female child must be put into a same-sex state and either masculinized or feminized (Strathern 1988; Lutkehaus 1995).

> Central to many male initiation ceremonies is the transformation of the initiate not from a "female" to a "male" state, but from a cross-sex to a same-sex one. . . . Male ritual does not produce "males" out of "females," but potential "fathers" out of "persons." What is produced is a sexually activated person, a potential reproducer, an incomplete person whose identity must be completed in relation with another. (Strathern 1988, quoted in Lutkehaus 1995:15)

In Strathern's view, initiation may well be a destructive rather than a constructive process, breaking down the identity of the androgynous child and re-forming it as a same-sex person with the power of sexual reproduction.

Initiation: The End of Childhood?

One of the problems of looking at the end of childhood in terms of initiation is, as Paul Roscoe (1995) points out, that it presupposes that categories such as childhood, adolescence, and adulthood are universal classifications, albeit with different manifestations. Charles Stafford, in his book on Chinese childhoods in Taiwan, suggests that being a child is in fact a life-long status. Marriage and one's own children may confer aspects of adulthood on a person, but there is a sense in which people remain "children", even *after* becoming adults by marrying and having children of their own. Just as "social inter-actions" and some of the problems of childhood seem to start before birth, certain of the responsibilities and risks of childhood seem to push into mid-life and beyond. Women in Angang frequently make enquiries at spirit medium altars about the health and prospects of their adult sons and daughters (many of whom live in other locations in Taiwan). Often they specifically ask local gods for long-distance intervention on their behalf. These "children" have many obligations towards their ageing parents, and it is in the interest of parents for them to receive spiritual protecting well beyond childhood. (1995:28)

The relationship between initiation and the end of childhood is a com-plex one, and there is ethnographic evidence which suggests that initia-tion may not be a single ritual event which marks the end of childhood but part of a series of processes which begin at puberty (however that is defined) and end many years later, after, for example, marriage or child-birth. Simon Ottenberg (1988), for example, points out that circumcision, while dramatic, may not be the defining psychological or developmental event in a boy's life. He argues that initiation should be looked at within the context of complete childhood experiences and seen as a continuation of previous patterns of socialization and child-rearing and their impact on gender and social solidarity. By viewing initiation as a cut-off point between childhood and adulthood, anthropologists have sometimes ignored the fact that in some instances, "rites for pubescent females and males are indigenously recognized as but the first in a sequence that con tinues long after the achievement of adolescence and adulthood, emically and etically defined" (Roscoe 1995:231). Thus Roscoe (1995) argues that among the Yangoru Boiken in Melanesia there are important parallels between wealth exchanges at a girl's first menstruation and those which occur at marriage, while in other contexts rituals that begin at first menarche are only the beginning of a series of rites that conclude when a young woman is formally betrothed at her future husband's house (Sexton 1995). Nancy Lutkehaus (1995) takes this one stage further by arguing that for a young Manam Island woman, even though puberty rites are a necessary condition for the transformation to adulthood, they are viewed as socially less significant than the rites practiced at marriage and at the birth of her first child.

If childhood is seen as ending after initiation, the problem remains as to why some societies continue to insist on other forms of ceremonies and rites of passage throughout life. A more nuanced approach would be to acknowledge that adult-making rituals continue throughout a person's life-cycle and that attaining full social personhood is an ongoing process. Patricia Townsend (1995) discusses initiation rites among the Melanesian Saniyo-Hiyowe and argues that rites of widowhood mirror puberty rites and can be seen as their inverse, symbolically deconstructing the nubility and fertility celebrated at puberty. Similarly, among the Yangoru Boiken, rites of passage during adolescence have to be seen as part of a much larger sequence, which starts with a woman's initiation and continues into the next generation when her own children are initiated (Roscoe 1995). Denise Fergie (1995), working with the Babae, also in Melanesia, analyzes three separate rites of passage, which, she argues, must be seen as one sequence. The first rituals celebrate child-bearing; the second set of rituals concern mortuary rites, performed at death; and the third sequence transforms a woman's individual and named spirit into a more generalized ancestor. As such, the three have to be understood in conjunction with each other, and focusing only on initiation as the end of childhood misses the greater significance of what Roscoe calls "the total ritual corpus – the sequence of sequences – [which] is also a kind of rite of passage, moving the individual through all of the culturally important dimensions and states of human existence" (1995:232). Maurice Bloch (1992) makes a similar point in his analysis of initiation among the Orokaiva of Papua New Guinea. He describes an elaborate ritual which begins when the community is invaded by people wearing masks decorated with feathers and pigs' tusks, who chase the children and shout at them, as if they are spirits. After the hunt, the children are taken into an initiation hut in the bush, where they are not allowed to eat normal food and, symbolically, are seen as dead. In the hut, they learn to play the sacred flutes, and conduct spirit dances. After several years, they return to the village as hunters, where once they had been prey. Here initiation is not part of a linear and teleological transformation from one state to another, but part of a continual exchange between the material and spiritual worlds, characterized by inversions of roles, changes in status, and the ultimate flexibility and transformation between adults, children, pigs, and spirits.

> Symbolically, emotionally and physically all the villagers accompany the children in their journey from the village to the bush; all therefore become, to a degree, hunted pigs or prey, and all are assimilated to the children as

they return as hunters. . . . Although in the initial hunt the adults of the village are associated with the invading spirits (after all it is they who represent them), there is also an element of themselves which is being chased round the village, since it is their children, part of themselves, who are hunted. Like the children, the adults are both hunted and hunters. And this is even true of the spirits. Like the children, they were driven into the bush by death, and like the children they will also return to the village as hunters. This will occur at the next initiation, when the masks will represent them violently crossing back over the boundary between the bush and the village.

All human generations, past, present and future, are therefore involved in this oscillating progressing spiral between bush and village, hunted and hunter, pig and spirit, both in the initiation ritual and always. (Bloch 1992:17)

In all these instances, to study only the initiation rites carried out in puberty is to miss the point that childhood is not always brought to an end by initiation, and that attaining social maturity can take a lifetime.

Conclusion

Adolescence, like childhood, is a much-contested state, which defies easy definition. There is undoubtedly a whole book to be written solely about this transitional and transformative stage, which is neither childhood nor adulthood. Initiation is a useful way of looking at the division between childhood and adulthood, but it does not always provide a definitive break. Although the meanings, functions, and symbolism of initiation ceremonies do not occupy the central place in anthropological theory and ethnographic description that they once did, by analyzing the main themes that anthropologists have previously identified in their studies, and by examining the various ways of understanding such rituals, it is clear that the transitions between childhood and adulthood have always been a concern to many anthropologists, even those with no stated interest in children and childhood. Childhood may not come to an end at initiation, but initiation does signal an important change in the status of children and the expectations placed on them. More generally, adolescence is best looked at as a transitional phase with elements of both adulthood and childhood, a time when children are unlearning some of their past behaviors, attitudes, and social statuses while learning new ones that will be needed in their future roles and lives. Whether adolescence is a time of constructing the adult social person or deconstructing the immature child, of making men and women or unmaking the androgynous child, whether it is a bridge between childhood and adulthood or simply one step of many throughout the life-cycle, it raises profound questions about the nature of childhood and the making of social maturity.

CONCLUSION

For over a century, anthropologists have discussed ideas about childhood and children's roles in social organization, although it is true that this work has often been sporadic and patchy, and for a fully comprehensive "anthropology of childhood" there were gaps that needed to be filled, questions to be asked, and new methods required for rounding out the study of childhood and making it part of the anthropological mainstream. The new child-centered anthropology of the last 30 years has gone a long way in addressing these problems and has revolutionized studies of children, enabling anthropologists to gain important new insights into children's lives and experiences. In particular its insights into children's own understandings of the realities of their lives have opened up new ways of thinking about children, and the important contribution that children themselves can make has been generally recognized. It has given the study of childhood a new impetus and legitimated it as a serious topic of research, showing that there can, and indeed should, be an anthropology of childhood and that it is a viable and dynamic area of specialization. What the new study of childhood has been less successful in doing is acknowledging its debt to the past and recognizing the strengths of previous works. It may be true that children's lives and worldviews were often overlooked, but ideas about childhood, even if they are articulated by adults, or only implicit in texts, do exist and can prove useful. I hope that this book has shown how contemporary studies of children can use, and build on, this previous work productively. As each of these chapters has shown, anthropological studies of pregnancy, birth, infancy, socialization, discipline, kinship, initiation, and life-cycles have much to contribute to the study of contemporary childhood and remain relevant to understanding children's lives.

Now that there is a large, and still growing, number of ethnographies of children, and their importance as active meaning-makers is acknowledged, it is time to hope that an anthropology of childhood will dissolve into mainstream anthropology and its concerns and interests be as central to the discipline as those of gender. There is an interesting parallel here with the work done on the new reproductive technologies. Despite a large canon of material on this subject, its importance lies not in that it forms a new subdiscipline of anthropology, but in that it has revitalized studies of kinship and addressed issues that had always been central to anthropological inquiry. Ideally an anthropology of childhood should do the same, and the study of children, their social worlds, the care they receive, and the contested nature of childhood should need no apology and should easily and lucidly relate to complementary and wide-ranging anthropological concerns of personhood, kinship, and social organization. Exploring ideas about childhood can be a way of examining boundaries and differences between children and adults, the living and the dead, and the fully and the potentially social. It can be a means of talking about the nature of children at all stages in their development: before birth, at birth and after birth, as part of this world, and also as part of other worlds. This book has attempted to look at what has been achieved so far, to acknowledge the importance of children, and to look forward to a time when the study of every aspect of the life-cycle is part of the mainstream.

Studying childhood is also a way of studying change, and it is often through looking at children's lives that these changes become most apparent. Political upheaval, globalization, economic development, and the spread of education and human rights have all had an impact on the ways in which children are understood and how they are treated. Chapter 6, for example, discussed the case of Tonga, where the harsh punishment and discipline of children has a long history but where, confronted with the human rights legislation adopted by the government, beatings of children are becoming less acceptable. Ideas about adoption and fosterage, as chapter 4 showed, also change in relation to external circumstances, and, even in communities with long cultural traditions of fosterage, ideas about who is the best person to care for a child, and where that child should be looked after, are under discussion. Similarly, Westernized concepts of adolescence are relatively new in many societies, and while adolescence has very different local manifestations, the adoption of the concept is a symptom of the impact of globalized ideas about education and modernization. This change is not limited to non-Western societies, and in Europe and North America children's lives have also altered dramatically in the last 50 years. Children are a cause for concern, and a focus for state intervention, in an unprecedented way and they have a social prominence far beyond that of previous generations. Politicians, of all convictions and all parties, now use the image of the child, and particularly the figure of the innocent child, to further their campaigns while simultaneously claiming to place the child above and beyond politics. As Henry Jenkins has written about North America:

> The dominant conception of childhood innocence presumes that children exist in a space beyond, above, outside the political; we imagine them to be noncombatants whom we protect from the harsh realities of the adult world, including the mud splattering of partisan politics. Yet, in reality, almost every major political battle of the twentieth century has been fought on the backs of our children, from the economic reforms of the Progressive Era (which sought to protect immigrant children from the sweatshop owners) and the social readjustments of the civil rights era (which often circulated around the images of black and white children playing together) to contemporary anxieties about the digital revolution (which often depict the wide-eyed child as subject to the corruptions of cybersex and porn websites). The innocent child carries the rhetorical force of such arguments; we are constantly urged to take action to protect our children. (1998:2)

The child is both reified and politicized, and one of the central contributions that anthropologists can bring to contemporary debates about childhood is their understanding that there is no such thing as "the child," and particularly not "the innocent child." There have been many examples given throughout this book that show quite clearly that the child is not defined by his or her innocence, and, indeed, the very sense of this term is questionable and capable of supporting several overlapping meanings. Using the term "childhood innocence" is loaded with culturally specific connotations. In the West the concept of a child's innocence is related to Christian notions of sin and redemption. It is also closely related to ideas about sexuality, so that an innocent child is a child who is unknowing about and uncorrupted by sex, a meaningless definition in other places outside the West. In other instances innocence means being shielded from certain types of knowledge, not only sexual but also knowledge of the outside world, particularly from violence or the negative images purveyed by television. The importance of an anthropological perspective on children's lives is that it shows so clearly that the concept of the innocent child, so important to national and international legislation, is but one cultural construct among many others. There is nothing natural in how children grow up, what they know, or the choice of topics from which they must be protected.

This is more than simply an academic exercise in cross-cultural comparisons. Another theme that has come out of this book is that how childhood is conceptualized has a direct impact on how children are treated. Loading connotations of innocence onto childhood can be extremely dangerous to children who do not conform. If children are not innocent, because they have experience of sex, because they have committed crimes, or because they have "guilty knowledge," they become problematic. It is only the right sort of children who can call on the protection and nurturance of adults, as Nancy Scheper-Hughes and Howard Stein argue: "It is the 'bad' (i.e. impulsive, lazy, aggressive, sexual) children who are being disciplined and purged (to a great extent representing the young members of already stigmatized and therefore suspect and vulnerable ethnic, racial and class minorities), and it is the 'good' (i.e. the innocent, a-sexual) children who are understood as being rescued" (1987:346). Anthropologists who have worked with vulnerable children outside the West, such as street children, child prostitutes, or child soldiers, have noted the same phenomenon, with children being judged by often alien standards of innocence and denied help if they fall short of an unfamiliar ideal.

It is not surprising, therefore, that studying children, their lives and representations, has become a highly political act. The rise of child-focused anthropology and its insistence on child informants comes out of changing ideas about childhood in the West and the reconfiguration of adult/child relationships. The idea of children as equal participants in society, with a voice worth hearing, is now commonplace, and ethnographies that treat children as insubstantial bystanders on the margins of society are seen as outdated and of limited use in understanding children's own worldviews. For child-centered anthropologists it has meant, in Robert LeVine's words, using "an anthropology of childhood as a political weapon against injustice" (2003:5) by reclaiming children from the ethnographic margins and taking their views seriously. It has meant examining the cultural politics of childhood, analyzing the impacts, both good and bad, of globalization, looking at how images and representations of the child are deployed, the effects this has on children's lives, and how children understand these changes. However, it is also important to remain aware that contemporary ways of studying children are as historically and culturally situated as any other. Many of the discussions of children found within previous ethnography did deny children's capabilities and potential, but these were products of their time. Children were of limited interest in the field because they were also of little concern at home. Just as it is important not to judge childhoods elsewhere by our own contemporary constructions of childhood, so it is vital not to dismiss previous ethnography because it is not informed by modern notions of equality between adults and children.

The concern in anthropology over children mirrors that of the broader concerns in Western societies. Indeed, within anthropology, and throughout the social sciences, it is very noticeable that there is now an increased focus on the earliest, rather than the final, part of the life-cycle and that there are very few ethnographies of the elderly or studies of ideas about old age. Again, this can be related to the ways that old people are conceptualized within Anglo-American societies and the consequent impact this has on the choice of ethnographic focus. Old people tend to be placed in the same position as children used to be: ignored, marginalized, viewed as economically useless and treated as being of limited interest. Anthropologists have examined death and funerary rituals, but the lives and experiences of older people, especially older women, remain relatively unexamined. It is possible to speculate that the next area of anthropological concern will be on those nearing the end of their lives, and that all the arguments about how anthropologists have ignored children will be revisited in reference to older people.

In the early years of the 21st century, however, it remains children, not the elderly, who are identified as the group most in need of social concern and intervention. Studies of childhood, especially of problematic childhoods, are increasingly tied to the need to act on behalf of children, and there has been a strong imperative amongst those who work with children to use their work to benefit children's lives. Partly because funding bodies increasingly demand that work be relevant and have some tangible benefit outside the academy and partly because childhood, and especially children in trouble or distress, remain highly emotive topics, the interplay between academic research and the promotion of children's well-being has become central to the study of childhood. Laurence Brockliss and George Rousseau, writing as historians but with an analysis equally pertinent to anthropologists, have argued for the need to engage critically with issues of childhood, not just as a way of filling the gaps left by previous historians, or as a bridge between previous eras and the contemporary world, but as a way of improving children's lives and contributing to their wellbeing.

> If we are to make the right decisions for the twenty-first century, we also need to consult the past to comprehend what happened to children in other revolutionary eras. The historical gaze is all the more crucial in this case in that the victimization of children in its many forms represents the one topic today we cannot quite bring ourselves to discuss calmly. It often seems to lie beyond all ordinary decency and to be the last aspect of modern life we have left to unpack. (2003:4)

Despite the many difficulties, I believe that childhood can be studied from a wide variety of perspectives, each of which can contribute to a fuller and more rounded anthropology of childhood. Childhood, its local manifestations, the ways in which societies adapt to their youngest members, the values they instill in them, and how they develop are all aspects of children's lives that need to be studied and understood if we are to learn how children grow up. All of the ethnographies discussed in this book have contributed to this picture and should be celebrated for what they can tell us about children's lives, even if the picture they give is not always as complete as we might like. Each one gives us valuable information about the lives of children as well as about the society to which they belong, and one cannot be understood without the other. Indeed, if there is one overriding conclusion from this book it is that the study of childhood need not be an exercise in looking for dichotomies. It is not necessary to understand children as either beings or becomings, active or passive, agentic or helpless, informants or the spoken for, the complete or the lacking. They, like adults, can be all of these things, and the best we can do is to analyze them within their own context, examining indigenous ideas about the relationships between adults and children and the consequent expectations placed on children. In all societies, children exist through relationships with others, both adults and other children, and we cannot understand their lives in isolation. Children can sometimes seem like small strangers to adult anthropologists, but they are worth drawing closer to and getting to know more fully.

BIBLIOGRAPHY

Aarre, K., 2000 Changing Attitudes towards Children in Care in Portugal in the 1990s: A Case Study of a Children's Home. Unpublished D.Phil. thesis, Oxford University.

Abrahams, R., 1972 Spirit, Twins, and Ashes in Labwor, Northern Uganda. *In* The Interpretation of Ritual: Essays in Honour of A. I. Richards. J. La Fontaine, ed. pp. 115–134. London: Tavistock.

Achebe, C., 1958 Things Fall Apart. London: Heinemann.

Achebe, C., 1980 Literary Insights into the *Ogbanje* Phenomenon. Journal of African Studies 7:31–38.

Achebe, C., 1986 The World of the *Ogbanje*. Enugu, Nigeria: Fourth Dimension Publishing.

Adler, P., and P. Adler, 1998 Peer Power: Preadolescent Culture and Identity. New Brunswick, NJ: Rutgers University Press.

Ahmed, S., J. Bwana, E. Guga, et al., 1999 Children in Need of Special Protection Measures: A Tanzanian Study. Dar es Salaam: UNICEF.

Alber, E., 2004 "The Real Parents Are the Foster Parents": Social Parenthood among the Baatombu in Northern Benin. *In* Cross-Cultural Approaches to Adoption. F. Bowie, ed. pp. 33–47. London: Routledge.

Anderson, A., 2004 Adoption and Belonging in Wogeo, Papua New Guinea. *In* Cross-Cultural Approaches to Adoption. F. Bowie, ed. pp. 111–126. London: Routledge.

Anderson-Levitt, K., 2005 The Schoolyard Gate: Schooling and Childhood in Global Perspective. Journal of Social History 38:987–1006.

Aptekar, L., 1988 Street Children of Cali. Durham, NC: Duke University Press.

Ardener, E., 1975 Belief and the Problem of Women. *In* Perceiving Women. S. Ardener, ed. pp. 1–17. London: J. M. Dent.

Ariès, P., 1979[1962] Centuries of Childhood: A Social History of Family Life. R. Baldick, trans. London: Penguin.

Ashley-Montague, M. F., 1937 Coming into Being among the Australian Aborigines: A Study of the Procreative Beliefs of the Native Tribes of Australia. London: Routledge.

Avedon, E., and B. Sutton-Smith, 1971 The Study of Games. London: Wiley.

Azu, D., 1974 The Ga Family and Social Change. Leiden: Afrika-Studiecentrum.

Baker, R., 1998 Negotiating Identities: A Study of the Lives of Street Children in Nepal. Unpublished Ph.D. thesis, University of Durham.

Baker, R., C. Panter-Brick, and A. Todd, 1996 Methods Used in Research with Street Children in Nepal. Childhood 3:171–193.

Bargach, J., 2002 Orphans of Islam: Family, Abandonment, and Secret Adoption in Morocco. Oxford: Rowman and Littlefield.

Barnes, P., and M.-J. Kehily, 2003 Play and the Cultures of Childhood. In Children's Cultural Worlds. M.-J. Kehily and J. Swann, eds. pp. 1–46. Chichester: John Wiley.

Barr, R., 1990 The Normal Crying Curve: What Do We Really Know? Developmental Medicine and Child Neurology 32:356–362.

Barr, R., M. Konner, R. Bakeman, and L. Adamson, 1991 Crying in !Kung San Infants: A Test of the Cultural Specificity Hypothesis. Developmental Medicine and Child Neurology 33:601–610.

Bascom, W., 1969 The Yoruba of Southwest Nigeria. New York: Holt, Rinehart and Winston.

Bastian, M., 2001 "The Demon Superstition": Abominable Twins and Mission Culture in Onitsha History. Ethnology 40:13–28.

Bates, D., 1938 The Passing of the Aborigines: A Lifetime Spent among the Natives of Australia. London: James Murray.

Beckerman, S., and P. Valentine, eds., 2002 Cultures of Multiple Fathers: The Theory and Practice of Partible Paternity in Lowland South America. Gainesville: University of Florida Press.

Beier, H. U., 1954 Spirit Children among the Yoruba. African Affairs 53:328–331.

Belaunde, L. E., 2001 Menstruation, Birth Observances and the Couple's Love amongst the Airo-Pai of Amazonian Peru. In Managing Reproductive Life: Cross-Cultural Themes in Fertility and Sexuality. S. Tremayne, ed. pp. 127–139. Oxford: Berghahn.

Benedict, R., 1932 Configurations of Culture in North America. American Anthropologist 34:1–27.

Benedict, R. 1934 Patterns of Culture. Boston: Houghton Mifflin.

Benedict, R., 1938 Continuities and Discontinuities in Cultural Conditioning. Psychiatry 1:161–167.

Benthall, J. 1992 A Late Developer? The Ethnography of Children. Anthropology Today 8(2):23–35.

Berlan, A., 2005 Education and Child Labour among Cocoa Producers in Ghana: The Anthropological Case for a Re-evaluation. Unpublished D.Phil. thesis, Oxford University.

Bernat, J. C., 1999 Children and the Politics of Violence in a Haitian Context: Statist Violence, Scarcity and Street Child Agency in Port-au-Prince. Critique of Anthropology 19:121–138.

Best, J., 1990 Threatened Children: Rhetoric and Concern about Child-Victims. Chicago: University of Chicago Press.

Bettelheim, B., 1955 Symbolic Wounds: Puberty Rites and the Envious Male. London: Thames and Hudson.

Beverly, E., and R. D. Whittemore, 1993 Mandinka Children and the Geography of Well-Being. Ethos 21:235–272.

Bird-David, N., 2005 Studying Children in "Hunter-Gatherer" Societies: Reflections from a Nayaka Perspective. In Hunter-Gatherer Childhoods: Evolutionary, Developmental and Cultural Perspectives. B. Hewlett and M. Lamb, eds. pp. 92–101. New York: Aldine.

Black, M., 1994 Home Truths. New Internationalist 252:11–13.

Blanchet, T., 1996 Lost Innocence, Stolen Childhoods. Dhaka: University of Dhaka Press.

Blanc-Szanton, C., 1985 Gender and Inter-Generational Resource Allocations: Thai and Sino-Thai Households in Central Thailand. In Structures and Strategies: Women, Work and Family in Asia. L. Dube and R. Palriwala, eds. pp. 79–102. New Delhi: Sage.

Bledsoe, C., 1990a The Politics of Children: Fosterage and the Social Management of Fertility among the Mende of Sierra Leone. In Births and Power: Social Change and the Politics of Reproduction. W. P. Handwerker, ed. pp. 81–100. Boulder, CO: Westview Press.

Bledsoe, C., 1990b No Success without Struggle: Social Mobility and Hardship for Foster Children in Sierra Leone. Man (N.S.) 25:70–88.

Bledsoe, C., 1992 The Cultural Transformation of Western Education in Sierra Leone. Africa 62:182–202.

Bloch, M., 1992 Prey into Hunter: The Politics of Religious Experience. Cambridge: Cambridge University Press.

Bloch, M., and S. Adler, 1994 African Children's Play and the Emergence of the Sexual Division of Labor. In Children's Play in Diverse Cultures. J. Roopnarine, J. Johnson, and F. Hopper, eds. pp. 148–178. Albany: State University of New York Press.

Bluebond-Langner, M., 1978 The Private Worlds of Dying Children. Princeton: Princeton University Press.

Bluebond-Langner, M., and J. Korbin, 2007 Challenges and Opportunities in the Anthropology of Childhood. American Anthropologist 109:241–246.

Blurton-Jones, N., K. Hawkes, and J. O'Connell, 2005 Older Hadza Men and Women as Helpers: Residence Data. In Hunter-Gatherer Childhoods: Evolutionary, Developmental and Cultural Perspectives. B. Hewlett and M. Lamb, eds. pp. 214–236. New York: Aldine.

Boas, F., 1916 New Evidence on the Instability of Human Types. Proceedings of the National Academy of Sciences of the United States of America 2:713–718.

Boas, F., 1974[1911] The Instability of Human Types. In The Shaping of American Anthropology, 1883–1911: A Franz Boas Reader. G. W. Stocking, ed. pp. 214–218. New York: Basic Books.

Boddy, J., 1989 Wombs and Alien Spirits: Women, Men, and the Zar Cult in Northern Sudan. Madison: University of Wisconsin Press.

Bodenhorn, B., 1988 Whales, Souls, Children and Other Things that are Good to Share: Core Metaphors in a Contemporary Whaling Society. Cambridge Anthropology 13:1–19.

Bohannon, L., 1954 Return to Laughter. London: Victor Gollancz.

Bourgois, P., 1998 Families and Children in Pain in the US Inner City. In Small Wars: The Cultural Politics of Childhood. N. Scheper-Hughes and C. Sargent, eds. 331–351. Berkeley: University of California Press.

Bowie, F., ed., 2004 Cross-Cultural Approaches to Adoption. London: Routledge.

Bowlby, J., 1953 Child Care and the Growth of Love. Harmondsworth: Penguin.

Boyden, J., 1997 Childhood and the Policy Makers: A Comparative Perspective on the Globalization of Childhood. In Constructing and Deconstructing Childhood: Contemporary Issues in the Sociological Study of Childhood. A. James and A. Prout, eds. pp. 190–299. London: Falmer Press.

Boyden, J., B. Ling, and W. Myers, 1998 What Works for Working Children. Florence: Rädda Barnen and UNICEF.

Brain, R., 1970 Child Witches. In Witchcraft Confessions and Accusations. M. Douglas, ed. pp. 161–182. London: Tavistock.

Briggs, J., 1970 Never in Anger: Portrait of an Eskimo Family. Cambridge, MA: Harvard University Press.

Briggs, J., 1991 Expecting the Unexpected: Canadian Inuit Training for an Experimental Lifestyle. Ethos 19:259–287.

Brockliss, L., and G. Rousseau, 2003 The History Child. Oxford Magazine, 0th Week, Michaelmas Term:4–7.

Brown, J., 1963 A Cross-Cultural Study of Female Initiation Rites. American Anthropologist 65:837–853.

Buckley, T., and A. Gottlieb, 1988 Blood Magic: The Anthropology of Menstruation. Berkeley: University of California Press.

Bukowski, W. M., A. F. Newcomb, and W. W. Hartup, 1996 The Company They Keep: Friendship in Childhood and Adolescence. Cambridge: Cambridge University Press.

Burbank, V. K., 1988 Aboriginal Adolescence: Maidenhood in an Australian Community. New Brunswick, NJ: Rutgers University Press.

Burman, E., 1996 Local, Global and Globalized: Child Development and International Child Rights Legislation. Childhood 3(1):45–66.

Burr, R., 2006 Vietnam's Children in a Changing World. New Brunswick, NJ: Rutgers University Press.

Burr, R., and H. Montgomery, 2003 Family, Kinship and Beyond. In Childhoods in Context. J. Maybin and M. Woodhead, eds. pp. 39–80. Chichester: John Wiley.

Burton, M., and D. White, 1987 Cross-Cultural Surveys Today. Annual Review of Anthropology 16:143–160.

Burton, R., and J. Whiting, 1961 The Absent Father and Cross-Sex Identity. Merrill-Palmer Quarterly of Behavior and Development 7(2):85–95.

Caplan, P., 1987 The Cultural Construction of Sexuality. London: Tavistock.

Carsten, J., 1991 Children in Between: Fostering and the Process of Kinship on Pulau Langkawi, Malaysia. Man (N.S.) 26:425–443.

Carvel, J., 2001 Nurses Upset over Foetus Disposals. Guardian, May 22.

Cassell, J., 1987 Children in the Field: Anthropological Experiences. Philadelphia: Temple University Press.

Caudill, W., and C. Schooler, 1973 Child Behavior and Child Rearing in Japan and the United States: An Interim Report. Journal of Nervous and Mental Disease 157:323–338.

Caudill, W., and H. Weinstein, 1969 Maternal Care and Infant Behavior in Japan and America. Psychiatry 32:12–43.

Cecil, R., 1996 An Insignificant Event? Literary and Anthropological Perspectives on Pregnancy Loss. In The Anthropology of Pregnancy Loss: Comparative Studies in Miscarriage, Stillbirth and Neonatal Death. R. Cecil, ed. pp. 1–16. Oxford: Berg.

Chagnon, N., 1968 Yanamamö: The Fierce People. New York: Holt, Rinehart and Winston.

Chappel, T. H. J., 1974 The Yoruba Cult of Twins in Historical Perspective. Africa 44:250–265.

Chen, X., D. French, and B. Schneider, 2006 Culture and Peer Relations. In Peer Relationships in Cultural Context. X. Chen, D. French, and B. Schneider, eds. pp. 3–20. Cambridge: Cambridge University Press.

Chin, E., 2001 Feminist Theory and the Ethnography of Children's Worlds: Barbie in New Haven, Connecticut. In Children and Anthropology: Perspectives for the 21st Century. H. Schwartzman, ed. pp. 129–148. Westport, CT: Bergin and Garvey.

Chisholm, J., 1983 Navajo Infancy: An Ethological Study of Child Development. New York: Aldine.

Chisholm, J., 1996 Learning "Respect for Everything": Navajo Images of Development. In Images of Childhood. C. P. Hwang, M. E. Lamb, and I. E. Sigel, eds. pp. 167–184. Hillsdale, NJ: Erlbaum.

Chodorow, N., 1978 The Reproduction of Mothering: Psychoanalysis and the Sociology of Gender. Berkeley: University of California Press.

Christensen, P., 1999 Vulnerable Bodies: Cultural Meanings of Child, Body and Illness. In The Body, Childhood and Society. A. Prout, ed., pp. 38–59. London: Macmillan.

Cicirelli, V., 1994 Sibling Relationships in Cross-Cultural Perspective. Journal of Marriage and the Family 56:7–20.

Cohen, S. 1973 Folk Devils and Moral Panics: The Creation of the Mods and Rockers. London: Paladin.

Collier, J., and S. J. Yanagisako, eds. 1987 Gender and Kinship: Essays Towards a Unified Analysis. Stanford: Stanford University Press.

Colson, E., 1960 The Social Organization of the Gwembe Tonga. Manchester: Manchester University Press.

Condon, R., 1987 Inuit Youth: Growth and Change in the Canadian Arctic. New Brunswick, NJ: Rutgers University Press.

Condon, R., 1990 The Rise of Adolescence: Social Change and Life Stage Dilemmas in the Central Canadian Arctic. Human Organization 49:266–279.

Condon, R., 1995 The Rise of the Leisure Class: Adolescence and Recreational Acculturation in the Canadian Arctic. Ethos 23:47–68.

Condon, R., and P. Stern, 1993 Gender-Role Preference, Gender Identity, and Gender Socialization among Contemporary Inuit Youth. Ethos 21:384–416.

Conklin, B., 2001 Consuming Grief: Compassionate Cannibalism in an Amazonian Society. Austin: University of Texas Press.

Conklin, B., and L. Morgan, 1996 Babies, Bodies, and the Production of Personhood in North America and a Native Amazonian Society. Ethos 24:657–694.

Corsaro, W., 1985 Friendship and Peer Culture in the Early Years. Norwood, NJ: Ablex.

Corsaro, W., 1988 Routines in the Peer Culture of American and Italian Nursery School Children. Sociology of Education 61:1–14.

Corsaro, W., 1992 Interpretative Reproduction in Children's Peer Cultures. Social Psychology Quarterly 55:160–177.

Corsaro, W., 2003 We're Friends, Right? Inside Kids' Culture. Washington, DC: Joseph Henry Press.

Corsaro, W., and D. Eder, 1990 Children's Peer Cultures. Annual Review of Sociology 16:197–220.

Corsaro, W., and T. Rizzo, 1998 Discussione and Friendship: Socialization Processes in the Peer Culture of Italian Nursery School Children. American Sociological Review 53:879–894.

Corsaro, W., L. Molinari, K. Hadley, and H. Sugioka, 2003 Keeping and Making Friends: Italian Children's Transition from Preschool to Elementary School. Social Psychology Quarterly 66:272–292.

Cowan, J., 1997 The Elements of the Aborigine Tradition. Shaftesbury: Element.

Cowan, J., M. B. Dembour, and R. Wilson, eds. 2001 Culture and Rights: Anthropological Perspectives. Cambridge: Cambridge University Press.

Crocker, W., and J. Crocker, 1994 The Canela: Bonding through Kinship, Ritual and Sex. Fort Worth, TX: Harcourt Brace College Publishers.

Culin, S., 1891 Street Games of Boys in Brooklyn. Journal of American Folklore 4(14):221–237.

Culin, S., 1898 American Indian Games. Journal of American Folklore 11(43):245–252.

Culin, S., 1899 Hawaiian Games. American Anthropologist 1:201–247.

D'Amato, J., 1993 Resistance and Compliance in Minority Classrooms. *In* Minority Education: Anthropological Perspectives. E. Jacob and C. Jordan, eds. pp. 181–207. Norwood, NJ: Ablex.

Davis, S. D., and D. Davis, 1989 Adolescence in a Moroccan Town: Making Social Sense. New Brusnwick, NJ: Rutgers University Press.

de Berry, J., 1999 Life after Loss: An Anthropological Study of Post-War Recovery, Teso, East Uganda, with Special Reference to Young People. Unpublished Ph.D. thesis, University of London.

de Boeck, F., 2005 The Divine Seed: Children, Gift and Witchcraft in the Democratic Republic of Congo. *In* Makers and Breakers: Children and Youth in Postcolonial Africa. A. Honwana and F. de Boeck, eds. pp. 188–214. Oxford: James Currey.

Delaney, C., 2000 Making Babies in a Turkish Village. *In* A World of Babies: Imagined Childcare Guides for Seven Societies. J. DeLoache and A. Gottlieb, eds. pp. 117–144. Cambridge: Cambridge University Press.

de Mause, L., 1974 The Evolution of Childhood. *In* The History of Childhood. L. de Mause, ed. pp. 1–73. New York: Psychohistory Press.

Demian, M., 2004 Transactions in Rights, Transactions in Children: A View of Adoption from Papua New Guinea. *In* Cross-Cultural Approaches to Adoption. F. Bowie, ed. pp. 97–110. London: Routledge.

Demos, J., and V. Demos, 1969 Adolescence in Historical Perspective. Journal of Marriage and the Family 31:632–638.

Descola, P., 1996 Spears of Twilight: Life and Death in the Amazon Jungle. London: HarperCollins.

Dettwyler, K., 1994 Dancing Skeletons: Life and Death in West Africa. Prospect Heights, IL: Waveland.

Diduk, S., 1993 Twins, Ancestors and Socio-Economic Change in Kedjom Society. Man (N.S.) 28:551–571.

Diduk, S., 2001 Twinship and Juvenile Power: The Ordinariness of the Extraordinary. Ethnology 40:29–43.

Diener, M., 2000 Gift from the Gods: A Balinese Guide to Early Child Rearing. *In* A World of Babies: Imagined Childcare Guides for Seven Societies.

J. DeLoache and A. Gottlieb, eds. pp. 91–116. Cambridge: Cambridge University Press.

Dirie, W., and C. Miller, 1999 Desert Flower: The Extraordinary Journey of a Desert Nomad. London: Virago.

Djamour, J., 1952 Adoption of Children among Singapore Malaysians. Journal of the Royal Anthropological Institute of Great Britain and Ireland 82:159–168.

Donnelly, M., 2005 Putting Corporal Punishment of Children in Historical Perspective. In Corporal Punishment of Children in Theoretical Perspective. M. Donnelly and M. A. Straus, eds. pp. 41–54. New Haven: Yale University Press.

Donnelly, M., and M. A. Straus, eds. 2005 Corporal Punishment of Children in Theoretical Perspective. New Haven: Yale University Press.

Dopamu, A., 2006 Change and Continuity: The Yoruba Belief in Life after Death [online]. [Accessed April 1, 2008]. Available from World Wide Web: http://www.metanexus.net/conferences/pdf/conference2006/Dopamu.pdf.

Driver, H., 1969 Girls' Puberty Rites and Matrilocal Residence. American Anthropologist 71:905–908.

Driver, H., 1971 Brown and Driver on Girls' Puberty Rites Again. American Anthropologist 73:1261–1262.

Du Bois, C., 1944 The People of Alor: A Social-Psychological Study of an East Indian Island. Minneapolis: Minnesota University Press.

Dunstan, G. R., 1988 The Human Embryo in the Western Moral Tradition. In The Status of the Human Embryo: Perspectives from Moral Tradition. G. R. Dunstan and M. Seller, eds. pp. 39–57. Oxford: Oxford University Press.

Eder, D., 1985 The Cycle of Popularity: Interpersonal Relations among Female Adolescents. Sociology of Education 58:154–165.

Edwards, C. P., 2000 Children's Play in Cross-Cultural Perspective: A New Look at the Six Cultures Study. Cross-Cultural Research 34:318–338.

Ehrenreich, B., and D. English, 1979 For Her Own Good: 150 Years of the Experts' Advice to Women. London: Pluto Press.

Einarsdóttir, J., 2000 "Tired of Weeping": Child Death and Mourning among Papel Mothers in Guinea-Bissau. Stockholm: Stockholm Studies in Social Anthropology.

El Saadawi, N., 1980 The Hidden Face of Eve: Women in the Arab World. London: Zed Books.

Embler, C., and M. Embler, 2005 Explaining Corporal Punishment of Children: A Cross-Cultural Study. American Anthropologist 107:609–619.

Ennew, J., 1980 The Western Isles Today. Cambridge: Cambridge University Press.

Ennew, J., 1986 The Sexual Exploitation of Children. Cambridge: Polity Press.

Ennew, J., 1993 Maids of All Work. New Internationalist, February:11–13.

Ennew, J., and V. Morrow, 2002 Releasing the Energy: Celebrating the Inspiration of Sharon Stephens. Childhood 9:5–17.

Ennew, J., and J. Swart-Kruger, 2003 Homes, Places and Spaces in the Construction of Street Children and Street Youth. Children, Youth and Environments [online], 13 (1) [Accessed April 1, 2008]. Available from World Wide Web: http://www.colorado.edu/journals/cye/13_1/Vol13_1Articles/CYE_CurrentIssue_ArticleIntro_Kruger_Ennew.htm.

Ephirim-Donkor, A., 1997 African Spirituality: On Becoming Ancestors. Trenton, NJ: Africa World Press.

Epstein, D., 1997 Cultures of Schooling/Cultures of Sexuality. International Journal of Inclusive Education 1:37–53.

Erikson, E. H., 1963 Youth: Change and Challenge. New York: Basic Books.

Erikson, E. H., 1968 Identity: Youth and Crisis. London: Faber and Faber.

Errington, S., 1987 Incestuous Twins and the House Societies of Insular Southeast Asia. Cultural Anthropology 2:403–444.

Evans-Pritchard, E. E., 1936 Customs and Beliefs Relating to Twins among the Nilotic Nuer. Uganda Journal 3:230–238.

Evans-Pritchard, E. E., 1951 Kinship and Marriage among the Nuer. Oxford: Oxford University Press.

Evans-Pritchard, E. E., 1956 Nuer Religion. Oxford: Clarendon Press.

Evans-Pritchard, E. E., 1965 The Comparative Method in Social Anthropology. In The Position of Women in Primitive Societies: And Other Essays in Social Anthropology. E. E. Evans-Pritchard, ed. pp. 13–36. London: Faber and Faber.

Fergie, D., 1995 Transforming Women: Being and Becoming in an Island Melanesian Society. In Gender Rituals: Female Initiation in Melanesia. N. C. Lutkehaus and P. B. Roscoe, eds. pp. 113–130. London: Routledge.

Ferme, M., 2001 The Underneath of Things: Violence, History, and the Everyday in Sierra Leone. Berkeley: University of California Press.

Fine, G. A., 1987 With the Boys: Little League Baseball and Preadolescent Culture. Chicago: University of Chicago Press.

Firestone, S., 1970 The Dialectic of Sex: The Case for Feminist Revolution. London: Jonathan Cape.

Firth, R., 1936 We, the Tikopia: A Sociological Study of Kinship in Primitive Polynesia. London: George Allen and Unwin.

Firth, R., 1956 Ceremonies for Children and Social Frequency in Tikopia. Oceania 27:12–55.

Firth, R., 1966 Twins, Birds and Vegetables: Problems of Identification in Primitive Religious Thought. Man (N.S.) 1:1–17.

Fock, N., 1963 Waiwai: Religion and Society of an Amazonian Tribe. Copenhagen: The National Museum.

Ford, N., and S. Saiprasert, 1993 Destinations Unknown: The Gender Construction and Changing Nature of the Sexual Lifestyles of Thai Youth. Paper presented at the Fifth International Conference on Thai Studies, SOAS, London.

Fordham, G., 1995 Whisky, Women and Song: Alcohol and AIDS in Northern Thailand. Australian Journal of Anthropology 6(3):154–177.

Fordham, G., 1998 Northern Thai Male Culture and the Assessment of HIV Risk: Towards a New Approach. Crossroads 12:77–164.

Fortes, M., 1949 The Web of Kinship among the Tallensi: The Second Part of an Analysis of the Social Structure of a Trans-Volta Tribe. Oxford: Oxford University Press.

Fortes, M., 1950 Kinship and Marriage among the Ashanti. In African Systems of Kinship and Marriage. A. R. Radcliffe-Brown and D. Forde, eds. pp. 252–284. Oxford: Oxford University Press.

Fortes, M., 1970 Social and Psychological Aspects of Education in Taleland. In From Child to Adult: Studies in the Anthropology of Education. J. Middleton, ed. pp. 14–74. New York: Natural History Press.

Fortes, M., 1974 The First Born. Journal of Child Psychology and Psychiatry 15(2): 81–104.

Foster, A. M., 1991 Women's Comprehensive Health Care in Contemporary Tunisia. Unpublished D.Phil. thesis, Oxford University.

Fox, R., 1983 The Red Lamp of Incest: An Enquiry into the Origins of Mind and Society. Notre Dame, IN: University of Notre Dame Press.

Franklin, S., 1995 Postmodern Procreation: A Cultural Account of Assisted Reproduction. In Conceiving the New World Order. F. Ginsburg and R. Rapp, eds. pp. 323–345. Berkeley: University of California Press.

Fraser, G., and P. Kilbride, 1980 Child Abuse and Neglect – Rare, but Perhaps Increasing, Phenomenon among the Samia of Kenya. Child Abuse and Neglect: The International Journal 4:227–232.

Freeman, D., 1983 Margaret Mead and Samoa: The Making and Unmaking of an Anthropological Myth. Cambridge, MA: Harvard University Press.

Freeman, D., 1999 The Fateful Hoaxing of Margaret Mead: A Historical Analysis of Her Samoan Research. Boulder, CO: Westview Press.

Freud, S., 1953a[1905] Three Essays on the Theory of Sexuality. In The Standard Edition of the Complete Psychological Works of Sigmund Freud, vol. VII. J. Strachey, ed. and trans. pp. 125–245. London: Hogarth Press.

Freud, S., 1953b[1913] Totem and Taboo: Some Points of Agreement between the Mental Lives of Savages and Neurotics. In The Standard Edition of the Complete Psychological Works of Sigmund Freud, vol. XIII. J. Strachey, ed. and trans. pp. 1–162. London: Hogarth Press.

Freud, S., 1964[1933] Anxiety and Instinctual Life (Lecture XXXII). In New Introductory Lectures on Psychoanalysis. W. J. H. Sprott, ed. and trans. pp. 107–143. London: Hogarth Press.

Friedenberg, E., 1973 The Vanishing Adolescent: Adolescence: Self-Definition and Conflict. In The Sociology of Youth: Evolution and Revolution. H. Silverstein, ed. pp. 109–118. New York: Macmillan.

Friedl, E., 1997 Children of Deh Koh: Young Life in an Iranian Village. Syracuse, NY: Syracuse University Press.

Friedl, E., 2004 The Ethnography of Children. Iranian Studies 37:655–663.

Furnham, A., 2005 Spare the Rod and Spoil the Child: Lay Theories of Corporal Punishment. In Corporal Punishment of Children in Theoretical Perspective. M. Donnelly and M. A. Straus, eds. pp. 134–150. New Haven: Yale University Press.

Furth, C., 1995 From Birth to Birth: The Growing Body in Chinese Medicine. In Chinese Views of Childhood. A. B. Kinney, ed. pp. 157–191. Honolulu: University of Hawaii Press.

Garbarino, J., 1999 Lost Boys: Why Our Sons Turn Violent and How We Can Save Them. New York: Free Press.

Gilmore, D., 1990 Manhood in the Making: Cultural Concepts of Masculinity. New Haven: Yale University Press.

Ginsburg, F., 1989 Contested Lives: The Abortion Debate in an American Community. Berkeley: University of California Press.

Gluckman, M., 1962 Les Rites de Passage. In Essays on the Ritual of Social Relations. M. Gluckman, ed. pp. 1–52. Manchester: Manchester University Press.

Goldstein, D. M., 1998 Nothing Bad Intended: Child Discipline, Punishment, and Survival in a Shantytown in Rio de Janeiro, Brazil. In Small Wars: The Cultural Politics of Childhood. N. Scheper-Hughes and C. Sargent, eds. pp. 389–415. Berkeley: University of California Press.

Gomme, A., 1898 The Traditional Games of England, Scotland, and Ireland: With Tunes, Singing-Rhymes, and Methods of Playing According to the Variants Extant and Recorded in Different Parts of the Kingdom. London: D. Nutt.

Gonçalves, M. A., 2001 O Mundo Inacabado: Ação e Criação em uma Cosmologia Amazônica – Etnografia Pirahã. Rio de Janeiro: Editora UFRJ.

Goodman, M. E., 1957 Values, Attitudes, and Social Concepts of Japanese and American Children. American Anthropologist 59:979–999.

Goodman, R., 1996 On Introducing the UN Convention on the Rights of the Child into Japan. In Case Studies on Human Rights in Japan. R. Goodman and I. Neary, eds. pp. 109–140. Richmond, Surrey: Curzon Press.

Goodman, R., 2000 Children of the Japanese State: The Changing Role of Child Protection Institutions in Contemporary Japan. Oxford: Oxford University Press.

Goodman, R., 2002 Child Abuse in Japan: "Discovery" and the Development of Policy. In Family and Social Policy in Japan: Anthropological Approaches. R. Goodman, ed. pp. 131–155. Cambridge: Cambridge University Press.

Goodwin, M. H., 1990 He-Said-She-Said: Talk as Social Organization among Black Children. Bloomington: Indiana University Press.

Goody, E., 1982 Parenthood and Social Reproduction: Fostering and Occupational Roles in West Africa. Cambridge: Cambridge University Press.

Goody, J., 1969 Adoption in Cross-Cultural Perspective. Comparative Studies in Society and History 11:55–78.

Goody, J., 1971 The Developmental Cycle in Domestic Groups. Cambridge: Cambridge University Press.

Goody, J., and E. Goody, 1967 The Circulation of Women and Children in Northern Ghana. Man (N.S.) 2:226–248.

Gottlieb, A., 1995 Beyond the Lonely Anthropologist: Collaboration in Research and Writing. American Anthropologist 97:21–26.

Gottlieb, A., 1998 Do Infants Have Religion? The Spiritual Lives of Beng Babies. American Anthropologist 100:122–135.

Gottlieb, A., 2000 Where Have All the Babies Gone? Toward an Anthropology of Infants (and Their Caretakers). Anthropological Quarterly 73(3):121–132.

Gottlieb, A., 2004 The Afterlife is Where We Come From: The Culture of Infancy in West Africa. Chicago: University of Chicago Press.

Graburn, N., 1987 Severe Child Abuse among the Canadian Inuit. In Child Survival: Anthropological Perspectives on the Treatment and Maltreatment of Children. N. Scheper-Hughes, ed. pp. 211–225. Dordrecht: D. Reidel.

Gravrand, H., 1983 La Civilisation Sereer: Cosaan (Les Origines). Dakar: Les Nouvelles Éditions Africaines.

Gregor, T., 1977 Mehinaku: The Drama of Daily Life in a Brazilian Indian Village. Chicago: University of Chicago Press.

Gregor, T., 1985 Anxious Pleasures: The Sexual Lives of an Amazonian People. Chicago: University of Chicago Press.

Gullestad, M., 1984 Kitchen Table Society: A Case Study of the Family Life and Friendships of Young Working-Class Mothers in Urban Norway. Oslo: Scandinavian University Press.

Gupta, A., 2002 Reliving Childhood? The Temporality of Childhood and Narratives of Reincarnation. Ethnos 67:33–55.

Halbmayer, E., 2004 "The One Who Feeds Has the Rights": Adoption and Fostering of Kin, Affines and Enemies among the Yukpa and other Carib-Speaking Indians of Lowland South America. In Cross-Cultural Approaches to Adoption. F. Bowie, ed. pp. 145–164. London: Routledge.

Hall, G. S., 1904 Adolescence: Its Psychology and Its Relations to Physiology, Anthropology, Sociology, Sex, Crime, Religion, and Education. New York: Appleton.

Hall, T., 2003 Better Times Than This: Youth Homelessness in Britain. London: Pluto Press.

Hall, T., and H. Montgomery, 2000 Home and Away: "Childhood," "Youth" and Young People. Anthropology Today 16(3):13–15.

Hallpike, C. R., 1979 The Foundations of Primitive Thought. Oxford: Clarendon Press.

Hamilton, A., 1981 Nature and Nurture: Aboriginal Child-Rearing in North-Central Arnhem Land. Canberra: Australian Institute of Aboriginal Studies.

Handler, R., 2004 Significant Others: Interpersonal and Professional Commitments in Anthropology. Madison: University of Wisconsin Press.

Hanks, J., 1963 Maternity and Its Rituals in Bang Chan. Data Paper 51, South East Asia Programme. Ithaca, NY: Cornell University.

Hardacre, H., 1997 Marketing the Menacing Fetus in Japan. Berkeley: University of California Press.

Hardman, C., 1973 Can There be an Anthropology of Childhood? Journal of the Anthropological Society of Oxford 4:85–99.

Hardman, C., 2000 Other Worlds: Notions of Self and Emotion among the Lohorung Rai. Oxford: Berg.

Harkness, S., and C. Super, 1983 The Cultural Construction of Child Development: A Framework for the Socialization of Affect. Ethos 11:221–231.

Harkness, S., and C. Super, 1985 The Cultural Context of Gender Segregation in Children's Peer Groups. Child Development 56:219–224.

Harkness, S., and C. Super, 1986 The Cultural Structuring of Children's Play in a Rural African Community. In The Many Faces of Play. K. Blanchard, ed. pp. 96–103. Champaign, IL: Human Kinetics Publishing.

Harner, M., 1969 The Jivaro: People of the Sacred Waterfalls. New York: Natural History Press.

Harris, J. R., 1998 The Nurture Assumption: Why Children Turn Out the Way They Do. New York: Free Press.

Harris, O., 1980 The Power of Signs: Gender, Culture and the Wild in the Bolivian Andes. In Nature, Culture and Gender. C. P. MacCormack and M. Strathern, eds. pp. 70–94. Cambridge: Cambridge University Press.

Hartup, W., 1983 Peer Relations. In Handbook of Child Psychology, vol. 4: Socialization, Personality and Social Development. E. M. Hetherington, ed. pp. 103–196. New York: Wiley.

Hawley, J., 1995 Ben Okri's Spirit-Child: Abiku Migration and Post-Modernity. Research in African Literatures 26:30–39.

Heald, S., 1982 The Making of Men: The Relevance of Vernacular Psychology to the Interpretation of a Gisu Ritual. Africa 52:15–36.

Heath, S. B., 1983 Ways with Words: Language, Life and Work in Communities and Classrooms. Cambridge: Cambridge University Press.

Hecht, T., 1998 At Home in the Street: Street Children of Northeast Brazil. Cambridge: Cambridge University Press.

Hendry, J., 1986 Becoming Japanese: The World of the Pre-School Child. Manchester: Manchester University Press.

Hendry, J., 1999 An Anthropologist in Japan: Glimpses of Life in the Field. London: Routledge.

Henry, P., G. Morelli, and E. Tronick, 2005 Child Caretakers among Efe Foragers of the Ituri Forest. *In* Hunter-Gatherer Childhoods: Evolutionary, Developmental and Cultural Perspectives. B. Hewlett and M. Lamb, eds. pp. 191–213. New York: Aldine.

Herdt, G., 1981 Guardians of the Flutes: Idioms of Masculinity. New York: McGraw-Hill.

Herdt, G., 1982a Rituals of Manhood: Male Initiation in New Guinea. Berkeley: University of California Press.

Herdt, G., 1982b Sambia Nose-Bleeding Rites and Male Proximity to Women. Ethos 10:189–231.

Herdt, G., 1993 Semen Transactions in Sambia Culture. *In* Ritualized Homosexuality in Melanesia. G. Herdt, ed. pp. 167–210. Berkeley: University of California Press.

Herdt, G., 1999 Sambian Sexual Cultures: Essays from the Field. Chicago: University of Chicago Press.

Hernandez, T., 1941 Children among the Drysdale River Tribes. Oceania 12:122–133.

Herron, R. E., and B. Sutton-Smith, 1971 Child's Play. London: Wiley.

Hewlett, B., 1991 Intimate Fathers: The Nature and Context of Aka Pygmy Paternal Infant Care. Ann Arbor: University of Michigan Press.

Hewlett, B., and M. Lamb, 2005 Emerging Issues in the Study of Hunter-Gatherer Children. *In* Hunter-Gatherer Childhoods: Evolutionary, Developmental and Cultural Perspectives. B. Hewlett and M. Lamb, eds. pp. 3–18. New York: Aldine.

Hilger, I., 1957 Araucanian Child Life and Its Cultural Background. Washington, DC: The Smithsonian.

Hinton, R., 2000 Seen But Not Heard: Refugee Children and Models for Intervention. *In* Abandoned Children. C. Panter-Brick and M. Smith, eds. pp. 199–212. Cambridge: Cambridge University Press.

Hirschfeld, L., 2002 Why Don't Anthropologists Like Children? American Anthropologist 104:611–627.

Hogbin, I., 1970a A New Guinea Childhood: From Weaning Till the Eighth Year in Wogeo. *In* From Child to Adult: Studies in the Anthropology of Education. J. Middleton, ed. pp. 134–162. New York: Natural History Press.

Hogbin, I., 1970b The Island of Menstruating Men: Religion in Wogeo, New Guinea. Scranton, PA: Chandler.

Holland, D., and M. Eisenhart, 1990 Educated in Romance: Women, Achievement, and College Culture. Chicago: University of Chicago Press.

Hollos, M., 2002 The Cultural Construction of Childhood: Changing Conceptions among the Pare of Northern Tanzania. Childhood 9:167–189.

Holmberg, A., 1969 Nomads of the Long Bow: The Siriono of Eastern Bolivia. New York: American Museum of Natural History.

Horton, R., 1961 Destiny and the Unconscious in West Africa. Africa 31: 110–116.

Huber, H., 1963 The Krobo: Traditional Social and Religious Life of a West African People. Bonn: Anthropos Institute.

Hugh-Jones, C., 1987 Children in the Amazon. *In* Children in the Field: Anthropological Experiences. J. Cassell, ed. pp. 27–64. Philadelphia: Temple University Press.

Hugh-Jones, S., 1979 The Palm and the Pleiades: Initiation and Cosmology in Northwest Amazonia. Cambridge: Cambridge University Press.

Hull, T., 1975 Each Child Brings Its Own Fortune: An Enquiry into the Value of Children in a Javanese Village. Unpublished Ph.D. thesis, Australian National University.

Hunt, D., 1970 Parents and Children in History: The Psychology of Family Life in Early Modern France. New York: Basic Books.

Huntsman, J., 1983 Complementary and Similar Kinsmen in Tokelau. *In* Sibling ship in Oceania: Studies in the Meaning of Kin Relations. M. Marshall, ed. pp. 79–103. Lanham, MD: University Press of America.

Hyman, I., and E. McDowell, 1979 An Overview. *In* American Education: Readings in History, Practice, and Alternatives. I. Hyman and J. Wise, eds. pp. 3–22. Philadelphia: Temple University Press.

Ilechukwu, S., 2007 *Ogbanje/Abiku* and Cultural Conceptualizations of Psychopathology in Nigeria. Mental Health, Religion and Culture 10:239–255.

Jackson, M., 1978 Ambivalence and the Last-Born: Birth Order Position in Convention and Myth. Man (N.S.) 12:341–361.

Jackson, P., 1989 Male Homosexuality in Thailand: An Interpretation of Contemporary Thai Sources. New York: Global Academic Publishers.

James, A., 1993 Childhood Identities: Self and Social Relationships in the Experience of the Child. Edinburgh: Edinburgh University Press.

James, A., 1995 Talking of Children and Youth: Language Socialization and Culture. *In* Youth Cultures: A Cross-Cultural Perspective. V. Amit-Talai and H. Wulff, eds. pp. 43–62. London: Routledge.

James, A., 1998 Play in Childhood: An Anthropological Perspective. Child Psychology and Psychiatry Review 3:104–109.

James, A., 2004 Understanding Childhood from an Interdisciplinary Perspective: Problems and Potentials. *In* Rethinking Childhood. P. Pufall and R. Unsworth, eds. pp. 25–37. New Brunswick, NJ: Rutgers University Press.

James, A., 2007 Giving Voice to Children's Voices: Practices and Problems, Pitfalls and Potentials. American Anthropologist 109:261–272.

James, A., and A. Prout, 1995 Hierarchy, Boundary and Agency in the Experience of Children: Towards a Theoretical Perspective. Sociological Studies of Children 7:77–99.

James, A., and A. Prout, eds., 1997 Constructing and Reconstructing Childhood: Contemporary Issues in the Sociological Study of Childhood. 2nd edition. London: Falmer Press.

James, A., C. Jenks, and A. Prout, 1998 Theorizing Childhood. Cambridge: Polity Press.

James, W., 2000 Placing the Unborn: On the Social Recognition of New Life. Anthropology and Medicine 7:169–189.

Jeffry, P., and R. Jeffry, 1996 Delayed Periods and Falling Babies: The Ethno-physiology and Politics of Pregnancy Loss in Rural North India. *In* The Anthropology of Pregnancy Loss: Comparative Studies in Miscarriage, Stillbirth and Neonatal Death. R. Cecil, ed. pp. 17–38. Oxford: Berg.

Jenkins, H., ed., 1998 The Children's Culture Reader. New York: New York University Press.

Jenks, C., 1996 Childhood. London: Routledge.

Johnson, M., 2000 The View from the Wuro: A Guide to Child Rearing for Fulani Parents. *In* A World of Babies: Imagined Childcare Guides for Seven Societies. J. DeLoache and A. Gottlieb, eds. pp. 171–198. Cambridge: Cambridge University Press.

Johnson, O., 1981 The Socioeconomic Context of Child Abuse in Native South America. *In* Child Abuse and Neglect: Cross-Cultural Perspectives. J. Korbin, ed. pp. 56–70. Berkeley: University of California Press.

Kaberry, P., 1936 Spirit-Children and Spirit-Centres of the North Kimberley Division, West Australia. Oceania 6:392–400.

Kaberry, P., 1939 Aboriginal Woman: Sacred and Profane. London: Routledge.

Kardiner, A., 1945 The Psychological Frontiers of Society. New York: Columbia University Press.

Kavapalu, H., 1993 Dealing with the Dark Side in the Ethnography of Childhood: Child Punishment in Tonga. Oceania 63:313–329.

Kavapalu, H., 1995 Power and Personhood in Tonga. Social Analysis 37: 15–28.

Kayongo-Male, D., and P. Walji, 1984 Children at Work in Kenya. Nairobi: Oxford University Press.

Kehily, M.-J., 2004 An Introduction to Childhood Studies. Maidenhead: Open University Press.

Kehily, M.-J., 2007 A Cultural Perspective. *In* Youth: Perspectives, Identities and Practices. M.-J. Kehily, ed. pp. 11–44. London: Sage.

Kehinde, A., 2003 Intertextuality and the Contemporary African Novel. Nordic Journal of African Studies 12:372–386.

Kellett, M., 2005 How to Develop Children as Researchers: A Step-by-Step Guide to Teaching the Research Process. London: Paul Chapman.

Key, E., 1909 The Century of the Child. London: G. P. Putnam and Sons.

Kidd, D., 1906 Savage Childhood: A Study of Kafir Children. London: Black.

Kirsch, A. T., 1982 Buddhism, Sex Roles and the Thai Economy. *In* Women of Southeast Asia. P. van Esterik, ed., pp. 16–41. DeKalb, IL, Center for Southeast Asian Studies, Northern Illinois University.

Kirsch, A. T., 1985 Text and Context: Buddhist Sex Roles/The Culture of Gender Revisited. American Ethnologist 12:302–320.

Knauft, B., 2003 What Ever Happened to Ritualized Homosexuality? Modern Sexual Subjects in Melanesia and Elsewhere. Annual Review of Sex Research 14:137–159.

Konner, M., 1972 Aspects of Developmental Ethology of a Foraging People. *In* Ethological Studies of Child Behaviour. N. Blurton-Jones, ed. pp. 285–304. Cambridge: Cambridge University Press.

Konner, M., 1976 Maternal Care, Infant Behavior and Development among the !Kung. *In* Kalahari Hunter-Gatherers: Studies of the !Kung San and Their Neighbors. R. Lee and I. DeVore, eds. pp. 218–245. Cambridge, MA: Harvard University Press.

Konner, M., 2005 Hunter-Gatherer Infancy and Childhood: The !Kung and Others. *In* Hunter-Gatherer Childhoods: Evolutionary, Developmental and Cultural Perspectives. B. Hewlett and M. Lamb, eds. pp. 19–64. New York: Aldine.

Korbin, J., 1977 Anthropological Contributions to the Study of Child Abuse. Child Abuse and Neglect: The International Journal 1:7–24.

Korbin, J., 1979 A Cross-Cultural Perspective on the Role of the Community in Child Abuse and Neglect. Child Abuse and Neglect: The International Journal 3:9–18.

Korbin, J., ed., 1981 Child Abuse and Neglect: Cross-Cultural Perspectives. Berkeley: University of California Press.

Kulick, D., 1992 Language Shift and Cultural Reproduction: Socialization, Self, and Syncretism in a Papua New Guinean Village. Cambridge: Cambridge University Press.

Kulick, D., and M. Willson, 1995 Taboo: Sex, Identity and Erotic Subjectivity in Anthropological Fieldwork. London: Routledge.

Laerke, A., 1998 By Means of Re-Membering: Notes on a Fieldwork with English Children. Anthropology Today 14(1):3–7.

La Fleur, W., 1992 Liquid Life: Abortion and Buddhism in Japan. Princeton: Princeton University Press.

La Fontaine, J. S., ed., 1978 Sex and Age as Principles of Social Differentiation. London: Athlone Press.

La Fontaine, J. S., 1986a An Anthropological Perspective on Children in Social Worlds. *In* Children of Social Worlds. M. Richards and P. Light, eds. pp. 10–30. Cambridge: Polity Press.

La Fontaine, J. S., 1986b Initiation. Manchester: Manchester University Press.

La Fontaine, J. S., 1988 Child Sexual Abuse and the Incest Taboo: Practical Problems and Theoretical Issues. Man (N.S.) 23:1–18.

La Fontaine, J. S., 1990 Child Sexual Abuse. Cambridge: Polity Press.

La Fontaine, J. S., 1992 Concepts of Evil, Witchcraft and the Sexual Abuse of Children in Modern England. Etnofoor: Journal of the Royal Dutch Anthropological Society 5:6–20.

La Fontaine, J. S., 1997 Are Children People? Paper presented at The Invisibility of Children Conference, Linköping University, Sweden.

La Fontaine, J. S., 1998 Speak of the Devil: Tales of Satanic Abuse in Contemporary England. Cambridge: Cambridge University Press.

Lanclos, D., 2003 At Play in Belfast: Children's Folklore and Identities in Northern Ireland. New Brunswick, NJ: Rutgers University Press.

Lancy, D., 1977 The Play Behavior of Kpelle Children During Rapid Cultural Change. In The Anthropological Study of Play: Problems and Perspectives. D. Lancy and B. A. Tindall, eds. pp. 72–79. New York: Leisure Press.

Lancy, D., 1996 Playing on the Mother-Ground: Cultural Routines for Children's Development. New York: Guilford Press.

Lancy, D., 2007 Accounting for Variability in Mother–Child Play. American Anthropologist 109:273–284.

Lancy, D., 2008 The Anthropology of Childhood: Cherubs, Chattel, Changelings. Cambridge: Cambridge University Press.

Lancy, D., and B. A. Tindall, eds., 1977 The Anthropological Study of Play: Problems and Prospects. New York: Leisure Press.

Langness, L. L., 1975 Margaret Mead and the Study of Socialization. Ethos 3:97–112.

Langness, L. L., 1981 Child Abuse and Cultural Values: The Case of New Guinea. In Child Abuse and Neglect: Cross-Cultural Perspectives. J. Korbin, ed. pp. 13–34. Berkeley: University of California Press.

Layne, L., 1996 "He Was a Real Baby with Real Things": A Material Culture Analysis of Personhood, Parenthood and Pregnancy Loss. Journal of Material Culture 5:321–345.

Layne, L., 2000 "How's the Baby Doing?" Struggling with Narratives of Progress in a Neonatal Intensive Care Unit. Medical Anthropology Quarterly 10:624–656.

Le, H.-N., 2000 Never Leave Your Little One Alone: Raising an Ifaluk Child. In A World of Babies: Imagined Childcare Guides for Seven Societies. J. DeLoache and A. Gottlieb, eds. pp. 199–220. Cambridge: Cambridge University Press.

Leach, E., 1964 Response to Raoul Naroll's "On Ethnic Unit Classification." Current Anthropology 5:299.

Leacock, E., 1981 Myths of Male Dominance: Collected Articles on Women Cross-Culturally. New York: Monthly Review Press.

Leiderman, H. P., and G. F. Leiderman, 1973 Polymatric Infant Care in the East African Highlands: Some Affective and Cognitive Consequences. Paper presented at the Minnesota Symposium on Child Development, Minneapolis, Minnesota.

Leis, N., 1982 The Not-So-Supernatural Power of Ijaw Children. In African Religious Groups and Beliefs. S. Ottenburg, ed. pp. 151–169. Meerut: Archana Publications.

LeVine, R., 1977 Child Rearing as Cultural Adaptation. In Culture and Infancy: Variations in the Human Experience. P. H. Leiderman, S. Tulkin, and A. Rosenfeld, eds. pp. 15–27. New York: Academic Press.

LeVine, R., 2003 Childhood Socialization: Comparative Studies of Parenting, Learning and Educational Change. Hong Kong: Comparative Education Research Centre.

LeVine, R., 2007 Ethnographic Studies of Childhood: A Historical Overview. American Anthropologist 109:247–260.

LeVine, S., and R. LeVine, 1981 Child Abuse and Neglect in Sub-Saharan Africa. In Child Abuse and Neglect: Cross-Cultural Perspectives. J. Korbin, ed. pp. 35–55. Berkeley: University of California Press.

LeVine, R., and R. New, eds., 2008 Anthropology and Child Development: A Cross-Cultural Reader. Oxford: Blackwell.

LeVine, R., and K. Norman, 2001 The Infant's Acquisition of Culture: Early Attachment Reexamined in Anthropological Perspective. In The Psychology of Cultural Experience. C. Moore and H. Mathews, eds. pp. 83–104. Cambridge: Cambridge University Press.

LeVine, R., S. Dixon, S. LeVine, et al., 1994. Child Care and Culture: Lessons from Africa. Cambridge: Cambridge University Press.

Levinson, D., 1989 Family Violence in Cross-Cultural Perspective. Newbury Park, CA: Sage.

Lewis, G., 1980 Day of Shining Red: An Essay on Understanding Ritual. Cambridge: Cambridge University Press.

Llewelyn-Davies, M., 1981 Women, Warriors and Patriarchs. In Sexual Meanings: The Cultural Constructions of Gender and Sexuality. S. B. Ortner and H. Whitehead, eds. pp. 330–358. Cambridge: Cambridge University Press.

Lubbock, J., 1978[1870] The Origin of Civilisation and the Primitive Condition of Man. Chicago: University of Chicago Press.

Lugalla, J., 2003 AIDS, Orphans, and Development in Sub-Saharan Africa: A Review of the Dilemma of Public Health and Development. Journal of Developing Societies 19:26–46.

Lutkehaus, N., 1995 Gender Metaphors: Female Rituals as Cultural Models in Manam. In Gender Rituals: Female Initiation in Melanesia. N. C. Lutkehaus and P. B. Roscoe, eds. pp. 183–204. London: Routledge.

McCabe, D., 2002 Histories of Errancy: Oral Yoruba *Abiku* Texts and Soyinka's "Abiku." Research in African Literatures 33:45–74.

McCallam, C., 1996 The Body That Knows: From Cashinahua Epistemology to a Medical Anthropology of Lowland South America. Medical Anthropology Quarterly 10:347–372.

Malinowski, B., 1922 Argonauts of the Western Pacific: An Account of Native Enterprise and Adventure in the Archipelagoes of Melanesian New Guinea. London: Routledge.

Malinowski, B., 1927 Sex and Repression in Savage Society. New York: Kegan Paul.

Malinowski, B., 1929 The Sexual Life of Savages in North-Western Melanesia: An Ethnographic Account of Courtship, Marriage and Family Life among the Natives of the Trobriand Islands, British New Guinea. London: Routledge and Sons.

Malinowski, B., 1948 Magic, Science and Religion and Other Essays. London: Souvenir Press.

Malinowski, B., 1960 A Scientific Theory of Culture and Other Essays. New York: Oxford University Press.

Malkki, L., and E. Martin, 2003 Children and the Gendered Politics of Globalization: In Remembrance of Sharon Stephens. American Ethnologist 30:216–224.

Mandela, N., 1994 Long Walk to Freedom: The Autobiography of Nelson Mandela. London: Little, Brown and Company.

Mandell, N., 1991 The Least-Adult Role in Studying Children. *In* Studying the Social Worlds of Children. F. Waksler, ed. pp. 38–59. London: Falmer Press.

Marano, H. E., 1999 The Power of Play. Psychology Today Magazine [online]. [Accessed April 1, 2008]. Available from World Wide Web: http://psychologytoday.com/articles/pto-19990701-000030.html.

Marglin, F. A., 1985 Wives of the God-King: The Rituals of the *Devadasis* of Puri. New Delhi: Oxford University Press.

Markowitz, F., and M. Ashkenazi, 1999 Sex, Sexuality and the Anthropologist. Urbana: University of Illinois Press.

Masson, J., 1984 Freud, the Assault on Truth: Freud's Suppression of the Seduction Theory. London: Faber.

Mayall, B., ed., 1994 Children's Childhoods: Observed and Experienced. London: Falmer Press.

Maybury-Lewis, D., 1974 Akwẽ-Shavante Society. Oxford: Oxford University Press.

Mayer, P., and I. Mayer, 1970 Socialization by Peers. *In* Socialization: The Approach from Social Anthropology. P. Mayer, ed. pp. 159–189. London: Tavistock.

Mead, M., 1949 Male and Female: A Study of the Sexes in a Changing World. London: Victor Gollancz.

Mead, M., 1971[1928] Coming of Age in Samoa: A Study of Adolescence and Sex in Primitive Societies. London: Pelican.

Middleton, J., ed., 1970. From Child to Adult: Studies in the Anthropology of Education. New York: Natural History Press.

Mills, A., 1994 Introduction. *In* Amerindian Rebirth: Reincarnation Belief among North American Indians and Inuit. A. Mills and R. Slobodin, eds. pp. 3–14. Toronto: University of Toronto Press.

Mitchell, L., and E. Georges, 1997 Cross-Cultural Cyborgs: Greek and Canadian Women's Discourses on Fetal Ultrasound. Feminist Studies 23:373–401.

Mobolade, T. 1973 The Concept of Abiku. African Arts 7:62–64.

Modell, J., 2002 A Sealed and Secret Kinship: The Culture of Policies and Practices in American Adoption. Oxford: Berghahn.

Montgomery, H., 2000 Becoming Part of This World: Anthropology, Infancy and Childhood. Journal of the Anthropological Society of Oxford 31:15–30.

Montgomery, H., 2001a Modern Babylon? Prostituting Children in Thailand. Oxford: Berghahn.

Montgomery, H., 2001b Imposing Rights? A Case Study of Child Prostitution in Thailand. *In* Culture and Rights: Anthropological Perspectives. J. Cowan, M.-B. Dembour, and R. Wilson, eds. pp. 80–101. Cambridge: Cambridge University Press.

Montgomery, H., 2003 Childhood in Time and Place. *In* Understanding Childhood: An Interdisciplinary Approach. M. Woodhead and H. Montgomery, eds. pp. 45–84. Chichester: John Wiley.

Moore, H., 1988 Feminism and Anthropology. Cambridge: Polity Press.

Morgan, L. M., 1997 Imagining the Unborn in the Ecuadoran Andes. Feminist Studies 23:322–350.

Morrison, T., 1973 Sula. New York: Knopf.

Morrison, T., 1987 Beloved. London: Chatto and Windus.

Morrow, V., 1995 Invisible Children? Toward a Re-Conceptualisation of Childhood Dependency and Responsibility. Sociological Studies of Children 7:207–230.

Morrow, V., 1996 Rethinking Childhood Dependency: Children's Contributions to the Domestic Economy. Sociological Review 44:58–77.

Morrow, V., and M. Richards, 1996 The Ethics of Social Research with Children: An Overview. Children and Society 10:90–105.

Morton, H., 1996 Becoming Tongan: An Ethnography of Childhood. Honolulu: University of Hawaii Press.

Morton, H., 2002 From *Mā'uli* to Motivator: Transformations in Reproductive Health Care in Tonga. *In* Birthing in the Pacific: Beyond Tradition and Modernity? V. Luckere and M. Jolly, eds. pp. 31–55. Honolulu: University of Hawaii Press.

Moskowitz, M., 2001 The Haunting Fetus: Abortion, Sexuality and the Spirit World in Taiwan. Honolulu: University of Hawaii Press.

Muecke, M. A., 1992 Mother Sold Food, Daughter Sells Her Body: The Cultural Continuity of Prostitution. Social Science and Medicine 35:891–901.

Murdock, G. P., 1949 Social Structure. New York: Macmillan.

Mussallam, B., 1990 The Human Embryo in Arabic Scientific and Religious Thought. In The Status of the Human Embryo: Perspectives from Moral Tradition. G. R. Dunstan and M. Seller, eds. pp. 32–46. Oxford: Oxford University Press.

Nations, M. K., and L. A. Rebhun, 1988 Angels with Wet Wings Won't Fly: Maternal Sentiment in Brazil and the Image of Neglect. Culture, Medicine and Psychiatry 12:141–200.

Needham, J., 1959 A History of Embryology. Cambridge: Cambridge University Press.

Nieuwenhuys, O., 1994 Children's Lifeworlds: Gender, Welfare and Labour in the Developing World. London: Routledge.

Nieuwenhuys, O., 1995 The Domestic Economy and the Exploitation of Children's Work: The Case of Kerala. International Journal of Children's Rights 3:213–225.

Nieuwenhuys, O., 1996 The Paradox of Child Labor and Anthropology. Annual Review of Anthropology 25:237–251.

Notermans, C., 2004 Fosterage and the Politics of Marriage and Kinship in East Cameroon. In Cross-Cultural Approaches to Adoption. F. Bowie, ed. pp. 48–63. London: Routledge.

Nuttall, M., 1994 The Name Never Dies. Greenland Inuit Ideas of the Person. In Amerindian Rebirth: Reincarnation Belief among North American Indians and Inuit. A. Mills and R. Slobodin, eds. pp. 123–135. Toronto: University of Toronto Press.

Nzewi, E. 2001 Malevolent Ogbanje: Recurrent Reincarnation or Sickle Cell Disease? Social Science and Medicine 52:1403–1416.

Oakley, A., 1994 Women and Children First and Last: Parallels and Differences between Children's and Women's Studies. In Children's Childhoods: Observed and Experienced. B. Mayall, ed. pp. 13–32. London: Falmer Press.

Ochs, E., 1982 Talking to Children in Western Samoa. Language in Society 11:77–104.

Ochs, E., 1988 Culture and Language Development: Language Acquisition and Language Socialization in a Samoan Village. Cambridge: Cambridge University Press.

Ochs, E., and B. Schieffelin, 1984 Language Acquisition and Socialization: Three Developmental Stories and Their Implications. In Culture Theory: Mind, Self, and Emotion. R. Shweder and R. LeVine, eds. pp. 276–320. Cambridge: Cambridge University Press.

O'Connell-Davidson, J., 2005 Children in the Global Sex Trade. Cambridge: Polity Press.

Ogbu, J., 1978 Minority Education and Caste: The American System in Cross-Cultural Perspective. New York: Academic Press.

Ogunjuyigbe, P., 2004 Under-Five Mortality in Nigeria: Perception and Attitudes of the Yorubas towards the Existence of *"Abiku."* Demographic Research 11(2):43–56.

Ogunyemi, C., 2002 An Abiku-Ogbanje Atlas: A Pre-Text for Rereading Soyinka's *Aké* and Morrison's *Beloved.* African American Review 36:663–678.

Okonkwo, C., 2004 A Critical Divination: Reading Sula as Ogbanje-Abiku. African American Review 38:651–668.

Okri, B., 1992 The Famished Road. London: Vintage.

Opie, I., 1993 The People in the Playground. Oxford: Oxford University Press.

Opie, I., and P. Opie, 1969 Children's Games in Street and Playground: Chasing, Catching, Seeking, Hunting, Racing, Dueling, Exerting, Daring, Guessing, Acting, Pretending. Oxford: Clarendon Press.

Opie, I., and P. Opie, 1997 Children's Games with Things: Marbles, Fivestones, Throwing and Catching, Gambling, Hopscotch, Chucking and Pitching, Ball-Bouncing, Skipping, Tops and Tipcat. Oxford: Oxford University Press.

Opie, I., and P. Opie, 2001[1959] The Lore and Language of Schoolchildren. Oxford: Oxford University Press.

Orchard, T., 2004 A Painful Power: Coming of Age, Sexuality and Relationships, and HIV/AIDS among *Devadasi* Sex Workers in Rural Karnataka, India. Unpublished Ph.D. thesis, University of Manitoba.

Ortner, S., 1974 Is Female to Male as Nature is to Culture? *In* Woman, Culture, and Society. M. Rosaldo and L. Lamphere, eds. pp. 67–87. Stanford: Stanford University Press.

Ottenberg, S., 1988 Oedipus, Gender and Social Solidarity: A Case Study of Male Childhood and Initiation. Ethos 16:326–352.

Paige, K. E., and J. M. Paige, 1981 The Politics of Reproductive Ritual. Berkeley: University of California Press.

Palmer, E., 2001 Born-Alive Bill Approved by Committee. CQ Weekly 59:1858.

Palmer, M., 1989 Civil Adoption in Contemporary Chinese Law: A Contract to Care. Modern Asian Studies 23:373–410.

Panter-Brick, C., 2000 Nobody's Children? A Reconsideration of Child Abandonment. *In* Abandoned Children. C. Panter-Brick and M. Smith, eds. pp. 1–26. Cambridge: Cambridge University Press.

Panter-Brick, C., 2001 Street Children and Their Peers: Perspectives on Homelessness, Poverty, and Health. *In* Children and Anthropology: Perspectives for the 21st Century. H. Schwartzman, ed. pp. 83–97. Westport, CT: Bergin and Garvey.

Panter-Brick, C., 2002 Street Children, Human Rights, and Public Health: A Critique and Future Directions. Annual Review of Anthropology 31:147–171.

Panter-Brick, C., and M. Smith, eds., 2000 Abandoned Children. Cambridge: Cambridge University Press.

Parker, R., 1991. Bodies, Pleasures and Passions: Sexual Culture and Contemporary Brazil. Boston: Beacon Press.

Parker, R., G. Herdt, and M. Carballo, 1991 Sexual Culture, HIV Transmission, and AIDS Research. Journal of Sex Research 28:77–98.

Parkin, D., 1985 Entitling Evil: Muslim and Non-Muslim in Coastal Kenya. In The Anthropology of Evil. D. Parkin, ed. pp. 224–243. Oxford: Blackwell.

Phongpaichit, P., 1982 From Peasant Girls to Bangkok Masseuses. Geneva: ILO.

Picone, M., 1998 Infanticide, the Spirits of Aborted Fetuses, and the Making of Motherhood in Japan. In Small Wars: The Cultural Politics of Childhood. N. Scheper-Hughes and C. Sargent, eds. pp. 37–57. Berkeley: University of California Press.

Plumb, J. H., 1975 The New World of Children in Eighteenth-Century England. Past and Present 67:64–95.

Poffenberger, T., 1981 Child Rearing and Social Structure in Rural India: Toward a Cross-Cultural Definition of Child Abuse and Neglect. In Child Abuse and Neglect: Cross-Cultural Perspectives. J. Korbin, ed. pp. 71–95. Berkeley: University of California Press.

Pollock, L. A., 1983 Forgotten Children: Parent–Child Relations from 1500 to 1900. Cambridge: Cambridge University Press.

Powdermaker, H., 1933 Life in Lesu: The Study of a Melanesian Society in New Ireland. London: Williams and Norgate.

Pufall, P., and R. Unsworth, 2004 Rethinking Childhood. New Brunswick, NJ: Rutgers University Press.

Punch, S., 2000 Children's Strategies for Creating Play Spaces: Negotiating Independence in Rural Bolivia. In Children's Geographies: Playing, Living, Learning. S. Holloway and G. Valentine, eds. pp. 48–62. London: Routledge.

Punch, S., 2001 Household Division of Labour: Generation, Gender, Age, Birth Order and Sibling Composition. Work, Employment and Society 15:803–823.

Qvortup, J., 2001 School-Work, Paid-Work and the Changing Obligations of Childhood. In Hidden Hands: International Perspectives on Children's Work and Labour. P. Mizen, C. Pole, and A. Bolton, eds. pp. 91–107. London: Routledge.

Radcliffe-Brown, A. R., and D. Forde, 1950 Introduction. In African Systems of Kinship and Marriage. A. R. Radcliffe-Brown and D. Forde, eds. pp. 1–85. Oxford: Oxford University Press.

Rapp, R., 1999 Testing Women, Testing the Fetus: The Social Impact of Amniocentesis in America. New York: Routledge.

Rasmussen, S. J., 1994 The Poetics of Childhood and Politics of Resistance in Tuareg Society: Some Thoughts on Studying "the Other" and Adult–Child Relationships. Ethos 22:343–372.

Raum, O. F., 1939 Female Initiation among the Chaga. American Anthropologist 41:554–565.

Raum, O. F., 1940 Chaga Childhood: A Description of Indigenous Education in an East African Tribe. Oxford: Oxford University Press.

Raum, O. F., 1970 Some Aspects of Indigenous Education among the Chaga. In From Child to Adult: Studies in the Anthropology of Education. J. Middleton, ed. pp. 91–108. New York: Natural History Press.

Read, M., 1968 Children of Their Fathers: Growing up among the Ngoni of Malawi. New York: Holt, Reinhart and Winston.

Reiter, R., 1975 Toward an Anthropology of Women. New York: Monthly Review Press.

Renne, E. P., 2001 Twinship in an Ekiti Yoruba Town. Ethnology 40:63–78.

Renne, E. P., 2002 The Fundamentals of Fertility: Cosmology and Conversion in a Southwestern Nigerian Town. Journal of the Royal Anthropological Institute (N.S.) 8:551–569.

Renne, E. P., 2005 Childhood Memories and Contemporary Parenting in Ekiti, Nigeria. Africa 75:63–82.

Renne, E. P., and M. Bastian, 2001 Reviewing Twinship in Africa. Ethnology 40:1–11.

Reynolds, P., 1991 Dance Civet Cat: Child Labour in the Zambezi Valley. Harare: Baobab Books.

Ribbens McCarthy, J., 1994 Mothers and Their Children: A Feminist Sociology of Childrearing. London: Sage.

Rigby, P., 1967 The Structural Context of Girls' Puberty Rites. Man (N.S.) 2:434–444.

Richards, A., 1956 Chisungu: A Girls' Initiation Ceremony among the Bemba of Northern Rhodesia. London: Faber and Faber.

Richards, A., 1970 Socialization and Contemporary British Anthropology. In Socialization: The Approach from Social Anthropology. P. Mayer, ed. pp. 1–32. London: Tavistock.

Rival, L., 1998 Androgynous Parents and Guest Children: The Huaorani Couvade. Journal of the Royal Anthropological Institute 4:619–642.

Rivière, P., 1974 The Couvade: A Problem Reborn. Man (N.S.) 9:423–435.

Roberts, J., M. Arth, and R. Bush, 1959 Games in Culture. American Anthropologist 61:597–605.

Roesch-Rhomberg, I., 2004 Korean Institutionalised Adoption. In Cross-Cultural Approaches to Adoption. F. Bowie, ed. pp. 81–96. London: Routledge.

Roopnarine, J., J. Johnson, and F. Hopper, eds., 1994 Children's Play in Diverse Cultures. Albany: State University of New York Press.

Roscoe, P., 1995 "Initiation" in Cross-Cultural Perspective. *In* Gender Rituals:
    Female Initiation in Melanesia. N. C. Lutkehaus and P. B. Roscoe, eds.
    pp. 219–238. London: Routledge.
Rosen, D., 2007 Child Soldiers, International Humanitarian Law, and the
    Globalization of Childhood. American Anthropologist 109:296–306.
Rossie, J.-P., 2005 Toys, Play, Culture and Society: An Anthropological Approach
    with Reference to North Africa and the Sahara. Stockholm: Stockholm
    International Toy Research Centre.
Rubin, G., 1989 Thinking Sex: Notes for a Radical Theory of the Politics of Sexuality.
    In Pleasure and Danger: Exploring Female Sexuality. C. Vance, ed. pp. 267–
    319. London: Pandora.
Ryan, F., 1994 From Rod to Reason: Historical Perspectives on Corporal
    Punishment in the Public School. Educational Horizons 72:70–77.
Sacks, K., 1974 Engels Revisited: Women, the Organization of Production,
    and Private Property. *In* Woman, Culture and Society. M. Rosaldo and
    L. Lamphere, eds. pp. 207–222. Stanford: Stanford University Press.
Saitoti, T. O., 1986 The Worlds of a Maasai Warrior: An Autobiography. New
    York: Random House.
Salomon, C., 2002 Obligatory Maternity and Diminished Reproductive Autonomy
    in A'jië and Paicî Kanak Societies. *In* Birthing in the Pacific: Beyond Tradition
    and Modernity? V. Luckere and M. Jolly, eds. pp. 79–99. Honolulu: University
    of Hawaii Press.
Santos-Granero, F., 2004 The Enemy Within: Child Sorcery, Revolution and
    the Evils of Modernization in Eastern Peru. *In* Darkness and Secrecy: The
    Anthropology of Assault, Sorcery and Witchcraft in Amazonia. N. Whitehead
    and R. Wright, eds. pp. 272–305. Durham, NC: Duke University Press.
Sapir, E., 1949 Selected Writings in Language, Culture, and Personality.
    Berkeley: University of California Press.
Schapera, I., 1927 Customs Relating to Twins in South Africa. Journal of the Royal
    African Society 26:117–137.
Schapera, I., 1971[1940] Married Life in an African Tribe. London: Faber and
    Faber.
Scheper-Hughes, N., 1987 Introduction: The Cultural Politics of Child Survival.
    In Child Survival: Anthropological Perspectives on the Treatment and
    Maltreatment of Children. N. Scheper-Hughes, ed. pp. 1–32. Dordrecht:
    D. Reidel.
Scheper-Hughes, N., 1992 Death without Weeping: The Violence of Everyday
    Life in Brazil. Berkeley: University of California Press.
Scheper-Hughes, N., 1995 "Who's the Killer?" Popular Justice and Human Rights
    in a South African Squatter Camp. Social Justice 22:143–164.
Scheper-Hughes, N., and C. Sargent, eds., 1998 Small Wars: The Cultural
    Politics of Childhood. Berkeley: University of California Press.

Scheper-Hughes, N., and H. Stein, 1987 Child Abuse and the Unconscious. *In* Child Survival: Anthropological Perspectives on the Treatment and Maltreatment of Children. N. Scheper-Hughes, ed. pp. 339–358. Dordrecht: D. Reidel.

Schildkrout, E., 1978 Roles of Children in Urban Kano. *In* Sex and Age as Principles of Social Differentiation. J. La Fontaine, ed. pp. 109–137. London: Athlone Press.

Schlegel, A., and H. Barry, 1991 Adolescence: An Anthropological Inquiry. New York: Free Press.

Schwartzman, H., 1976 The Anthropological Study of Children's Play. Annual Review of Anthropology 5:289–328.

Schwartzman, H., 1978 Transformations: The Anthropology of Children's Play. New York: Plenum Press.

Schwartzman, H., 2001 Children and Anthropology: A Century of Studies. *In* Children and Anthropology: Perspectives for the 21st Century. H. Schwartzman, ed. pp. 15–37. Westport, CT: Bergin and Garvey.

Scrimshaw, S., 1978 Infant Mortality and Behavior in the Regulation of Family Size. Population and Development Review 4:383–403.

Scrimshaw, S., 1984 Infanticide in Human Populations: Societal and Individual Concerns. *In* Infanticide: Comparative and Evolutionary Perspectives. G. Hausfater and S. B. Hrdy, eds. pp. 439–462. New York: Aldine.

Scrimshaw, S., and D. March, 1984 "I Had a Baby Sister But She Only Lasted One Day." Journal of the American Medical Association 251:732–733.

Sexton, L., 1995 Marriage as the Model for a New Initiation Ritual. *In* Gender Rituals: Female Initiation in Melanesia. N. C. Lutkehaus and P. B. Roscoe, eds. pp. 205–218. London: Routledge.

Seymour, S., 1999 Women, Family, and Child Care in India: A World in Transition. Cambridge: Cambridge University Press.

Shostak, M., 1983 Nisa: The Life and Words of a !Kung Woman. New York: Vintage Books.

Small, M., 1998 Our Babies, Ourselves: How Biology and Culture Shape the Way We Parent. New York: Anchor.

Sobo, E. J., 1996 Cultural Explanations for Pregnancy Loss in Rural Jamaica. *In* The Anthropology of Pregnancy Loss: Comparative Studies in Miscarriage, Stillbirth and Neonatal Death. R. Cecil, ed. pp. 39–58. Oxford: Berg.

Sofaer Derevenski, J., 2000 Children and Material Culture. London: Routledge.

Solberg, A., 1997 Negotiating Childhood: Changing Constructions of Age for Norwegian Children. *In* Constructing and Reconstructing Childhood. 2nd edition. A. James and A. Prout, eds. pp. 126–144. London: Falmer Press.

Soyinka, W., 1981 Aké: The Years of Childhood. London: Rex Collings.

Spencer, B., and F. J. Gillen, 1899 The Native Tribes of Central Australia. London: Macmillan.

Spencer, B., and F. J. Gillen, 1927 The Arunta: A Study of a Stone Age People. London: Macmillan.

Spencer, P., 1965 The Samburu: A Study of Gerontocracy in a Nomadic Tribe. London: Routledge and Kegan Paul.

Stack, C., 1974 All Our Kin. New York: Basic Books.

Stafford, C., 1995 The Roads of Chinese Childhood: Learning and Identification in Angang. Cambridge: Cambridge University Press.

Steinberg, L. D., and S. B. Silverberg, 1986 The Vicissitudes of Autonomy in Early Adolescence. Child Development 57:841–851.

Stephens, S., ed., 1995a Children and the Politics of Culture. Princeton: Princeton University Press.

Stephens, S., 1995b The "Cultural Fallout" of Chernobyl Radiation in Norwegian Sami Regions: Implications for Children. In Children and the Politics of Culture. S. Stephens, ed. pp. 292–318. Princeton: Princeton University Press.

Stevens, P., 1977 Studies in the Anthropology of Play: Papers in Memory of B. Allan Tindall. New York: Leisure Press.

Strathern, M., 1988 The Gender of the Gift: Problems with Women and Problems with Society in Melanesia. Berkeley: University of California Press.

Straus, M., and M. Donnelly, 2005 Theoretical Approaches to Corporal Punishment. In Corporal Punishment of Children in Theoretical Perspective. M. Donnelly and M. A. Straus, eds. pp. 41–53. New Haven: Yale University Press.

Sutton-Smith, B., 1959 The Games of New Zealand Children. Berkeley: University of California Press.

Sutton-Smith, B., 1972 The Folkgames of Children. Austin: University of Texas Press.

Sutton-Smith, B., 1977 Play as Adaptive Potentiation: A Footnote to the 1976 Keynote Address. In Studies in the Anthropology of Play. P. Stevens, ed. pp. 232–237. New York: Leisure Press.

Sutton-Smith, B., 1997 The Ambiguity of Play. Cambridge, MA: Harvard University Press.

Sutton-Smith, B., and D. Kelly-Byrne, 1983 The Masks of Play. In The Masks of Play. B. Sutton-Smith and D. Kelly-Byrne, eds. pp. 184–199. New York: Leisure Press.

Talle, A., 2004 Adoption Practices among the Pastoral Maasai of East Africa: Enacting Fertility. In Cross-Cultural Approaches to Adoption. F. Bowie, ed. pp. 64–78. London: Routledge.

Tanabe, S., 1991 Spirits, Power and the Discourse of Female Gender; the Phi Meng Cult of Northern Thailand. In Thai Constructions of Knowledge. M. Chitakasem and A. Turton, eds. pp. 183–212. London: SOAS.

Tantiwiramanond, D., and S. Pandey, 1987 The Status and Role of Women in the Pre-Modern Period: A Historical and Cultural Perspective. Sojourn 2:125–149.

Thitsa, K., 1980 Providence and Prostitution: Image and Reality for Women in Buddhist Thailand. London: Change International.

Thorne, B., 1993 Gender Play: Girls and Boys in School. Buckingham: Open University Press.

Tober, D., 2004 Children in the Field and Methodological Challenges of Research in Iran. Iranian Studies 37:643–654.

Tolfree, D., 1995 Roofs and Roots: The Care of Separated Children in the Developing World. Aldershot: Arena.

Toren, C., 1990 Making Sense of Hierarchy: Cognition as Social Process in Fiji. London: Athlone Press.

Toren, C., 1993 Making History: The Significance of Childhood Cognition for a Comparative Anthropology of Mind. Man (N.S.) 28:461–478.

Toren, C., 2007 Sunday Lunch in Fiji: Continuity and Transformation in Ideas of the Household. American Anthropologist 109:285–295.

Townsend, P. 1995 The Washed and the Unwashed: Women's Life-Cycle Rituals among the Saniyo-Hiyowe of East Sepik Province, Papua New Guinea. In Gender Rituals: Female Initiation in Melanesia. N. C. Lutkehaus and P. B. Roscoe, eds. pp. 165–182. London: Routledge.

Tucker, B., and A. Young, 2005 Growing up Mikea: Children's Time Allocation and Tuber Foraging in Southwestern Madagascar. In Hunter-Gatherer Childhoods: Evolutionary, Developmental and Cultural Perspectives. B. Hewlett and M. Lamb, eds. pp. 147–171. New York: Aldine.

Turnbull, C., 1961 The Forest People. New York: Simon and Schuster.

Turnbull, C., 1994 The Mountain People. London: Pimlico.

Turner, E., 1994 Beyond Inupiaq Reincarnation: Cosmological Cycling. In Amerindian Rebirth: Reincarnation Belief among North American Indians and Inuit. A. Mills and R. Slobodin, eds. pp. 67–81. Toronto: University of Toronto Press.

Turner, V., 1967 The Forest of Symbols: Aspects of Ndembu Ritual. Ithaca, NY: Cornell University Press.

Turner, V., 1969 The Ritual Process: Structure and Anti-Structure. London: Routledge and Kegan Paul.

Tylor, E., 1879 Geographical Distribution of Games. Fortnightly Review XXV:23–30.

Tylor, E., 1913[1871] Primitive Culture: Researches into the Development of Mythology, Philosophy, Religion, Language, Art and Custom. London: John Murray.

Vance, C., 1991 Anthropology Rediscovers Sexuality: A Theoretical Comment. Social Science and Medicine 33:875–884.

van Esterik, P., 1996 Nurturance and Reciprocity in Thai Studies: A Tribute to Lucien and Jane Hanks. In State, Power and Culture in Thailand. E. P. Durrenberger, ed. pp. 22–46. New Haven: Yale University Press.

van Gennep, A., 1960[1909] The Rites of Passage. M. Vizedom and G. Caffee, trans. Chicago: University of Chicago Press.

Vann, R., 1982 The Youth of Centuries of Childhood. History and Theory 21:279–297.

Wade, P., 1993 Sexuality and Masculinity in Fieldwork among Colombian Blacks. In Gendered Fields: Women, Men and Ethnography. D. Bell, P. Caplan, and W. Karim, eds. pp. 199–214. London: Routledge.

Wagatsuma, H., 1981 Child Abandonment and Infanticide: A Japanese Case. In Child Abuse and Neglect: Cross-Cultural Perspectives. J. Korbin, ed. pp. 120–138. Berkeley: University of California Press.

Wagley, C., 1977 Welcome of Tears: The Tapirapé Indians of Central Brazil. New York: Oxford University Press.

Wake, C. S., 1878 The Evolution of Morality. London: Trübner and Co.

Waksler, F. C., 1991 Studying Children: Phenomenological Insights. In Studying the Social Worlds of Children: Sociological Readings. F. C. Waksler, ed. pp. 60–69. London: Falmer Press.

Wedgwood, C., 1938 The Life of Children in Manam. Oceania 9:1–29.

Weeks, J., 1981 Sex, Politics and Society: The Regulation of Sexuality since 1800. New York: Longman.

Weisner, T., and R. Gallimore, 1977 My Brother's Keeper: Child and Sibling Caretaking. Current Anthropology 18:169–190.

White, M., 1993 The Material Child: Coming of Age in Japan and America. New York: Free Press.

Whiting, B., 1963 Six Cultures: Studies of Child Rearing. New York: Wiley.

Whiting, B., and C. P. Edwards, 1988 Children of Different Worlds: The Formation of Social Behavior. Cambridge, MA: Harvard University Press.

Whiting, B., and J. Whiting, 1987 Foreword. In Inuit Youth: Growth and Change in the Canadian Arctic. R. Condon. pp. xiii–xx. New Brunswick, NJ: Rutgers University Press.

Whiting, J., 1961 Socialization Process and Personality. In Psychological Anthropology: Approaches to Culture and Personality. F. Hsu, ed. pp. 355–380. Homewood, IL: Dorsey Press.

Whiting, J., 1977 A Model for Psychocultural Research. In Culture and Infancy: Variations in the Human Experience. P. H. Leiderman, S. Tulkin, and A. Rosenfeld, eds. pp. 29–48. New York: Academic Press.

Whiting, J., 1994 Fifty Years as a Behavioral Scientist: Autobiographical Notes. In Culture and Human Development: The Selected Papers of John Whiting. E. H. Chasdi, ed. pp. 14–44. Cambridge: Cambridge University Press.

Whiting, J., and I. Child, 1953 Child Training and Personality: A Cross-Cultural Study. New Haven: Yale University Press.

Whiting, J., R. Kluckhohn, and A. Anthony, 1958 The Function of Male Initiation Ceremonies at Puberty. In Readings in Social Psychology.

E. E. Maccoby, T. M. Newcomb, and E. L. Hartley, eds. pp. 359–370. New York: Holt, Rinehart and Winston.

Willis, P., 1977 Learning to Labour: How Working Class Kids Get Working Class Jobs. London: Saxon House.

Wilson, M., 1950 Nyakyusa Kinship. *In* African Systems of Kinship and Marriage. A. R. Radcliffe-Brown and D. Forde, eds. pp. 111–139. Oxford: Oxford University Press.

Wolf, M., 1972 Women and the Family in Rural Taiwan. Stanford: Stanford University Press.

Woodhead, M., 1999 Combating Child Labour: Listen to What the Children Say. Childhood 6:27–49.

Wu, D., 1981 Child Abuse in Taiwan. *In* Child Abuse and Neglect: Cross-Cultural Perspectives. J. Korbin, ed. pp. 139–165. Berkeley: University of California Press.

Wulff, H., 1995 Inter-Racial Friendship: Consuming Youth Styles, Ethnicity and Teenage Femininity in South London. *In* Youth Cultures: A Cross-Cultural Perspective. V. Amit-Talai and H. Wulff, eds. pp. 63–80. London: Routledge.

Zelizer, V., 1985 Pricing the Priceless Child: The Changing Social Value of Children. New Haven: Yale University Press.

INDEX